CONTINUOUS QUALITY IMPROVEMENT

A Manufacturing Professional's Guide

By
William Winchell

Richard Perich
Administrator

Published by

Society of Manufacturing Engineers
One SME Drive, P.O. Box 930
Dearborn, Michigan 48121

CONTINUOUS QUALITY IMPROVEMENT

A Manufacturing Professional's Guide

Copyright © 1991
Society of Manufacturing Engineers
Dearborn, Michigan

First Edition

Fourth Printing

Library of Congress Catalog Card Number: 91-60113
International Standard Book Number: 0-87263-401-9
Manufactured in the United States of America

Preface

Making good quality products is now a license to stay in business. In a like context, continuous improvement is absolutely necessary for a business to survive over the long term. Gaps in quality among competitors have disastrous results for the follower. In the past decade, many companies have downsized or gone out of business where gaps in quality were perceived to exist by customers. Only through continuous improvement can these gaps be eliminated.

This book is about continuous improvement. It is a comprehensive coverage of the factors necessary to have continuous improvement. Much of this concerns a basic cultural change in the way a company does business. How to plan, organize, and train for improvement is discussed. Also covered are important areas such as team building, setting priorities, goal setting, problem solving, and rewarding performance. Tips on getting "buy-in" and avoiding failure are also in this book. Basic tools found useful in continuous improvement are illustrated. The appendix includes many forms that may be helpful in this effort. For those that may want to explore specific areas, many of the chapters include a Bibliography which list many sources that may be consulted.

Much of this book is based on personal experience during my industrial career; particularly the GM-10 product development program. Concepts developed in GM-10 are widely used in many other continuous improvement efforts today. I wish to thank my associates at GM-10 for these experiences. Also influential were my associates in professional societies, such as the American Society for Quality Control and the Society of Manufacturing Engineers. Their thoughts, in a forum enhancing critical thinking, helped shape the concepts brought out in this book. Thanks as well to the academic institutions I have been associated with that encourage such efforts.

A number of companies generously allowed us to use their forms and questionnaires in this publication. Special thanks to:

American Supplier Institute
Ann Arbor Consulting Associates, Inc.
Boothroyd Dewhurst, Inc.
Charney and Associates
Chrysler Corporation
Ford Motor Company
General Motors Corporation
Industrial Technology Institute

Thanks also to Edith Holmes for her paper on the ISO 9000 standards in Appendix B.

The journey for continuous improvement is long and hard. But it is absolutely necessary. I wish you well.

William Winchell
Purdue University

Table of Contents

Chapter 1
Introduction.. 1

Chapter 2
What is Quality?.. 9

Chapter 3
What Is a Quality System?...................................... 29

Chapter 4
Continuous Quality Improvement................................. 49

Chapter 5
Tools For Continuous Quality Improvement....................... 69

Chapter 6
The Need for Buy-In... 101

Chapter 7
Planning For Improvement...................................... 123

Chapter 8
Organizing For Improvement.................................... 151

Chapter 9
Training For Improvement 173

Chapter 10
Team Building... 195

Chapter 11
Setting Priorities.. 209

Chapter 12
Goal Setting.. 221

Chapter 13
Problem Solving... 231

Chapter 14
Rewarding Performance... 241

Chapter 15
Avoiding Failure.. 251

Chapter 16
Keeping It In Perspective..................................... 261

Chapter 17
Summary... 275

Appendix A.. A-1
Appendix B.. B-2

CHAPTER 1

INTRODUCTION

In this chapter. . .

NEED FOR CONTINUOUS QUALITY IMPROVEMENT

QUALITY AND PRODUCTIVITY

COMPANY CULTURAL INFLUENCE

1
Introduction

This book is about quality from the viewpoint of the manufacturing professional. Those in manufacturing have a major impact on the quality of products because of their focus on the factory floor. The factory floor is the place where what is needed by the customer takes final form.

But form alone is not enough for customers. They expect form to meet their needs without flaws. Flaws perceived by the user of the product are often not related to dimensions or materials. For example, product users may only care about the results--how well the performance of the product meets their needs. Also of great concern is how long the product lasts.

Traditionally, the sales or marketing function was responsible for identifying the needs of customers. Product engineering interpreted these needs into dimensions and materials to be used by manufacturing to assure performance and durability. It was often a major challenge for manufacturing to follow the directions given by product engineering. Tolerances, for example, were often less than could be met by the inherent process capability of the factory floor. The result was much rework, scrap and customer disappointments.

Severe competitive pressures at the beginning of the 1980s inspired new approaches for many companies. Much of this pressure concerned perceived better quality and lower prices from offshore producers. For the manufacturing professional, these new approaches meant getting directly involved with marketing and development efforts for new products. By the end of the past decade, dramatic improvements in satisfying customers were seen. The new approaches worked.

Many people saw their role in manufacturing grow, bringing about new challenges. Those involved in the new roles looked beyond the factory floor. Interpersonal relations and teams made up of people from several functional areas were the key to successful efforts. Manufacturing professionals were involved in all the major activities in a company. Some activities helped in identifying customer needs and solving design problems. Those directly involved in production contributed to improving quality.

"Profile 21: The Manufacturing Engineer in the 21st Century," a study commissioned by the Society of Manufacturing Engineers, indicates that the role of the manufacturing professional will continue to expand. This expansion will be driven by increased product sophistication. Also contributing, will be the increasing emphasis on the global nature of manufacturing. Manufacturing strategies like customer satisfaction issues, will be market-driven rather than technology driven. The customer will play an increasing role in strategic decisions affecting product design and manufacturing. Designers will look more closely at features demanded by customers and will offer a broader range of product variation. Overriding all the product related manufacturing issues will be a demand from the manufacturer and consumer for product quality.

NEED FOR CONTINUOUS QUALITY IMPROVEMENT

Quality is a competitive advantage in the marketplace. This means a company must have the same or better quality than its competitors. The quality of competitors, however, is constantly improving. This situation keeps a company improving quality continuously to remain a viable force in the marketplace.

Huge differences in quality between imports and domestic products were seen in the early 1980s. This gap in quality provides an important lesson for manufacturing companies. Gaps in quality between competitors mean a substantial competitive advantage to the quality leader. Too great a gap could result in the quality follower losing market share or going out of business. Once a gap in quality is recognized by customers, it will take a long time for the quality follower to regain needed confidences in the marketplace.

Imports to the United States during the 1980s grew steadily for many products. Much of the gains by imports were due to customers making a purchase decision based on comparing products from different manufacturers. The customer then decided which had the greatest value.

The automotive industry is a good example. Domestic models in 1980 suffered from marginal drivability and an increasing frequency of repairs during the warranty period. Japanese imports had as little as 25% of the problems during warranty and drove better.

The handwriting was on the wall. It became a battle for survival. The largest domestic producer of vehicles stopped producing small cars in the United States relying on imports for that market segment. Its market share plummetted from 44% to 36% by the end of the decade.

This nose-dive in market share occurred in spite of a formidable quality improvement program throughout the decade. The program helped gradually close the gap in quality. At the end of the decade there was almost no difference in quality between domestic and imported cars. Yet, market share was still not regained.

The damage was done. Huge profits were lost because of the decline in market share. The battle for survival, consisting of a massive quality improvement program and new technology, required an investment of billions of dollars. Small car manufacturing was no longer being done in the United States. This company may never regain its former stature.

Once customer perceptions about inferior quality are formed they are hard to change. Many companies, like the example just mentioned, improved tremendously during the last decade. Repair records verify dramatic improvement. But Gallup Poll results in 1988, sponsored by the American Society for Quality Control, indicated that the perception of quality of American products didn't change in three years. It often takes time for a customer to change perceptions about quality. To speed a change in perception, some companies are communicating quality improvements and the status of the product quality in advertisements.

Good news came from a 1989 Gallup survey, also sponsored by the American Society for Quality Control. A majority of executives believes that companies in the United States are gaining on foreign competitors in terms of quality. Over half the executives are pleased with their quality strategies. They also feel their companies have achieved significant results in terms of profitability and market share through using these strategies. In addition, three quarters of the executives feel their major competitors in the future will be American companies and not offshore producers.

The message is clear. Companies can no longer tolerate adverse gaps in product quality between their products and those of their competitors. To prevent this, a viable program of continuous improvement must be developed and put into practice.

QUALITY AND PRODUCTIVITY

There is direct relationship between quality and productivity. Better quality increases the productivity of an organization. To succeed in the marketplace, whether it is domestic or international a company must be efficient at making high quality products. Many companies found that it pays to invest effort during development to assure a quality product. This avoids the high cost of repairing products in the hands of customers. Unhappy customers may not buy products from that company again.

Productivity is a key factor in the competitive advantage long enjoyed by the United States. For nearly 100 years, gains in productivity in the United States were more than any other country in the world. During the 1960s, Japan and Europe started having larger increases in productivity than the U.S. This has eroded the lead in productivity that the U.S. once had.

It is important that a strong competitive manufacturing base be maintained. Without exports that are manufactured, there will be insufficient income to pay for desirable imports. Also, a strong manufacturing base is critical to national security as a producer of military equipment.

In the past, productivity gains resulted from better technology. Lately, there is an increasing awareness that up to 80% of the gains of technology may be possible just through better attention to business basics. This is at the heart of any continuous improvement effort.

Productivity, in simplistic terms, can be defined as the value of the output of a company divided by the value of the input to produce that output. A manufacturing company may use revenue as the value of the output. Cost may be used as the value of the input. For the example labeled as "CURRENT" in Figure 1-1, productivity equals the revenue divided by cost (100/80) or 1.25.

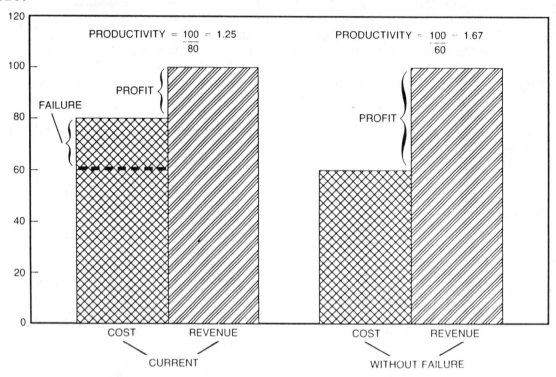

Figure 1-1. The relationship between quality and productivity.

Quality, for simplicity, can be defined as the cost of product failures divided by revenue. Failures could be within the plant and include such things as rework, scrap, reinspection and sorting. Other failures occur after shipping to the customer and may be due to warranty claims, customer complaint handling and field service. Failure costs are typically high for any firm and a high priority in a quality improvement program. Recently, a well known manufacturer indicated that their cost of failures was 20% of revenues.

Figure 1-1 also illustrates the potential productivity improvement through making quality better. For the example labeled "WITHOUT FAILURE," it is assumed that failure costs are 20% of revenue. If failures could be eliminated, cost would decrease by 25%. Productivity would equal revenue divided by cost (100/60) or 1.67. Note also that profits double from that in the example labeled "CURRENT." The potential gain in productivity through eliminating failure costs is 33.6%.

Obviously, the potential gain in productivity through quality improvements is very attractive. The direct relationship between quality and productivity has important implications in maintaining a strong competitive position for a company.

COMPANY CULTURAL INFLUENCE

In the past decade, many companies restructured and down-sized operations. Gone are companies that could not compete successfully.

Among many of those that survived, there is a common ingredient. They recognized that they must change. This change involved the basic way they conducted their business. Culture within many companies changed dramatically. For most companies, the new culture is still evolving.

Much of the change involved humanizing the workplace. Workers during the 1980s were much different from their predecessors. More are now involved in administration. Unskilled labor accounts for only 30% of the work force down from 50% in the 1960s. Women in the work force increased from 16% in the 1940s to 42%. The employees with only an 8th grade education dropped to 6% from 30% in 1950. College graduates now comprise 40% of the work force. The workers are well informed and much more technically oriented. They are also less willing to work in a hierarchical, autocratic business setting.

Because of this, many companies have modernized their style of management. Self-management is widely practiced rather than rigid supervision. A team approach involving interested parties is used to solve problems instead of taking the problems to management for solution. In many plants, workers are allowed to stop production lines to assure consistent quality. They also can switch tasks with others to prevent boredom. The role of management has changed to that of a facilitator to help employees make improvements. The result is better decisions and workers who feel that they are making a positive contribution.

Other major changes have taken place in the work environment. There is now a customer centered mentality. It is widely recognized that meeting the needs of the customer is the only way to survive in the marketplace.

There is also a recognition that you fix processes and not people. People want to do a good job and sometimes can't due to factors beyond their control.

Also, there is an awareness that better solutions are drafted by those involved in the process rather than management. If people are involved as team players with others in a process, there is high likelihood that a viable solution will be found.

The last observation is that the only competitive strategy for a company is continuous improvement. Those believing in continuous improvement recognize that the journey will be long and hard and probably never end.

In summary, the change in culture of many companies was vital in improving quality. Many believe this change of culture permitted manufacturing in the U.S. to maintain its competitive posture against imports during the last decade. The culture change is also the common thread among many chapters in this book.

BIBLIOGRAPHY

Bergstrom, Robin P., "Portrait of a Profession in Change." Manufacturing Engineering, December 1988, p. 44.

Consumer's Perceptions Concerning the Quality of American Products and Services. Milwaukee: American Society for Quality Control, 1988.

Patterson, Tim, "Humanizing the Workplace." World, May 1986. p. 24.

Quality: Executive Priority or Afterthought? Milwaukee: American Society for Quality Control, 1989.

CHAPTER 2

WHAT IS QUALITY?

In this chapter. . .

QUALITY PRIOR TO THE LAST DECADE

PRODUCT QUALITY

OTHER CONCEPTS OF QUALITY
1. Internal Customers
2. Quality of Tooling amd Equipment
3. Quality of the Measurement Devices
4. Quality of the Work Force

2
What Is Quality?

QUALITY PRIOR TO THE LAST DECADE

The meaning of quality, prior to the last decade, focused on the factory floor. For many companies, a product was considered good quality if it was passed by the final inspector. The inspector often practiced much leeway in making this decision. Tolerances were often not met and much discretion was used. When the inspector did not want to make the decision, written deviations were used. These required signatures by management. Deviations became numerous in many companies.

Tolerances were being second-guessed by the inspector and those signing the deviations. Clearly, where this happened, process capability on the factory floor was not good enough to meet the tolerances. Many tolerances were based on tradition; those used on similar parts in the past. What is even more alarming is that most of those making decisions about what is good or bad really lacked direct contact with the customer.

Inspectors were in a bad position. They were, in reality, traffic cops. Bad parts were directed to disposal. Good parts were directed to the customer. When inspectors rejected something, they were often thought of as the "bad guy." Peer pressure was terrific. The name of the game was to get production past the inspector. The inspector was really held responsible for quality, yet had little control over it. A commonly accepted cliche is you can't inspect quality into a product. Quality really depends on how well the product is designed and processed.

Often, there was little rapport between product design and manufacturing. Product designers often avoided issues and told manufacturing they must make the product as specified. Complicating the issue, was the fact that product designers did not really trust manufacturing. They felt if they widened tolerances to match process capability, even greater liberties toward what was acceptable would be taken by those on the factory floor. During this time, unilateral actions by manufacturing to improve process capability by changing the process were mostly unsuccessful. Management often struggled with justification issues and was unable to fund the needed changes. The above scenario was widespread in domestic companies prior to the last decade. Consumers tolerated marginal product quality from domestic companies because they had no choice. This changed when better quality products, often at lower prices, became available from offshore producers. Loyalty to "made-in America" products prevented a stampede of imports from occurring. But the die was cast. Sales of domestic companies softened. Domestic companies realized they had to change their way of doing business to compete.

For suppliers to companies producing directly for the consumer market, it was a double hit. First, domestic companies ordered less from suppliers. Second, domestic companies started ordering from offshore producers to get better quality and lower prices.

Quality became the dominant issue. Understanding what quality is became a high priority. The focus for product quality needed to be changed from the factory floor to the customer. The process by which quality is achieved needed to be understood.

There is a common theme to the thinking of the quality gurus of the 1980s-- Deming, Juran, Crosby, Feigenbaum, and others. They all express a strong agreement that quality must be a fundamental business strategy for a company to survive. This new strategy was seen as the driver of an immense culture change in companies. Real change in culture is often a painful experience. It forces all employees to adopt new roles. Long-term employees may feel uncomfortable in new roles that often result in more participation and responsibility. For management, the change is particularly difficult, since it seemingly reduces power and authority. A different style of management is necessary involving everyone in decision making.

The process to assure quality products involves everyone in a company. In the decade just completed, giant strides were made in creating widespread understanding of these concepts and the start of cultural changes in many companies. Many ideas while not new, were misunderstood by domestic producers before entering the battle for survival.

PRODUCT QUALITY

It is now widely believed by those in industry that quality is meeting the needs of the customer. The focus on the customer is important. It is the customer that defines quality expectations in the marketplace.

In a sense, quality is like beauty. The judgment about whether something is of good quality is in the eyes of the beholder. In an age of consumerism, those who buy products are becoming increasingly sophisticated. This is forcing the manufacturer to pay closer attention to what the customer thinks.

For suppliers of companies making consumer products, this has severe implications. More than ever before, suppliers must thoroughly understand the application of their product. Even more important, they must deal with how their portion fits in with the general strategy of getting customer satisfaction. This takes a close working relationship, which may be described as a partnership among companies. The success of a supplier really depends on how the products entering the consumer marketplace are perceived by the final customer. If there is wide acceptance, the supplier will likely prosper. If not, survival may be questionable.

According to the American Society for Quality Control, "quality is the totality of features and characteristics of a product or service that bear on its ability to satisfy given needs." The definition implies that the needs of the customer are the "drivers" of quality. It also implies that satisfaction of those needs really determines whether quality is met.

Consumers, for the most part, do not really care about specifications. They have their individual perceptions of what a product should be like. They evaluate whether quality has been met by how the product differs from what they think it should be like.

A way of understanding these perceptions is to consider that a consumer may look at quality in four ways. These are "function," "use features," "perception features" and "price." This relationship is shown in Figure 2-1.

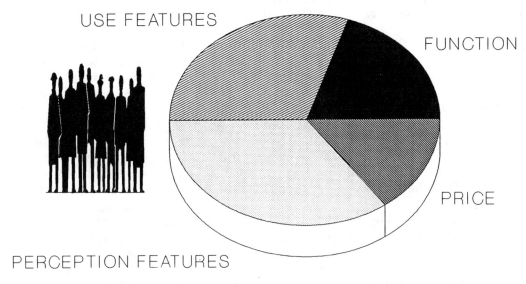

Figure 2-1. Customer perceptions of quality.

"Function" relates to the ability of the product to do the job for which it was purchased. Using an auto, for example, one function is that it goes from starting point A to destination B whenever desired. Consumers are also concerned with how long it will do the function without failing. This is a measure of reliability or durability of the product.

"Use features" relate to how the consumer interfaces with the product. In a car, for example, this may be how comfortable the seats are and how accessible the controls are.

"Perception features" relate to the customer appeal, or how the consumer feels about the "excitement" of the product. For a car enthusiast, it may be that a vehicle has all the available technical advances.

"Price" is, in reality, a trade-off with the other ways a customer perceives quality. It is the value the customer places on the product to determine whether a purchase is made. A car designed with the latest technical advances would cost more than one designed for basic transportation. If the extra cost of the technically advanced car is within the added value the customer perceives, then a sale is likely. If the added cost is not justified in the mind of the customer, a sale is not likely.

The relative weight given by the consumer to these four areas shifts constantly. Some of the dynamic nature of this depends on the environment. In a robust environment, the added cost of the technically advanced car may be perceived as justified by more consumers. It also depends upon the demographics of the market segment to which the product is being sold. A retired person has different needs than a young person just starting a career. A company must continuously study the needs of consumers to provide a product that is perceived as being of good quality.

A study showed that about 80% of the perception of customer satisfaction depends upon whether a product meets the true needs of the customer. Meeting these needs depends on correct assessment of the needs, relevant design of the product, capable processing, and safe delivery to the customer. All this must be accomplished in a timely fashion.

The remaining 20% of the perception of customer satisfaction depends upon how well a company handles complaints and solves problems. The study found most companies spend nearly all customer service time fixing problems. Little time is spent finding out why the problems occurred in the first place. This lack of effort meant many problems occurred repeatedly. The penalties on a company for lack of customer satisfaction are severe. The study showed that for every five customers who have a problem, one customer is lost forever. By losing this customer, 20% of your potential future repeat sales disappears. Even worse, an unhappy customer tells others about the problem. This secondary effect could impact future sales even more.

Figure 2-2 illustrates the relationship between perceived customer satisfaction and repeat sales of a product. Interestingly, the potential profit lost or gained by how the customer feels about a product is huge. It often is far greater than a company's expenses for quality. Additional sales gained by better quality being recognized by the customer results in a huge profit potential. Conversely, if bad quality is perceived, sales will be lost and the future of a company is in question.

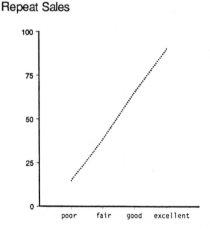

Figure 2-2. Expected repeat sales for customer quality perception levels.

Compounding the damage is that only 5% of customer problems is known to the manufacturer. Customers do not complain for three reasons: one is that the customer perceives it to be too much trouble. The second reason is that the customer feels no one cares and it is a waste of time. The third reason found in the study was a perception that no viable process for making complaints exists. Unfortunately, these views are probably well founded.

The study showed that for low priced items, an unhappy consumer may just throw the product away over one-third of the time. One-half of the customers may go back to a retailer. The retailer typically does not tell the manufacturer about the specific problem. Where there is an exchange of product, the product may be returned to the manufacturer. But, the chances of the manufacturer finding something wrong with it are slight. The problem is usually assumed to be something else and is not really solved. From the study, a company may well assume that for every known problem, there are 19 more. This is a sobering thought for a company battling to survive.

However, many companies after recognizing the situation are putting new systems in place. These companies actively seek out all the customers having problems. They know that many problems are not directly tied to the product. For example, some are due to confusion on the part of the customer. When cleared up by the manufacturer, loyalty is retained. Future customer literature is changed to encourage reading by the customer and to address areas that may be confusing. Other companies reportedly give a blank check to the customer service department to deal with consumer problems. By this, a strong statement is made to consumers that the company is dedicated to solving each problem. Customer satisfaction rose dramatically at almost no increase in cost.

A vision of what is really causing customers to be unhappy is slowly being formed through studies. Currently, the cause is almost equally divided among the systems that companies use, the employees in those systems and the customer. The answer seems to lie in improved systems that tolerate slip-ups by the employees and the customer. The key to customer satisfaction is doing it right the first time. If this does not happen, a speedy resolution of the problem is absolutely necessary. If a person has a problem resolved, they will tell five persons good things about the product. The study showed that it is critical to find all those that have problems and resolve them.

Once customer needs are identified, they are transformed into product features and characteristics. At this stage, the product is described in general terms. For example, the gasoline mileage or the expected life of the product may be determined. Next, the features and characteristics are transformed into design and product specifications. In this stage, drawings are made. Both transformations are difficult tasks, since both are iterative processes. A need cannot be satisfied by itself but must be counterbalanced with other needs. Also, each customer is somewhat different and the design must be tolerant of these differences. A composite of product features and characteristics, taken as a whole, really satisfies the needs of a broad range of customers.

The product design and specifications are in terms of performance requirements and manufacturing directions. Drawings with tolerances are the basis for manufacturing to conform to the design. How well performance requirements are met is evaluated by laboratory and field tests during the development of the product. Also evaluated during this time is whether the product can be made as specified by the manufacturing directions. Changes in the product and process are usually made during the development phase. This is also an iterative process fine-tuning anticipated results.

Prediction of whether the product will meet the needs of the customer is possible during the development phase. Needed adjustments can be made. But, the accuracy of the prediction is contingent on how well the needs of the customer were translated in the various phases. If it was not done correctly, customers will likely not be happy when they buy the products.

The useful life of the product and its dependability are usually also of concern. The bathtub curve is often used to illustrate failure patterns of products during their lifetime, as shown in Figure 2-3. The time segment marked "A" is called the "infant mortality period." Failures occurring very early in the use of the product are in this segment. Typically, these failures are due to manufacturing defects or are the result of misuse or misapplication. The time segment marked "B" is called the "constant failure-rate period." Failures in this segment may be due to design or unforeseen changes in environment. Also, failures could reflect accidents. These accidents may be unavoidable. On the other hand, some accidents may have been avoided by proper maintenance. The time segment marked "C" is called the "wearout period." Failures occur because the parts are reaching the end of their useful life.

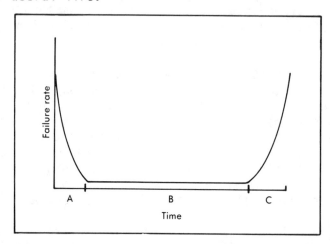

Figure 2-3. Failure rate versus time curve. (From *Tool and Manufacturing Engineers Handbook*)

Another consideration is that the product can be used safely. Also important are ease of performing maintenance, availability of spare parts and service facilities. Clear operating instructions are necessary. It is also very desirable to have a built-in tolerance so that misuse or misapplication will not cause problems. This could avoid injury to the user, a loss of performance, or premature failure.

Product designs should address an appropriate market segment of customers. For example, customers in a lower-price market segment for appliances may not need the additional features found in higher-priced appliances. For some customers, it may be a balance between the financially affordable and the operationally adequate. Some features are equally desirable to customers of both lower and higher-price models. An example is the expected life of a product.

Important are what levels of features, cost, quality and service are being offered by the competition. This technique is widely known as "benchmarking." Through this, goals can be established that are achievable. For many companies, this has been a valuable source of intelligence about levels of improvement necessary to remain competitive. Marketing advantages also can be assessed. Visits to companies can be identified to gain a first-hand view of how new levels of performance are achieved.

Identifying the needs of customers is often complex. In mass marketing situations, where many customers are provided with equivalent products, mail surveys have been useful. In contractual situations, the customer is sometimes not the ultimate user. In this case, the needs of both the immediate customer and the ultimate user of the product should be identified. The needs of customers constantly change. This requires that the identification of needs be updated regularly.

OTHER CONCEPTS OF QUALITY

An important concept of quality is that everyone in an organization is both a supplier to others in the organization and a customer. They receive input from others, process it and pass it along to the next internal customer. Only a small fraction of those in any organization pass their output to the external customer.

Although the external customer is important, the quality of a product depends on the quality of output passed along each internal customer. This concept does not distinguish between white and blue collar workers. Each contributes to the quality of the product. Also, the collective effectiveness of each employee really determines the competitiveness of the company in the marketplace.

Measures of performance, both in quality and quantity terms, are often created for each employee. Where the process recognizes that the internal customers are really teams of employees, these performance measures relate to team performance. In this way, the means of satisfying internal customers are identified and quantified. It is important that these performance measures support the goals of the entire organization. Each has an operational definition of quality and can evaluate the contribution that is made. Usually, employees in each process make up the performance measures. In a way, each team or individual employee is an entrepreneurship creating an improved quality of work life.

QUALITY OF TOOLING AND EQUIPMENT

The key to making products conform to designs is the quality of the tools and equipment producing the designs. Extensive acceptance testing is often done by the builder and the purchaser to assure performance and capability before installation in production. After installation, maintenance is required regularly to keep in "as-new" condition. Predictive maintenance programs are highly effective. Companies may use two main measures of performance to evaluate the quality of tooling and equipment availability and process capability.

Availability has a close relationship with reliability. Getting the desired reliability during operation assures required production levels can be obtained during the life of the manufacturing system. For existing equipment, this can be found easily. All that is required is the various length of times that the system operated without failing and the times to repair when it did fail. For new equipment and tools, this evaluation is done during the extensive acceptance testing. Deteriorating performance can be corrected prior to installation in production. Availability is the percent that a system is operating when called upon to run. Not having perfect performance is due to the time taken to repair a breakdown. This can be also stated as:

$$\text{Availability} = \frac{\text{MTBF} - \text{MTTR}}{\text{MTBF}} \times 100$$

MTBF = mean time between failure.
MTTR = mean time to repair.

The relationship is illustrated in Figure 2-4. If the MTBF = 100 hours and MTTR = 5 hours then the availability will be:

$$\text{Availability} = \frac{100 - 95}{100} \times 100 = 95\%$$

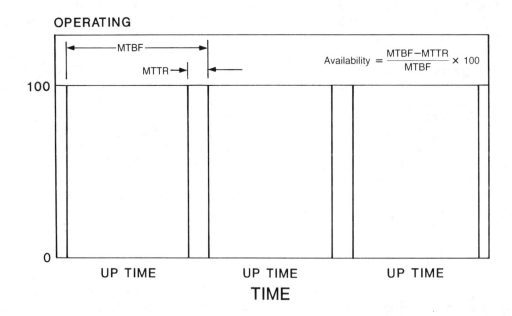

Figure 2-4. Relationship of mean time between failure, mean time to repair and availability.

Part No. & Name		Char. Measured
12345 SHAFT		DIAMETER
Operation No. & Desc. 10 TURN GRIND		Date 7/5/90

SAMPLE DATA:

No.	Value	No.	Value	No.	Value	No.	Value	No.	Value
1	16	21	16	41	16	61	10	81	17
2	15	22	15	42	15	62	17	82	16
3	17	23	17	43	16	63	15	83	17
4	14	24	16	44	15	64	16	84	10
5	10	25	10	45	17	65	15	85	16
6	17	26	15	46	14	66	15	86	17
7	15	27	16	47	16	67	16	87	16
8	16	28	17	48	13	68	14	88	16
9	16	29	16	49	17	69	17	89	14
10	15	30	17	50	15	70	17	90	16
11	14	31	15	51	14	71	15	91	17
12	16	32	16	52	16	72	15	92	16
13	10	33	14	53	15	73	16	93	16
14	16	34	17	54	17	74	16	94	10
15	15	35	10	55	15	75	14	95	16
16	17	36	17	56	16	76	17	96	16
17	16	37	15	57	10	77	10	97	14
18	15	38	15	58	17	78	16	98	16
19	17	39	16	59	10	79	17	99	16
20	16	40	16	60	16	80	16	100	16

Remarks: STRAIGHT LINE SIDE 1 INDICATES NORMALITY
& NO

TALLY SHEET:

VALUE		11	12	13	14	15	16	17	18	19	20	21	22		
TALLY				I	LHT IIII	LHT LHT LHT LHT LHT	LHT LHT LHT LHT LHT LHT II	LHT LHT LHT LHT II	LHT LHT						
FREQUENCY				1	9	25	32	23	10	0					

Figure 2-5. Data collection for capability analysis. (*Courtesy of Ford Motor Company*)

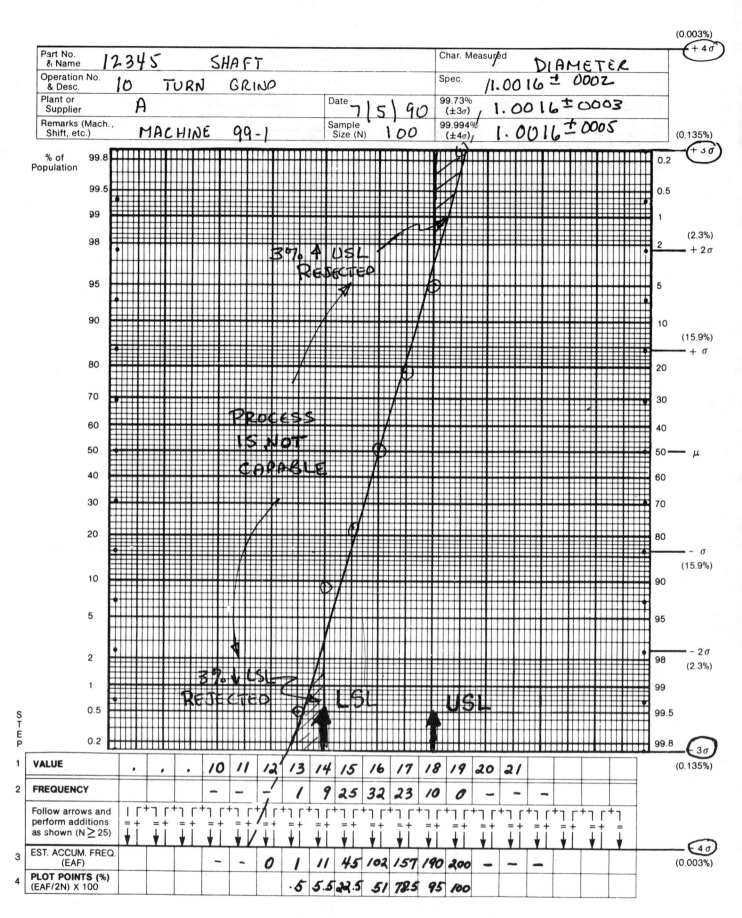

Figure 2-6. Capability analysis sheet. (*Courtesy of Ford Motor Company*)

Process capability, broadly speaking, is an assessment of the stability of the process and the ability of the process to meet needed tolerances on critical characteristics. If a process is stable, it will likely result in a near normal distribution of the critical characteristics. Also, there will be a minimum of variation among parts run on different machine cycles and the process will not drift over time. Otherwise, the evaluation is aborted and fixes made. Such evaluations are made in steps. Typically, a short-term process performance is scheduled first requiring data from 25 groups of parts. A short-term evaluation is shown in Figure 2-5 and Figure 2-6. Both of these forms are repeated in the Appendix. If successful, a long-term process performance may be scheduled lasting at least 25 working days. The long-term evaluation is done using control charts which are described in Chapter 5. Depending upon results and the criticality of the characteristics, control charts could be incorporated in the process indefinitely.

A widely used index for evaluating capability is the process capability index C_{pk}. This index indicates both the variability and the centering of the process with respect to the tolerance.

$$C_{pk} = \frac{USL - \overline{X}}{3S} \text{ or } \frac{LSL - \overline{X}}{3S} \text{ whichever is the least absolute value.}$$

USL = upper specification limit
LSL = lower specification limit
$\overline{X}$ = sample average
S = standard deviation of the sample data

This relationship is illustrated in Figure 2-7. The higher the value of C_{pk} the better is the capability. Though the variation is identical, the process that is not centered has the lower process capability index as seen in Figure 2-8.

LSL = 6mm   USL = 14mm

4s   4s

$\overline{X}$ = 10 mm
S = 1 mm

$$C_{pk} = \frac{USL - \overline{X}}{3S} = \frac{14 - 10}{3 \times 1} = 1.33$$

$$C_{pk} = \frac{LSL - \overline{X}}{3S} = \frac{6 - 10}{3 \times 1} = 1.33$$

$$C_{pk} = \text{minimum} = 1.33$$

Figure 2-7. C_{pk} with centered process.

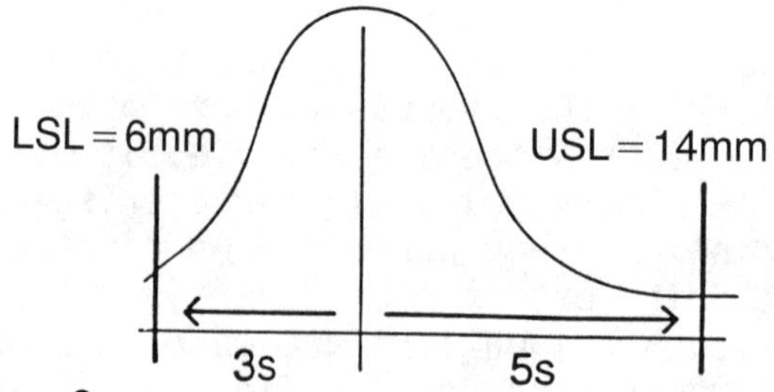

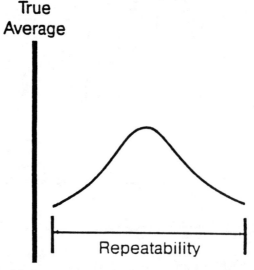

$$LSL = 6mm \qquad USL = 14mm$$

$$\overline{X} = 9$$
$$S = 1$$

$$C_{pk} = \frac{USL - \overline{X}}{3S} = \frac{14 - 9}{3 \times 1} = 1.6$$

$$C_{pk} = \frac{LSL - \overline{X}}{3S} = \frac{6 - 9}{3 \times 1} = 1.0$$

$$C_{pk} = \text{minimum} = 1.0$$

Figure 2-8. C_{pk} with off-centered process.

QUALITY OF THE MEASUREMENT DEVICES

In the past, measurements were commonly accepted as correct. The pursuit of improved quality has proven this to be a fallacy. In fact, the first step recommended in pursuing a processing error is to check the measuring device. To assure accuracy, calibration of each device to known standards on a preplanned schedule is mandatory in almost all companies. Besides accuracy, other factors that cause variation are repeatability, reproducibility, stability and linearity of the device. A variation in readings can be caused by wear, deterioration, or changing environmental conditions, such as temperature or humidity.

Currently, most variation is likely to be caused by the factors of repeatability and reproducibility. Repeatability is variation due to the device itself. It is the measurement obtained when one operator uses the same gage for measuring the identical characteristics of the same parts. This is illustrated in Figure 2-9. Reproducibility is variation caused by

Figure 2-9. Gage repeatability. *(Courtesy of General Motors Corporation)*

22

the persons operating the device. This is illustrated in Figure 2-10. It is the variation of the average of measurements made by different operators using the same gage when measuring identical characteristics of the same parts. Generally, the variation due to repeatability and reproducibility should be less than 10% of the tolerance of the dimension measured. Often, it is more. A worksheet for making this analysis is shown in Figure 2-11.

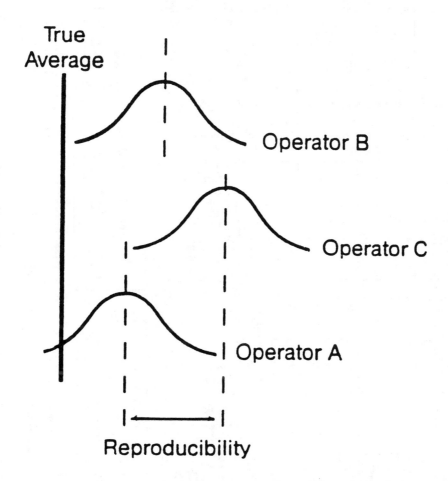

Figure 2-10. Gage reproducibility. *(Courtesy of General Motors Corporation)*

Further explanation of Figure 2-11 is presented in the next several paragraphs (sections VARIABLE GAGE STUDY FOR REPEATABILITY AND REPRODUCIBILITY (LONG METHOD) and CONDUCTING THE STUDY) from the General Motors Statistical Process Control Manual.

VARIABLE GAGE STUDY FOR REPEATABILITY AND REPRODUCIBILITY (LONG METHOD)

The long method of variable gage study can determine errors of gage repeatability and reproducibility (R&R) separately. Study results can also provide information concerning the causes of gage error.

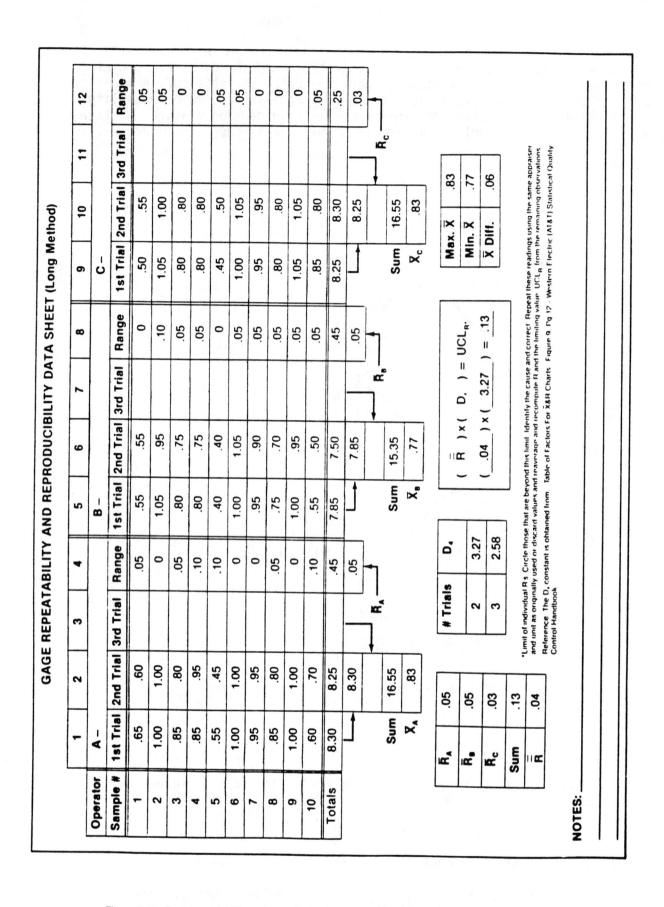

Figure 2-11. Gage repeatability and reproducibility report. *(Courtesy of General Motors Corporation)*

24

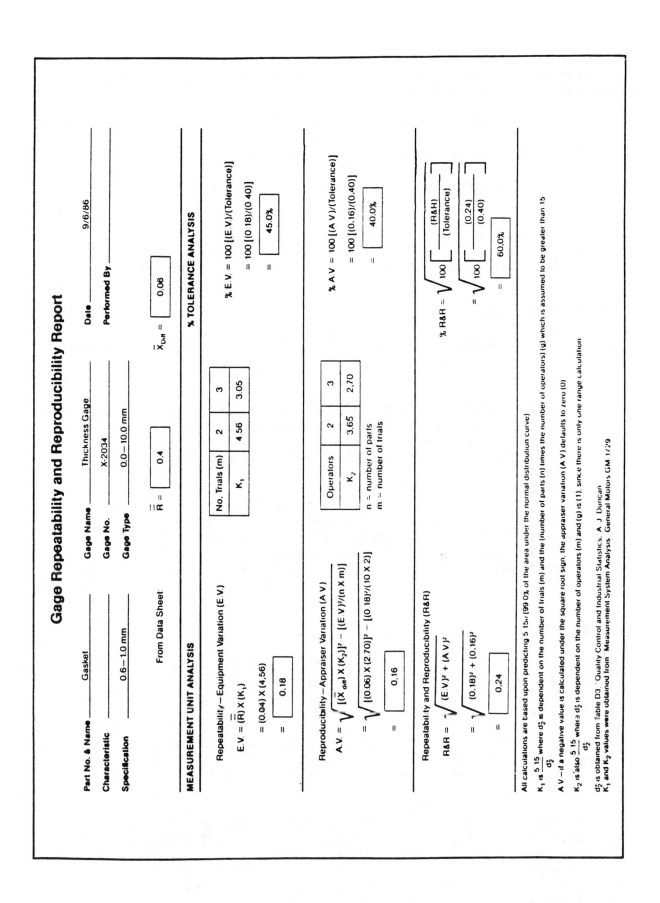

Figure 2-11. Gage repeatability and reproducibility report. *(Courtesy of General Motors Corporation)*

For example, if lack of reproducibility is large compared to repeatability, then possible causes could be:

1. The operator is not properly trained in how to use and read the gage instrument;
2. Calibrations on the gage dial are not clear.

If lack of repeatability is large compared to reproducibility, the reasons may be:

1. The gage instruments need maintenance;
2. The gage should be redesigned to be more rigid;
3. The clamping or location for gaging needs to be improved.

CONDUCTING THE STUDY

Even though the number of operators, the number of trials and the number of parts may be varied, one should conduct the study according to the following steps:

1. Refer to operators A, B, and C, and number the parts 1 through 10 so that the numbers are not visible to the operators.
2. Calibrate the gage.
3. Let Operator A measure 10 parts in a random order and enter the results in Column 1.
4. Repeat step 3 with Operators B and C.
5. Repeat the cycle, with 10 parts measured in another random order, for the number of trials required.
6. Steps 3 through 5 may be modified for large size parts, unavailability of parts or when operators are on different shifts.
7. Using the form shown in Figure 2-10, enter the observations on one side and calculate Gage R & R using the formulas shown in Figure 2-11.

QUALITY OF THE WORK FORCE

The most critical factor in assuring quality is the quality of the work force. One report says that when looking at the work force in the United States, there is good and bad news. One-third of the work force is better educated than elsewhere in the world. One out of five adults has four years of college or better. The remaining two-thirds of the work force could have better education, more skills and improved motivation. Regarding education, one of five adults cannot read, write or count on a seventh grade level. This situation is expected to continue well into the future if drastic action is not taken.

Many companies are involved in improving this situation. Long time employees not having basic skills are receiving lessons in basic math and reading. One large electronic manufacturer is spending several hundred million dollars for both blue and white collar workers education in basic skills. Training is done extensively directed toward improving the work force in such things as continuous improvement efforts. Regarding motivation, culture is changing in companies to allow everyone in an organization to play a bigger part in their own destiny. A large portion of the remainder of this book is devoted to this subject.

In the next chapter, the quality system in operation in a company will be discussed.

BIBLIOGRAPHY

Bolton, Caroline and Winchell, William, "Can Quality Cost Dimension Customer Satisfaction?" Quality Congress Transactions. Milwaukee: American Society for Quality Control, 1989.

Burke, Michael I., "How Quality is Factored in the Design Process." Automotive Engineering, October 1989, p. 65.

Choate, Pat, "Where Does Quality Fit in with the Competitiveness Debate?" Quality Progress, February 1988, p. 25.

General Motors Statistical Process Control Manual. Detroit: General Motors Corp.

Goodman, John, "The Nature of Customer Satisfaction." Quality Progress, February 1989.

Juran, J.M., Editor, Quality Control Handbook, 4th ed. New York: McGraw Hill, 1988.

McBride, Vernon, "In Today's Market, Quality is Best Focal Point for Upper Management." Industrial Engineering, July 1986, p. 51.

TESQA, Tooling and Equipment Quality Assurance. Detroit: Chrysler Corp., January 1989.

Veilleux, Raymond F. and Wick, Charles, Tool and Manufacturing Engineers Handbook, 4th ed., Volume 4: Quality Control and Assembly. Dearborn, MI: Society of Manufacturing Engineers, 1984.

CHAPTER 3

WHAT IS A
QUALITY SYSTEM?

In this chapter. . .

CONSIDERATIONS

1. Prevention of Defects
2. Customer Focus
3. Total Involvement
4. Selection and Training
5. Standards
6. Legal Liability

DEFINING A QUALITY SYSTEM

MANAGEMENT

MARKETING

PRODUCT DEVELOPMENT

SUPPLIERS

MATERIAL

MANUFACTURING

SERVICE

AUDITS

Appendix information

Cost of quality worksheet
(Courtesy Charney & Associates, Inc.) A-1--A-2

Form used to evaluate quality systems of tool and equipment suppliers
(Courtesy of Chrysler Corporation) A-3--A-12

Design failure mode and effects analysis
(Courtesy of Chrysler Corporation) A-13

Process failure mode and effects analysis
(Courtesy of Chrysler Corporation) A-14

Capability analysis chart
(Courtesy of Ford Motor Company) A-15--A-16

3
What Is a Quality System?

This chapter defines and describes quality systems. A system is a group of
related activities working together toward a common goal. By activities
working together, better results are obtained. Classically, a system
interacts with the environment. It also can regulate and adjust itself.
The American Society for Quality Control defines a quality system as "the
collective plans, activities, and events that are provided to ensure that a
product, process, or service will satisfy given needs." The activities that
typically make up a quality system are shown in Figure 3-1. They include
the quality subsystems of management, marketing, product development,
suppliers, materials, manufacturing and service. When operating alone, the
priorities of each activity may conflict. Working together, activities can
better achieve common goals. Bringing all subsystems into unison is the job
of management.

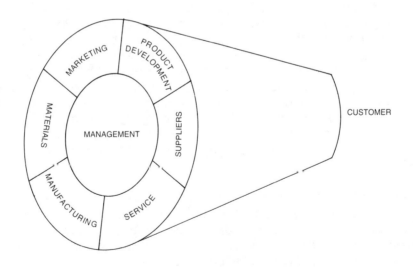

Figure 3-1. Typical activities found in a quality system.

The goal for a quality system is to ensure that the product meets the needs
of the customer. For a quality system, the environment the system interacts
with is the customer of the product. Being self-regulated relates to the
capability to maintain a quality level that has been reached. The ability

of the system to adjust relates to its capability to improve upon the current quality level. The ultimate goal of any quality system should be no unhappy customers. The makeup of a quality system is different in every company. The sophistication of a system depends upon what is needed to achieve the goals of the quality system. A supplier not producing directly for a consumer market may not need as complete a marketing quality subsystem as a company that does. Similarly, a company which only has to meet contract requirements will have a different quality system than a mass marketer. For those in manufacturing, certain operations on the floor must be viewed as components of the larger quality system. These operations are part of the system to achieve the quality goals of the company. For example, all workers must understand how they help in meeting the needs of the customers.

CONSIDERATIONS

The quality system must consider many factors. Among the important ones are:

* Prevention of defects;
* Customer focus;
* Total involvement;
* Selection and training;
* Standards;
* Legal liability.

PREVENTION

Many quality systems in the past were designed to "sort" good products from bad. This was usually done by the final inspector. It was often not done during the various processing steps further weakening the quality effort. Those products judged to be bad had to be reworked to meet specifications. If they could not be reworked, they were scrapped. This type of system is known as a "detection/correction" system. With this system, problems were not found until they were inspected. Problems not caught by the inspector were shipped. This caused unhappy customers. Because of the nature of humans, the effectiveness of the sorting operations was often less than 90%. This meant at least one out of every 10 bad parts reached the customer. The old cliche "You can't inspect quality into your product" was proven repeatedly.

Quality systems that are preventive in nature are now widely in place. These systems help prevent problems from occurring in the first place. This is done by placing emphasis on proper planning and problem prevention early in the product cycle. The various elements of this type of system are described later in this chapter.

CUSTOMER FOCUS

The final word on how well a product meets needs is given by customers and users. The perceptions formed are also influenced by the offerings of competitors. They are formed over the life of the product, not just when it was purchased.

Being aware of customers' needs is important. In addition, focusing the attention of employees in a company on customers and users and their needs is absolutely essential. This is vital to having an effective quality system. For example, group discussions focus on needs to be satisfied by product designs. In this way, the risk--that the product is viewed by employees as only an inanimate object--is minimized.

TOTAL INVOLVEMENT

Quality cannot be obtained by focusing on inspection, product design, or operator education alone. Important as each of these elements may be, improved quality occurs from a balanced effort throughout the company. Quality activities must exist in all functions: marketing, product development, manufacturing, accounting, etc. These activities must work in harmony with each other as a finely-tuned entity to satisfy the needs of customers and users.

Quality can be attained only through the participation of everyone in the company. Management, together with white-and blue-collar workers, must act as allies in the pursuit of improvement. This partnership also should extend to suppliers and maybe customers. This broad participation requires a change in culture in most companies. It will not work unless it is ingrained in the way a company conducts its business. Organizationally, this means doing away with the "top-down" autocratic form of management. Artificial walls between departments stifle teamwork and must be removed. Employee involvement teams have made impressive strides in improving quality.

The use of product development teams is growing in many companies. These teams are assembled early in the product development cycle. They are composed of members from each function working on developing and manufacturing the product. When suppliers are selected, they join the team. Teams have been very successful in the early identification of problems. Also, they have succeeded in finding timely solutions prior to production.

SELECTION AND TRAINING

The top officer in successful companies is often regarded as a "change agent." The person driving "change" must have stature and credibility. This is vital to overcoming resistance to change and entrenched ideas. The leader must make everybody understand that changes must be made to stay competitive. Also, the leader must be able to inspire personnel in the company to be willing to change.

Successful companies also set goals; but goals require resources. The resources are people and the tools they require. Improvement teams, using people from various functions, are used by many companies. Once the teams and tools have been selected, the company can start training.

This training may take many forms. Some larger companies own quality
·training institutes. Others begin with off-site workshops conducted by
quality experts for management and the staff. In-house training for others
is done on subjects related to the objectives to be achieved. Other
training can be given for specific topics, such as statistical process
control (SPC). Training needs must be looked at frequently and new courses
offered.

STANDARDS

The consequences of not being aware of industry standards can be tragic to a
company. Standards exist for many industrial and business needs. They
include such things as design, procurement, manufacturing, and quality
control. Also, standards may be available for the product, its service and
ease of repair.

The subject matter of industrial standards is very broad. Standards can
cover size and strength characteristics, or performance in terms of quality,
reliability, and safety. They also can address assembly methods and control
procedures. Standards also cover packaging, shipping, and identification of
parts. Other standards cover warnings, labels, and instructions. Some
standards are defined in various federal and state laws, and by
international bodies. Many standards are set by committees under the
guidance of groups. These groups include the ASQC, ANSI and others.
Standards for quality are listed in Table 3-1.

Table 3-1. Standards for Quality Control

Standard Number	Standard Title
ANSI/ASQC A3	Quality Systems Terminology
ANSI/ASQC C1 (ANSI Z1.8)	Specifications of General Requirements for a Quality Program
ANSI/ASQC Z1.15	Generic Guidelines for Quality Systems
ANSI/ASQC E2	Guide to Inspection Planning
MIL-Q-9858A	Quality Program Requirements
MIL-I-45208A	Inspection System Requirements
MIL-STD-45662	Calibration System Requirements
·ISO/DIS 8402	Quality Assurance Vocabulary
ISO/DIS 9000	Guide to Quality Management and Quality Assurance Standard
ISO/DIS 9001	Quality Systems: Assurance Model for Design/Development, Production, Installation and Servicing Capability
ISO/DIS 9002	Quality Systems: Assurance Model for Production and Installation Capability
ISO/DIS 9003	Quality Systems: Assurance Model for Final Inspection and Test Capability
ISO/DIS 9004	Guide to Quality Management and Quality System Elements

It is important for companies to develop their workmanship standards to
judge whether a product is of acceptable quality. These are especially
useful when visual judgments are required. They provide a means by which a
comparison can be made.

LEGAL LIABILITY

Various theories of legal liability have developed over the years. These permit the purchaser or user of a product to recover damages from a manufacturer or supplier. The major theories are negligence, breach of express warranty, breach of implied warranty, and strict liability. A suit grounded on negligence generally means that reasonable and prudent care has not been taken in manufacturing the product. A breach of express warranty may exist when representations are made, often in advertisements or sales agreements, that the product does not meet. Cases of breach of implied warranty had their beginning when a disclaimer of warranty in a sales agreement by a manufacturer was ignored by the court. Strict liability can occur when a defect exists in a product that makes it unreasonably dangerous to use and causes harm. Customers and users can be better protected and the risk of legal liability for a manufacturer can be minimized through a properly designed quality system. Such a system must deal with safety considerations.

DEFINING A QUALITY SYSTEM

The quality system of a company can be defined in terms of costs for each quality activity. Quality cost techniques identify costs associated with activities and events taking place in the quality system. Four major categories for quality costs are:

* Prevention--costs incurred in planning, implementing, and maintaining a quality system that will ensure conformance to quality requirements at economical levels. An example of prevention cost is <u>training</u> in the use of SPC.
* Appraisal--costs incurred in determining the degree of conformance to quality requirements. An example of appraisal cost is <u>inspection</u>.
* Internal failure--costs arising when products, components, and materials fail to meet quality requirements prior to shipping to the customer. An example of internal failure cost is <u>scrap</u>.
* External failure--costs incurred when products fail to meet quality requirements after shipping to the customer. An example of external failure cost is <u>warranty claims</u>.

A Cost of Quality Worksheet can be found in the Appendix.

Each major cost category has many specific activities that can be used in detailing a quality system. Many manufacturers change the terms found in the literature to the language used in their companies. Prevention and appraisal costs can be viewed as inputs into the quality system. These costs are normally budgeted and controlled by management. Based on how well prevention is applied, internal and external failures will occur. The internal and external failures can be viewed as outputs of the system. This relationship is illustrated in Figure 3-2.

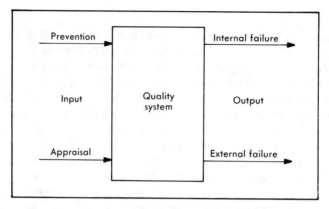

Figure 3-2. Relationship of the basic quality cost categories.

Quality cost can help provide a focus to a quality council. The council, used by many companies, is made up of the leaders of each functional area in a company. This group can make strategic and tactical decisions for improving quality based upon the information provided. Improvement teams are staffed by the quality council to meet specific objectives. These teams are composed of members from each functional area concerned with the specific objective.

The quality council can use quality cost reports to point out strengths and weaknesses of a quality system. They also can describe the benefits and ramifications of changes in terms that everyone can understand--dollars. Return-on-investment models and other financial analyses can be constructed directly from quality cost data to justify needed changes. The quality council also can use this information to rank problems in order of priority. Improvement teams can then seek out root causes, and solutions. Results can be tracked to help efforts head in the right direction. Companies using quality cost recognize the value of this information to those making improvements.

A quality system is the framework for each quality activity. The major parts of the system can be classified:

* Management
* Marketing
* Product development
* Suppliers
* Material
* Manufacturing
* Service
* Audits

MANAGEMENT

Quality management is the "nerve center" of the quality system. It provides leadership to the quality effort. It makes sure that all activities in the system are working together toward a common goal. Strategic planning and staffing improvement efforts are part of quality management. The senior officers of a company are responsible for it. Often, it is managed through a quality council made up of those persons leading the various functional departments. In this way, barriers between departments are broken down. Each function has a part of the decision process and a "buy-in" to the approach.

In the past, the strategy of many companies was driven by product design and technology alone. Erratic quality occurred because product designs were changed when it was too late to order or rebuild needed equipment. Often a company was forced to make do with what was on hand. Much of the time customers were delighted with the product advances. Conversely, at times they were not pleased with the quality of the product.

The strategy of many companies is changing. Management now sees that quality must be on an equal footing with other factors in driving the strategy for a company. More than ever, good quality is absolutely required to sell products. Without it, a company can not be competitive in today's world marketplace.

Strategic planning for most companies now means that the business plan must meet the other strategic driving forces without quality suffering. For many companies, simultaneous engineering of products and processes through product development teams allows this to happen. Processing problems can be solved before the product is released for production. These problems are now handled when design changes are made, increasing the time available for developing solutions. With this approach, customer needs and requirements can be integrated into the planning early in the product development cycle. A quality policy should be adopted to describe the company's strategy in pursuing quality. This policy should be approved by and released under the signature of the chief executive officer of the company. An example of typical quality policy is as follows:

> "It is the policy of Corning to achieve total quality performance in meeting the requirements of external and internal customers. Total quality performance means understanding who the customer is, what the requirements are, and meeting those requirements, without error, on time, every time."

Key performance measurements are created for each objective and goal of the company. These may include such measures as customer satisfaction levels and process capability. Performance measures set through benchmarking what other companies do are reachable. They have already been met by another company.

A quality business plan should be prepared. The purpose of this plan is to meet the quality policy, goals and objectives of the company. This plan is really a part of the company business plan. The quality plan should detail how quality activities of the company will be started or improved. Resources required and the plans for timely deployment need to be included.

The quality policy and quality system should be documented in a quality manual. This manual should be available to all employees. It should also contain quality planning guidelines with specifics for each product line.

MARKETING

Marketing quality plays a critical role in the quality system. This is where the needs of the customer or user are identified. For those companies making products directly for the consumer market, this is done through a variety of techniques. Clinics may be used early in the product cycle involving small groups of consumers who observe and try out the product. Surveys, either by mail or telephone, reach a larger group of likely consumers. Current products are carefully examined against what customers think about them. This may involve products being sold by both the company and its competitors. For companies supplying mass marketers, this analysis is difficult. Often, these suppliers do not depend solely upon the mass marketer for this information. They seek their information directly from the ultimate user to sharpen their competitive position.

Based on the needs, a product definition is drafted. This may include such factors as performance, size, and weight. For an electrical motor, it includes measures of power requirements, starting and running torques. It also may include the safety certifications required. Other factors may be style or aesthetics and packaging requirements. Not included are specific details of the design or process for making the motor. This is up to product development and manufacturing engineers.

For companies dealing with the consumer market, advertising is usually the responsibility of marketing. For suppliers to other companies, statements may be made during sales contacts. These sales contacts may include, besides marketing, product and manufacturing engineers. It is important that the customer or user not be misled by advertising or statements. Misled customers often are not happy. The quality system should provide for review of what and how information is communicated about the product. The message to customers must be accurate, clear, and complete.

PRODUCT DEVELOPMENT

The quality of the product development effort is also critical. This is where the product is taken from an idea to a form that meets both company goals and customer expectations. It is where the needs of the customer are translated into drawings and specifications. Many inputs are required to develop new designs and specifications. The product definition from the marketing area is an important input. Other considerations are the quality policy, goals, and objectives of the company. Also, what is happening on products similar to the new design is important. Answers to these questions can identify improvements that are needed. Experience on past products should be fully used to prevent previous problems from recurring. A detailed design and associated validation plan should be prepared to ensure that the necessary steps are taken.

The product development team must agree on what is in the drawing and in the specifications. For many companies, this team is made up of members from marketing, product design, manufacturing, and other interested parties. The use of ANSI Y14.5M, "Geometric Dimensioning and Tolerancing," helps in clearly communicating product needs. For more information on geometric dimensioning and tolerancing, refer to Chapter 4, "Dimensional Metrology and

Geometric Conformance," of the Tool and Manufacturing Engineers Handbook (TMEH), Volume 4.

After the design and specifications are done, the design validation phase begins. This is where confidence is gained that the design will meet specific objectives. Many improvements in the product design and specifications are found necessary during validation. Analytical approaches include calculations by others not involved in the project. This verifies that original calculations were correct.

Also used are design failure mode and effects analysis (DFMEA), fault tree analysis, and hazard analysis. An example of DFMEA is shown in Figure 3-3, and a blank form appears in the Appendix. Note that part of the DFMEA is a risk assessment of the failure mode. Any failure mode found in a DFMEA may lead to a design change to stop the failure mode from occurring. If a design change is not fruitful, a manufacturing solution is sought. The manufacturing process and quality procedures are changed to lessen the risk. Third party independent evaluations are also used to verify original calculations that the design is based on.

Other validations are done by testing prototypes that represent the design. This testing usually checks both performance and durability issues. An adequate number of samples should be available to provide statistical confidence in the results. The tests should simulate the conditions expected when the product is used by the customer. Tests should only be done on prototypes made to the latest changes. After analyzing test results, needed changes should be made in the design promptly.

The design should be reviewed frequently by the product development team. Issues that should be covered include expectations for customer satisfaction and process capability. Addressing all the problem areas in the review is critical. For example, capability of the process should be such that the tolerances on the drawing can be met. If that is improbable, other solutions need to be found. Rebuilding or buying equipment may be necessary. Perhaps the design could be changed to be more tolerant of the inherent capability of the process. Finding solutions at this time is much better than waiting until the product is in production.

A market readiness review is of great importance before release for production. The objective is to see if production and field service is ready. This review should include availability of customer manuals and location of field service offices. Also important is training of field service people, and stocking of spare parts.

Controls must be provided so that the design and specifications released to production are the same as those that were validated. These controls also should provide a method for making changes to the design. The method should allow changes to be scheduled in advance. Also, there must be a means to verify that the changes were made. Obsolete drawings and specifications should be promptly removed from work areas.

DESIGN
FAILURE MODE AND EFFECTS ANALYSIS

Subsystem/Name ___Rear Axle Housing Shaft___ (1) Final Design Deadline ___1/2/84___ (6)

Model Year/Vehicle(s) ___1985/E-Body___ (2) Prepared by ___John B. Dole___ (7)

Primary Design Responsibility ___Dept. 5000, Chassis Systems___ (3) Reviewed by ___E.D. Smith___ (8)

Other Depts Involved ___Warranty, Manufacturing___ (4) FMEA Date (Orig.) ___1/2/82___ (Rev.) ___10/12/83___ (9)

Plants (and/or Supplier(s) Involved ___Plant A & Supplier XYZ___ (5) Page ___ of ___

P = Probability (Chance) of Occurence (1)
S = Seriousness of Failure to the Vehicle (2)
D = Likelihood that the Defect will Reach the Customer (3)
R = Risk Priority Measure (PxSxD) (4) (5)

1 = very low or none 2 = low or minor 3 = moderate or significant 4 = high 5 = very high or catastrophic

(10) NO.	(11) PART NAME, PART NO. & PROCESS	(12) FUNCTION PART & PROCESS	(13) FAILURE MODE	(14) MECHANISM(S) & CAUSES(S) OF FAILURE	(15) EFFECT(S) OF FAILURE	(16) CURRENT CONTROLS	(17) P.R.A.				(22) RECOMMENDED CORRECTIVE ACTION(S)	(23) ACTION(S) TAKEN	(24) P.R.A.				(25) RESPONSIBLE DEPARTMENT (INDIVIDUAL)
							(18) P	(19) S	(20) D	(21) R			P	S	D	R	
1	Tube - Rear Axle Housing - 2562-xx	Support to rear axle assy	• Fracture	• Inadequate wall thickness	• Loss of rear brakes/loss of vehicle control	None	2	5	5	50	Run general and rough road durability at minimum thickness	Product change to increase wall thickness Approval 4/83	1	5	3	15	EQ&R (J.L. Smith) SQA (J.L. Smith)
				• Inadequate material		None	1	5	5	25	Material's engineering approval required before drawing release	Approved 6/83	1	5	2	10	Engg. (J.J. Smith)
			• Loose press fit to center section	• Tolerance stack-up		Spec. 2562	3	5	5	75	Revalidated as minimum thickness	Product change to increase tube O.D. by .062 Approved 6/83	1	5	2	10	SQA (J.L. Smith) EQ&R (J.J. Smith)
			Yield	• Improper mat'l.	• Accel brg. wear • Improper vehicle attitude	None	1	3	5	15	Material's engineering approval required before drawing release	Same as earlier	1	3	2	6	Engg. (J.J. Smith)
				• Inadequate wall thickness		None	2	3	5	30	Same durability test as listed earlier	Same as earlier	1	3	3	9	EQ&R (J.J. Smith) SQA (J.L. Smith)

84-485-2100

Figure 3-3. An example of a design failure mode and effects analysis.

(Courtesy of Chrysler Corporation)

SUPPLIERS

In many companies, suppliers contribute up to 70% of the value of the product. This indicates that the success of a company is linked to its suppliers. The suppliers are really an extension of the company and partners in the effort. In recognition of this, some companies award long-term contracts and sole supplier status. The procedure used to select suppliers is critical. This procedure should require on site surveys of the supplier to find out if parts can be made with needed quality. Results of this should be checked against the quality history of the supplier and the experience of other customers. A form used by a major company to evaluate the quality systems of suppliers of tools and equipment can be found in the Appendix.

All engineering, production, and quality requirements should be mutually agreed to by the supplier and purchaser. These requirements must be documented in contract specifications, drawings, and purchase orders.

The responsibility for the quality of the material purchased should be placed on the supplier. This matches responsibility for quality with the entity that has control of it. Where suppliers also design the part, they usually assume the responsibility for performance and durability objectives. The supplier also may furnish prototype parts for the development phase. A joint agreement on the changes required in the supplier's quality system should be reached before buying prototype production parts.

The quality capability of each supplier should be periodically reevaluated. Source surveillance visits also should be scheduled based on observed incoming quality performance. How the supplier is faring on a formal supplier rating system also may help in deciding the timing of visits. Other factors to be considered are the complexity of the item and the quantity purchased. Some companies have found formal certification of the quality system of a supplier to be effective in maintaining high quality. A clear agreement is necessary about the methods by which conformance to requirements will be verified for incoming material. In the initial stages of production, a special procedure may be necessary to qualify the supplier's production process. For regular shipments, conformance could be based on quality information from the supplier. Verification of this information can be done by several means. For example, the purchaser may audit by doing inspections at the supplier, or audit by occasionally doing receiving inspections.

Disputes with suppliers should be handled in a businesslike manner. Talking before problems occur can reduce conflicts.

MATERIAL

Many product quality problems can be traced to improper handling and storage during the shipping of material from suppliers. It also happens during manufacturing of the product and shipment to the customer. The risk of damage continues until the product is placed into service. Damage is caused by many things, such as vibration, shock, and even vandalism. It can be reduced by planning and use of special shipping containers.

Another factor in reducing damage is clear and detailed written procedures for handling, packing, and storing. To minimize further problems, controls must be in place so damaged goods are not used.

Identification of the product should be on the shipping carton or container and on the product itself. The marking should be legible, durable, and remain intact for a reasonable time. This identification, with adequate records, helps in tracing the location of the product, should it require repair or recall. Doing this cuts the number of product recalls and unhappy customers.

MANUFACTURING

If marketing and the product development teams are successful, manufacturing needs only to make the product to the drawing. Products made by manufacturing to properly developed designs and specifications will meet the needs of the customers.

To help get consistent quality, there should be a "manufacturing quality plan" (MQP). The plan is part of the quality business plan previously mentioned. It differs in that it is specific to a product and is very detailed. The plan shows who has responsibility and authority for various tasks. It lists quality objectives, acceptance criteria, and timing. Also included are details concerning processing, tools, gages, and equipment. Specific procedures are covered for process validation methods, specific testing, and in-process controls. Also included are gage controls, inspection needs, and auditing methods. In addition, the plan addresses the activities of the quality system for that product. The MQP is designed to match system responsibilities with control and accountability. For example, manufacturing has to make the part to the design. In this context, manufacturing is held responsible for the quality of the product. Production operators, not inspectors, do SPC charts. The operator can most quickly adjust the process or get the machine or tooling fixed.

The plan must address problems found during design validation. The need for preventing a potential failure mode is pointed out on the DFMEA. Prevention may be by design of the processes, control of the processes, or inspections.

After doing a DFMEA, some companies use a "failure prevention analysis" (FPA) to pinpoint where action by manufacturing is necessary. Means are then identified to prevent the failure modes from occurring. Other companies use a method known as "seriousness classification of characteristics" to find out the critical features of the design. Controls are placed in the process for the critical features. These classifications typically fall into three or four categories. A typical classification method is shown in Table 3-2 on the next page.

Another valuable input into the MQP is the process failure mode and effects analysis (PFMEA). This technique checks the manufacturing process for potential failure modes and their causes. Its purpose is to identify and eliminate potential failure modes in the process. If this cannot be done, the objective is to minimize the risk of those failure modes remaining.

Table 3-2. A Typical Seriousness Classification of Characteristics

Type	Title	Description
I	Critical	Could cause safety consequence or complete loss of function.
II	Serious	Could cause major degradation of function or major loss in appearance.
III	Moderate	Could cause degradation of function.

Actions that may be taken include process redesign, process control, and changes in the design of the product. Figure 3-4 shows a PFMEA form; a blank form is in the Appendix.

Another key input for the MQP is current capability studies on the machines and processes being used. A capability study helps find out if tolerances can be met. An example is in Appendix A. This information can help in deciding where new or rebuilt equipment and tools are required. Process and machine capability studies are discussed in Chapter 2 of Tool and Manufacturing Engineers Handbook (Fourth edition), Volume 4.

Gage capability studies also help in deciding if new or rebuilt gages are required. A gage capability study finds the reproducibility and repeatability of a gage. When inspection and testing equipment are part of production equipment, gage capability studies also must be done. Validation of the process and gages is scheduled prior to start of production. This ensures that the process can make the product. It also provides confidence that the gages are capable of checking the product to specifications. Process and gage validation is much broader in concept than process or gage capability studies. Often, it includes product durability and functional testing. Also, an intense check of the readiness of the entire quality and manufacturing system is done at this time. When the process and gages have been successfully validated, production can begin.

Controls during production should proceed according to the MQP. The quality system should guarantee that the required production operations are done in the specified manner and sequence. Documented work instructions should define what each operator must do. These instructions also contain the criteria for quality standards. SPC charts should be used by production operators to help reduce variability on critical dimensions. The use of SPC charts is discussed in Chapter 2 of TMEH, Volume 4.

PROCESS
FAILURE MODE AND EFFECTS ANALYSIS

Subsystem/Name _____ *Axle Housing*

Model Year/Vehicle(s) _____ *1990*

Primary Design Responsibility _____ *Power Train*

Other Depts Involved _____ *SQA Manufacturing, Process & Reliability*

Plants (and/or Supplier(s) Involved _____ *Chrysler and Tubing Supplier*

Final Design Deadline _____ *December 1986*

Prepared by _____ *A.B. Jones*   Signature _____

Reviewed by _____ *A.B. Smith*   Signature _____

FMEA Date (Orig.) *3/15/86* _____ (Rev.) *5/15/86*

P = Probability (Chance) of Occurence

S = Seriousness of Failure to the **Vehicle**

D = Likelihood that the Defect will Reach the **Customer**

R = Risk Priority Measure (PxSxD)

1 = very low or none   2 = low or minor   3 = moderate or significant   4 = high   5 = very high or catastrophic

NO.	PART NAME PART NO. & PROCESS	FUNCTION PART & PROCESS	FAILURE MODE	MECHANISM(S) & CAUSES(S) OF FAILURE	EFFECT(S) OF FAILURE	CURRENT CONTROLS	P.R.A.				RECOMMENDED CORRECTIVE ACTION(S)	ACTION(S) TAKEN	P.R.A.				RESPONSIBLE DEPARTMENT (INDIVIDUAL)
							P	S	D	R			P	S	D	R	
13	-Axle tube -T1234 -Grinding operation -Centerless grinder no. 2	-Press fit tube for integrity of housing assembly -Grind the O.D. & the corner radius	Oversize diameter	• Measurement error -Master out of calibration -Measuring equipment malfunction -Improper use of gauge	-No build condition -Improper fit -Requires excessive force in assy -Possible flange cracks -High scrap. -Low production -Could reach in the field & fail	-2 pcs. checked per hour -Gauge calibration every two weeks -Inadequate operator training or instructions	3	5	3	45	-Implement X-R chart after proving process potential of CP 1-33 -Check gauge to a master every shift & record the results -Conduct gauge R&R to see if gauge is capable -Train use of gauge & variable chart	-Capability study conducted 6/86 -Operator trained in gauge check & calibration 5/86 -Gauge R&R done. -Gauge improvement order released 6/86	1	5	2	10	-SPC coordinator -Plant quality engineer
				• New operator -Limited set up knowledge -Limited machine knowledge -Overadjustment based on one piece sample -Limited SPC charting knowledge	Same as above.	-Foreman approves the setup -Foreman changes the settings on the machine	3	5	3	45	-OJT with formal SPC training as a prerequisite for job -Display set up instructions on the equipment -Do's & don'ts list	-Operator scheduled for formal SPC 8/86 -Set up instructions posted 7/86 -Do's & don'ts list posted & reviewed with all operators 7/86	2	5	2	20	-SPC training coordinator -Manufacturing & process engineering

Figure 3-4. A form used for process failure mode and effects analysis. *(Courtesy of Chrysler Corporation)*

Special processes, such as chemical cleaning, may affect product characteristics in ways that cannot be easily measured. Checks are made on the equipment used in the special process. Sometimes it may be desirable to provide for operator certification. Also used in these situations are checks on the medium involved in processing, such as solution control for pH.

It is important to control gages and measuring equipment. These checks ensure that the devices are calibrated regularly. Readings from gages and measuring equipment are checked for accuracy using certified standards. The frequency of calibration should be such that each can be adjusted, repaired, or replaced prior to becoming inaccurate. If inaccuracy is found, it may be necessary to recheck items previously processed. Calibration also should be done on gages that are part of production tools and equipment.

Nonconforming material must be kept clearly marked and segregated in a designated holding area. This material may be scrapped, reworked, or returned to the supplier. If the material is reworked, it must be reinspected. Decisions regarding this material should be made by a group of people chosen by management. In some companies, this body is called the material review board (MRB). A major objective of the MRB is to correct problems, and to avoid them in the future.

Changes to the process or gages must be carefully controlled and documented. Changes must be carefully evaluated for their effect on quality. Any revisions should be documented in the MQP. Also, the need for revalidation of the process or gages prior to implementation must be determined. Inspection may be classified as receiving, in-process, or final. Testing also may be done during each of these steps. As mentioned previously, receiving inspection is one of several ways of verifying the supplier's performance. If receiving inspection is done, the use of acceptance sampling is normally preferred. Records of a supplier's quality history help decide the level of inspection required. Tests, such as chemical analysis, also may be done at this time. A receiving inspection facility should have quarantine areas for both unchecked and rejected material. This prevents their accidental use in production.

In-process inspection or testing should be used at critical spots in the process. Checks should be close to the point of processing. Often, inspection is done by the machine operator. Results may be used to make SPC charts and keep the machine in adjustment. It also may be done automatically by a machine. The automatic checking stations could drive adaptive controls that minimize variability. For more information on automatic gaging and process control, refer to Chapter 3, "Inspection Equipment and Techniques," of TMEH, Volume 4.

Often used prior to starting production is setup and first piece inspection. Although diminishing, there are still applications where fixed inspection stations are placed at intervals throughout the process. Also, applications still exist where roving inspectors monitor specified operations.

SERVICE

When the customer or user receives the product, it should be accompanied by instructions for use, such as owners' manuals. Assembly instructions are usually necessary when the product is delivered in kit form. Other products need warning labels. These help prevent misuse or misapplication of the product. This material should inform the user in "plain" English.

Product revisions should be validated, as was done on the original product, to ensure that the revision yields the desired results. Special tools required for installation should be easily obtained.

Means for servicing the product should be provided. It should be easily maintained. Necessary parts and materials for maintenance should be readily available. This ensures a minimum of downtime for the user. A service manual, for which the procedures have been validated, should be available. The user should be informed of service facilities and how to obtain parts. Special tools required for service should be readily available and validated that they will do the task. Measuring and testing equipment used in installation and servicing should meet the same standards as production equipment. It must also be maintained and calibrated with the same diligence as the equipment used in production.

Timely and meaningful information on field failures and customer perceptions should be fed back to appropriate parties in the company. At least some users should be contacted after receiving the product, to learn if their quality and performance expectations were met.

Continual feedback from users should be analyzed for significance. This means summarizing data in various ways. Summarizing could be by product or type of application. The information for this summary can be obtained from such things as the failure analysis of returned materials, service contact reports, and complaints. A separate tracking system may be necessary sometimes for the evaluation of the safety performance of the product. Other feedback may be available from trade associations, government bodies, or insurance companies. This information should help in efforts to prevent problems from recurring.

AUDITS

Audits must be done to help find where improvements can be made. These audits should evaluate the effectiveness of the quality system. Other audits, such as on product quality, are also regularly conducted by all companies. In many companies, auditing is done by those in the quality function.

The next chapter discusses what continuous improvement means.

BIBLIOGRAPHY

"An Automotive Systems Approach." Automotive Engineering, February 1989.

Burke, Michael I., "How Quality is Factored in the Design Process."
Automotive Engineering, October 1989, p. 65.

Cary, Mark et al., "The Customer Window 1986." Quality Progress, June 1987,
p. 37.

"General Motors Statistical Process Control Manual." General Motors
Corp.

Juran, J.M., Editor, Quality Control Handbook, 4th ed. New York: McGraw
Hill, 1988.

Peach, Robert W., ISO 9000 Series Quality Management and Quality Assurance.
Milwaukee: American Society for Quality Control, 1990.

Principles of Quality Cost, 2nd ed. Milwaukee: American Society of Quality
Control, 1990.

"Quality Systems Terminology." American National Standards
Institute/American Society for Quality Control (ANSI/ASQC) A3-1987.

TESQA, Tooling and Equipment Quality Assurance. Detroit: Chrysler Corp.
January 1989.

Veilleux, Raymond F. and Wick, Charles, Tool and Manufacturing Engineers
Handbook, 4th ed., Volume 4: Quality Control and Assembly. Dearborn, MI:
Society of Manufacturing Engineers, 1984.

CHAPTER 4

CONTINUOUS QUALITY IMPROVEMENT

In this chapter. . .

BROAD CONCEPT OF CONTINUOUS IMPROVEMENT

CURRENT OPPORTUNITIES FOR IMPROVEMENT

FOCUSES OF CONTINUOUS IMPROVEMENT

CONTINUOUS IMPROVEMENT OF ORGANIZATIONS

CONTINUOUS IMPROVEMENT OF PROCESSES

CONTINUOUS IMPROVEMENT OF INDIVIDUALS

INSIGHTS FOR IMPROVEMENT

CUSTOMER SATISFACTION

HUMAN RESOURCE UTILIZATION

QUALITY RESULTS

LEADERSHIP

STRATEGIC QUALITY PLANNING

INFORMATION AND ANALYSIS

APPROACH FOR IMPROVEMENT
1. Plan
2. Do
3. Check
4. Action

Appendix information

Ladder of cultural change A-17

Performance indexing (Courtesy of Charney & Associates, Inc.) A-18

Locating performance measurements worksheet A-19

4
Continuous Quality Improvement

The improvement of quality has been sought by manufacturers for a long time. The path seeking improvement is marked by many thrusts. Some earlier ones started in the 1960s were quality control (QC), quality assurance (QA), and product assurance (PA); then came total quality control (TQC) and company wide quality control (CWQC). Today, there is total quality management (TQM).

Companies in business for any length of time embarked on a series of thrusts to improve quality. Despite these efforts, companies today may spend over one-fourth of their revenue to find and correct quality problems. Because of product failures, customers are getting products not up to par and seeking other sources. The survival of many companies depends on correcting this situation.

BROAD CONCEPT OF CONTINUOUS IMPROVEMENT

The concept of continuous improvement is the strategy that companies must adopt. Knee-jerk reactions to problems are no longer sound. It is an established fact that inspection has little effect on quality. Companies must be involved in an ongoing effort to seek better levels of performance. Once new levels are reached, the effort must continue toward the next level. The journey for continuous improvement is expected by many to last forever.

Improvement efforts must be broad and applied to everything. Continuous improvement is far more than just improving the quality of products. For example, it could relate to improving cash flow through better customer billing methods, or reducing the lead time required to develop a product. Quality improvement is only part of the broader improvement effort. Continuous improvement mandates that there must be a basic change in the way that we think, learn, govern and operate any organization. Many efforts of the past to improve quality were fruitless because this basic change did not happen.

CURRENT OPPORTUNITIES FOR IMPROVEMENT

The MIT Commission on Industrial Productivity recently made some profound findings about American industry. They relate directly to why past thrusts for improvement did not fulfill hopes.

First, the commission found that many American organizations have outdated strategies. These companies still have a short-term focus. Near-term results, such as sales targets next month, are the sole consideration, instead of improving the processes that allow the outcomes to be possible. Quality is often not considered unless problems occur. Long-term plans to improve quality are not developed. Companies that are making great strides in competitiveness recognize that quality is a driving force in strategic planning. These companies also recognize that change requires a large effort over a long time.

Second, the commission found that cooperation among departments is lacking in many companies. Because of this, solutions may be developed that may not be the best decisions for the company. They may only be best for the department that is most persuasive. For example, the company may have a design that is very appealing, but it cannot be produced without extensive rework. With little accord between product design and manufacturing, the company is stuck with a big problem. If the functions worked more closely together, the design might be modified to be easier to make and still attractive to the customer. Some companies are using teams made up of members from various functions; these teams are very successful in breaking down barriers among departments.

Third, the commission discovered that many companies did not take full advantage of the abilities of their personnel. Companies that involve their entire work force in decision-making are making giant strides in improving competitiveness. Those not committed to employee involvement find that solutions often are not successful. Workers on the factory floor probably know more about the causes of problems than those in the offices. Not seeking the help of the workers on the floor is often fatal. In the past decade, there were companies that felt that technology alone was the answer. Now, it is widely believed that gains made through employee involvement are greater.

A fourth observation by the commission was that there are too many functional illiterates in the work force. This was felt to be due to an obsolete educational system. By upgrading the level of literacy, a company can improve its ability to compete. Many companies are working with schools to improve the situation. Meanwhile, other companies are investing sizable training funds to upgrade the math and reading levels of workers on the payroll. Other specialized training, such as SPC, is being done on a vast scale.

FOCUSES OF CONTINUOUS IMPROVEMENT

The most successful continuous improvement efforts do not focus on the product. This approach has not worked well in the past. Improvements were generally short-lived and not effective, because permanent solutions were not obtained. Permanent solutions often require a basic change in how the business is run. This involves both business processes and company organization.

Today, it is thought that continuous improvement can be obtained by focusing on three factors: the organization, the processes involved with the organization, and concerned individuals. Processes can be classified as business or manufacturing. Figure 4-1 shows this relationship. These three factors are the real focuses of improvement. Collectively, they make up the system that influences the quality of the product.

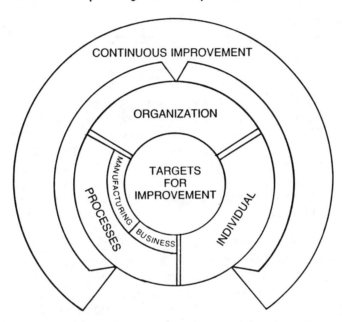

Figure 4-1. Relationship of targets for continuous improvement.

The focuses exist both inside and outside a company. For example, a supplier is external to a company. In reality, the supplier is part of the organization that influences quality. Recognizing this, many companies refer to a supplier as a partner. The processes used by the supplier extend to and are integral with those in the buying company. Individuals from the supplier are concerned in these processes.

The customer, who is also external to a company, plays a critical part in focusing quality direction. If the customer is another company, strong direction is given by the customer's requirements for quality products. For companies selling directly to the consumer market, the direction is more subtle. For these companies, it is critical to seek out the perceptions of customers. A few companies consider customers as part of the organization that influences quality. By doing this, they include the parties that really decide if quality exists.

To show the relationships among the real focuses of improvement--the individual, the processes, and the organization--consider what may happen when a product fails. The scenario can be the same whether the failure occurs in the plant or when the product is used by the customer. If a failure occurs, an improvement is needed in one or more of the focuses.

Assume that a failure happens because an assembly was not put together correctly. Considering the individual, this may be because the operator was not instructed adequately.

Looking at the process, improvements may be needed in both manufacturing and business processes. Perhaps the business process of materials delivery is providing wrong but look-alike parts to the operator. Also, the assembly process may not have the proper fixtures to prevent putting together wrong parts. Another possibility is that the business process of product development did not make a design that prevented incorrect assembly.

Regarding the organization, the culture may be driven around the need to make production schedules despite all obstacles. Because of this, the climate in the company may have led the operator to compromise quality for quantity.

For continuous improvement, efforts must be focused on all three objectives. Past quality improvement efforts focused on the individual after analyzing the product. The individual was usually someone on the factory floor. In the example just given, the operator possibly would be retrained and the problem considered solved; but what happens when the operator is sick or transferred? The new operator may make the same mistake. Although it is important to start with individuals, permanent solutions are often not reached with this approach.

Usually, an individual can provide valuable input leading to permanent solutions. These often require changes in the process and organization. Perhaps a combination of changing fixtures and product design can lead to an enduring solution to the problem. Also, seeking solutions in the process and organization can suggest more individual improvements. Training in design for assembly for a product development engineer may be appropriate. Training in quality for the plant manager may start needed changes in the organization, also.

CONTINUOUS IMPROVEMENT OF ORGANIZATIONS

Many will agree that a drastic change in culture is necessary to improve the organization of most companies. These changes require a big shift in the way things are done. This is the most difficult part of continuous improvement and takes a long time. A few companies started the transition in the early 1980s, and the end is not in sight--but the rewards so far have exceeded the expectations of everyone. Some believe the end will never be reached, because of the need to adapt constantly to the dynamic world that we operate within.

Formally, culture is made up of the values and beliefs shared by most members of an organization. Beliefs are assumptions about what is true. Values are opinions about what is worthwhile or desirable. To survive, there must be a culture within a company dedicated to quality as viewed by the customer. There also must be a dedication to continuous improvement in everything. This culture must have clear values and beliefs driving its behavior, since behavior is the foundation by which the company is managed and seen by everyone.

One way to look at the cultural change required is by seeing it as a ladder as shown in Figure 4-2. This figure is revised and reprinted in the Appendix for further use by the reader. Though described as a ladder, the changes need not be made one step at a time or in the sequence shown. Stages at each step may be pursued together. Also, all the steps may not be necessary and additional steps may be added to meet the unique needs of each company.

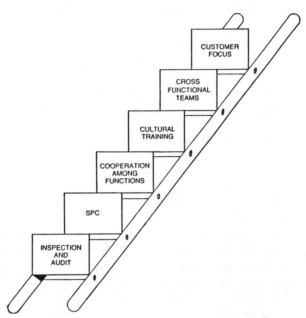

Figure 4-2. Ladder of cultural change in an organization.

To illustrate the cultural change, a hypothetical situation is described. At the bottom rung, a company that relies heavily on inspection and auditing by QC is shown. Little prevention activity to avoid problems is practiced. The company realizes it must change to survive. They know because the companies that they supply told them they must change. At this point, they really have no vision of what they must do. If they did, they would see that they must be customer-driven as shown on the top rung of the ladder.

The company reached the second rung on the ladder when SPC was adopted. The work concerned with SPC was done by QC. It made their customers happy for a while, but the company could see little improvement to offset the added cost. Adjustments were then made in the approach. The work for SPC was shifted from QC to the operator. Some improvements were obtained, but not enough. The company realized that the operator could only correct perhaps 15% of the problems; the rest were due to things that others in the company controlled.

More adjustments were made. Different functions started working more closely together. The company was now on the third rung of the ladder. Responsibility was matched with control by the shift of inspection to manufacturing. Marketing worked closer with product development to help with the design. Engineers from manufacturing got involved with looking at products early in the design phase. Things were getting better for this company, but it was still struggling to survive.

Then management got interested in changing the culture of the company. Other companies involved in this approach appeared to be making progress.

Training was set up for the top people in the organization. The company was now on the fourth rung of the ladder. Top management learned they must be the innovators of change. They must have a vision of what the company should be like. From this vision, they must prepare plans to get there. The most difficult change is in the area of behavior. This must correlate to the values and beliefs required in the new culture. Management's actions will be closely watched by everyone. Others will adjust their values and beliefs according to what they observe.

Top management learned, during the training, that typical values and beliefs of companies involved in a cultural change include:

* The entire organization must focus on customers and their needs. The judgment of the quality of products is in the eyes of the final customer.
* There must be a strong focus by the organization on each employee. Through serving its own employees well, a like behavior is carried over to its customers. Efforts must be made to develop a work force with high motivation.
* There also must be strong emphasis on safety in everything the company does. This includes its products and facilities. Also of concern is the safety of the community in which it resides.
* Prevention of problems must be another area of focus for the company. For this, the company needs to continuously improve the ability of its individuals, processes and organization.
* A strong emphasis must be placed on teamwork. Solutions by a team are usually better than those developed separately.
* There must be total involvement of everyone in an organization regularly. Each employee should participate in problem solving and continuous improvement. Decision-making should be done on the lowest level by those involved in the process. Those closest to problems can make good solutions.
* Every employee in the company must be able to speak the truth without fear of punishment. Continuous improvement efforts will not succeed without open discussions of the issues.

The changing of any company to these values and beliefs is a difficult task. Much patience and persistence is needed. Each process within a company, whether done by blue or white-collar workers, must be looked at and improved. Barriers and resistance to change must be handled delicately. The pace must be such that it doesn't overtax the organization.

After training, management of the hypothetical company decided to plan how they would go ahead. They recognized that changes must start with them. Through their behavior, the right values and beliefs will trickle down through the organization. First on the list was a review of the mission statement to see if it matched the desired values and beliefs. Next, the strategic plan was reviewed to adjust it for required changes. Goals were set for achievement of the needed changes.

In the next step, the organization of the company was reviewed. It was decided that a continuous improvement steering committee was required. This would be made up of leaders of various functional areas. In this way, any conflicts in goals could be resolved. Also, those involved could reach a consensus about the focus of improvement efforts. Finding ways of making the identified improvements would be up to improvement teams.

The improvement teams are made up of members from each functional area. The make-up of each team depends upon the project assigned by the steering committee. Implementation of this approach will allow the company to reach the fifth rung of the ladder shown in Figure 4-2. This is where cross-functional teams are used to obtain improvements.

The company is now one step from the top rung of the ladder--but it is a giant step. The last rung denotes that the desired belief and value system is in place. This means that the behavior of most people in the organization reflects the new culture. Reaching this point takes dedication from everyone. Management must provide leadership in changing behavior. Resources must be provided, particularly for massive and continuous training.

Cross-functional improvement teams must change and fine-tune various processes to reflect the new value system. Most individuals in the company must see the need for change and reflect new values in their behavior. The way this is done is different for each company. There is no "canned approach" to be emulated. Much of it depends on the personalities involved.

The change in culture is worth it. No company has reported that they have completed the change to a new culture. Those that are close report the following results:

* Increased market share. After a long erosion in market share to off-shore producers, Xerox recently regained four points. Independent testers say the reliability of Xerox products has greatly improved. Xerox won the Malcolm Baldrige National Quality Award in 1989 for improvement of quality.
* Cost reductions. The Signets Company reported that over four years they saved one-third of pretax profits because of quality improvements. For every dollar invested, seven dollars were saved.
* Lower throughput time. One company reported that time between order placement and shipment to the customer was significantly reduced. For this company, quality improvements cut this time from two weeks to four days.
* Management is easier. As errors are eliminated, one company found that precious time and resources are saved. Plans can be made and executed without time out for "firefighting."
* Communications are better. Feedback is sought for making improvements and is more objective. Personal attacks and infighting were at a minimum in one company.
* Employees are happier. One company reported that all employees feel that they contribute to the improvement of quality and they like it.

CONTINUOUS IMPROVEMENT OF PROCESSES

High priority for making improvements focuses on processes. An organization is made up of many processes, of both a business and manufacturing nature. In general, this is where lasting solutions are best made. Improving the organization is necessary to have the climate favorable for a company to do the right things--but this improvement takes a long time.

For processes, changes that last can be made quickly. Probably 85% of the problems in a company are due to inadequate processes. Much of the necessary improvement is in the business processes, not in those processes making the product. The small remainder of problems can be corrected by working solely with individuals within the processes.

There are surprisingly large numbers of business and manufacturing processes in a company. For the most part, business processes are run by white-collar workers who support selling or scheduling the product. Others are concerned with the design of the product and production equipment. Manufacturing processes are usually run by blue-collar workers who make the product.

Determining how critical a process is may be easier for manufacturing than for business processes. Techniques such as DFMEA and PFMEA can be used for manufacturing processes. A consensus of the members of a steering committee may be the best way of identifying critical business processes. Although there can be a large number of these processes, often less than 30 are critical to a company.

At this point, the steering committee can rate how the company performs on each critical process. One basis for the rating is how each process supports the values and beliefs envisioned for the company. Based on the analysis, specific goals can be assigned for cross-functional improvement teams.

The setting of clear goals that are realistic but challenging is the starting point of quality improvement. Motorola, another winner of the Malcolm Baldrige Quality Award, achieved its goal of a ten-fold increase in quality over a five-year period. Benchmarking the performance of other companies is often useful in setting the goals to a realistic level. For example, a competitor may have 30% fewer field problems. For this company, a reduction in field failures by 30% would be realistic. Achievement of this goal also would be necessary to remain competitive in the marketplace.

Conceptually, a process is an activity that transforms inputs into outputs. Simply, inputs could be people, material, equipment and information. Inputs are mostly received from other processes within a company. The output from each process is either a product or a service. The output is furnished to a customer. Within a company, there are many processes intricately linked together, as shown in Figure 4-3. Each successive process is a customer for the preceding process. In a like manner, the preceding process is a supplier to the following process.

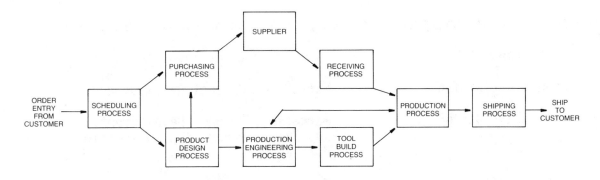

Figure 4-3. The processes within a system for delivering consumer goods.

Collectively, the processes form the system that delivers products to customers of the company. The output of the last process in the chain is delivered to the customer who placed the order with the company. A process is usually represented by an input-output box, as shown in Figure 4-4. Within the process there may be many operations dedicated to making a transformation. These operations may be in several different functions of a company.

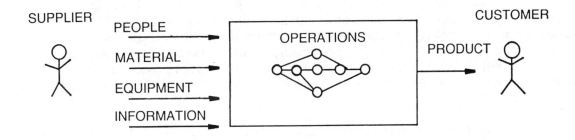

Figure 4-4. Illustration of a conceptual process.

Take, for example, the product design process shown in Figure 4-3. This process is a customer of the scheduling process. It also is a supplier to both the purchasing process and production engineering process. The scheduling process must furnish information about detailed customer needs. How thoroughly this job is done has a lot to do with the effectiveness of the design process. Each process acts as a link in an intricate chain. The chain is only as good as the weakest link. Priority for quality improvement should be given to the weakest link. Reaching solutions is often complex because each process may involve several functional areas in a company. Under these circumstances, no one functional area feels an "ownership" of the process. Usually there is a total lack of ownership, which is why many problems occur.

The operations in the product design process can be viewed simply as:

Step	Functions Involved
1. Product Definition	Marketing, Product Development
2. Preliminary Design	Marketing, Product Development, Suppliers, Production Engineering, Purchasing
3. Design Review	Marketing, Product Development, Suppliers, Production Engineering, Production, Purchasing
4. Validation	Product Development, Quality
5. Final Design	Marketing, Product Development, Suppliers, Production Engineering, Production, Purchasing
6. Release for Production	Marketing, Product Development, Suppliers, Production Engineering, Production, Purchasing

There are seven functional areas involved in the process. Getting an improvement in the process is complex. No one functional area is the natural owner of the entire process. Many companies have solved this dilemma by using cross-functional improvement teams. Members of the team represent each functional area in the process. The team is recognized as the natural owner of the process. Consensus is sought to obtain the best solution for the company.

A popular strategy for improving processes is to evaluate variations in the parameters of the process. This holds true for both manufacturing and business processes. Performance measures are sought for the process to be improved. For a manufacturing process, they may be such things as downtime or level of inventory. A business process such as product design, may make a number of changes after release for production. Changes in design after tooling is complete are usually very disruptive. There is also a large risk of making a mistake.

The performance measures may be chosen at the output of the process. In this way, the measures reflect what the entire process is doing. Appendix 8 shows a worksheet for locating performance measurements. For many companies, the measure of the output is the key issue in process performance.

In a process where operations are done by different functional areas, additional measures may be identified. Usually, these measures are at the interfaces between two functional areas, as shown in Figure 4-5. Many companies have found that most problems occur at these interfaces. Often, these problems are due to confusion between the functional areas about what is required. This confusion can be cleared up in team meetings after being pointed out.

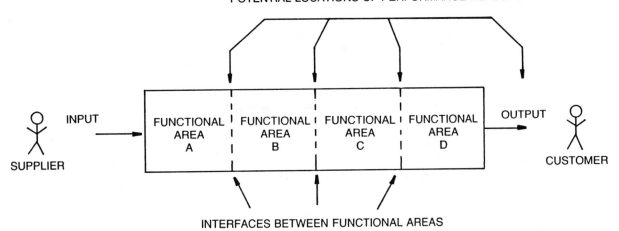

Figure 4-5. Location of performance measures within a process.

Properly selected measures will vary over time. The variation will be
stable if it is due to the inherent nature of the process. It will not be
stable if it is due to something else (such as workers not paying
attention). When plotted on SPC charts, this will be clear.

A major auto producer used this approach in a product design process. There
were 17 designers involved. Management was not pleased with the large
number of design changes after release to production. SPC charts showed
that there was only one designer who needed individual help. The other 16
were victims of the process. Though unacceptable, they could do no better
until the design process was changed. Dramatic improvements came about
through rethinking the process.

This example shows the advantages of improving processes. Without this
analysis, the designers would, rightly, become more frustrated. Pressure
would undoubtedly be used on each designer to improve performance. If the
process was not changed, most of them would fail. They would be unhappy and
productivity would likely suffer.

There are other ways of showing process measures so they can be analyzed for
improvement. Various means of doing this will be discussed in the next
chapter. One of these methods is shown in the Appendix and marked
"Performance indexing."

CONTINUOUS IMPROVEMENT OF INDIVIDUALS

In the past, the major focus for quality improvement was the individual.
The cause of a problem was usually traced to a person, and pressure was
applied for improvement. Sometimes this included disciplinary action. Now,
it is widely recognized that most individuals try to do high quality work,
but are blocked from doing so by the organization or the process they work
within. For example, only a small portion of the problems pointed out by
SPC can be solved solely by the operator. The bulk of the problems require
a change in the process or organization.

To a large extent, individuals mirror the organization or process they work
in. A human receives input, produces the understood output, and changes
actions based upon any feedback, as shown in Figure 4-6.

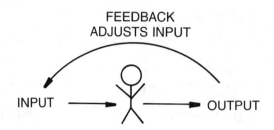

Figure 4-6. How an individual in a process reacts.

To help an individual get high-quality performance, a standard of what is
expected for output is needed. The standard should be customer-driven, and
supported by the process. To develop the standard, it is necessary to
understand what is needed by the customer, how this need can be satisfied
and measured, and the limits acceptable to the customer. This must be
clearly conveyed in some type of documentation. Also desirable in the
standard is what the customer can expect if acceptable limits are not
maintained. Conveying this to the individual is particularly challenging;
feedback to the individual is vital to the improvement of quality. It
can be internal feedback, with individuals checking their output against the
standard, or external feedback from others, particularly customers. Often,
what is shown in the standard may need additional clarification.
Modifications in the resources available to the individual may have to be
made. The way feedback is given is critical. For example, if workers are
struggling with quality problems and management complains that they are
falling behind, the wrong "signal" is given--it may be seen as a strong
statement that getting the product out is more important than quality.

To obtain the best quality, individual strengths should be matched to the
needs of the job. Training should be done before placing a person on the
job. The training objectives should include a clear understanding of the
quality standards and how to measure them. The person also should
understand what must be done if acceptable limits are not obtained. More
companies are insisting that the operation be shut down until quality issues
are resolved. Other important considerations are whether a person is
mentally, physically and emotionally fit to do the job. Additional training
may be in order. Many companies are providing basic math and reading
classes to those who need help. Physical impairments often can be handled
by modifying workstations. In a few situations, it may be that the employee
should be assigned elsewhere. When improvements are required from
individuals during production, the same type of training mentioned above
should be repeated. Talking to the individuals to find out their ideas
could be an immense help. Most often the fix requires changing the process,
not the individual.

INSIGHTS FOR IMPROVEMENT

The Malcolm Baldrige National Quality Award provides insight into what is needed for continuous quality improvement. This award was created in 1987 by U.S. Public Law 100-107. Its purpose is to stimulate and reward companies for improving the quality of their goods and services. The application for the award has guidelines and criteria that can provide a benchmark for companies to judge how they are organized for quality improvement.

The guidelines and criteria form the foundation of an effective improvement effort. As shown in Figure 4-7, there are seven categories of effort supporting continuous improvement; some are considered more critical than others, and are given different points or weights in recognition of this. In reality, an effective effort cannot exist without all seven components pulling together.

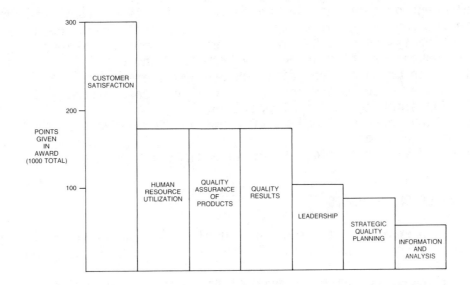

Figure 4-7. Major components of effort for continuous quality improvement.

CUSTOMER SATISFACTION

The component given the largest weight in the award is customer satisfaction. This category accounts for almost one-third of the total points allowed in the award, showing its importance. Criteria about this category reflect how a company addresses customer requirements and service relationships. Key factors are:

* Knowledge of customer requirements and expectations through interviews, surveys and other means. A deep understanding of customers is needed so their wants can be turned into products.
* Effective management and improvement of relations with customers. This would include providing customers with easy access to the company for help. An important element is establishing a long-standing relationship going beyond selling the product.

* Standards for the servicing of customers. This would include response time and other key service performance indicators.
* Commitment to customers on warranties.
* Complaint resolution procedure for customers and feedback of difficulty to company for preventing future problems.
* Measurement of the satisfaction of customers.
* Improvement of customer satisfaction.
* Comparison of customer satisfaction with competitors.

HUMAN RESOURCE UTILIZATION

This category is next in importance. It deals with how a company manages its human resources to reach full potential. Also, it pertains to the involvement of everyone in quality efforts. Major factors concern:

* Human resource planning to support quality goals.
* Involvement of employees in improvement using teams with members from different functional areas and suppliers. Also, providing a suggestion system or other means of making input to management.
* Education and training in quality knowledge and skills. Important is training in problem identification and improvement skills.
* Performance measurements for the identification of teams and individuals making quality improvements.
* Recognition for contributions of teams and individuals by both management and peers.
* Health and safety considerations in quality improvements.

QUALITY ASSURANCE OF PRODUCTS

This category concerns the existence of a quality system within the company for design and control of products. Factors within this category include:

* Customer needs converted to product and process requirements.
* Control of business and manufacturing processes so that products meet design plans or specifications.
* Continuous improvement of products and processes.
* Activity in assessing the quality of products and processes. This concerns both manufacturing and business processes.
* Documentation existing to support the quality system.
* Control and improvement of the quality of the material provided by suppliers.
* A focus on preventing mistakes, not merely correcting them.

QUALITY RESULTS

This category relates to having tangible improvements in terms of quality measures. The measures are derived from customer needs and from business operations. Key factors are:

* Improvement trends in product and service quality measures.
* Comparisons with quality results of competitors.

* Improvement trends in quality measurements of business processes.
* Improvement trends in quality measurements of suppliers.

LEADERSHIP

This relates to the culture of the company. The ability of top management to create values and spread them through the company is a major part of this category. Important factors are:

* Leadership of the senior executives in developing and personally maintaining an environment for quality excellence. This involves such things as being active in the planning, and recognizing achievers.
* Existence of organization values within the company.
* The integration of these values with the management style.
* The extension of quality leadership to the community in which the company resides.
* Reinforcing throughout the company the concept that customer satisfaction is the top company goal and that improving quality is the way to get it. This commitment must run from the top of the organization to the bottom.
* A partnership with customers and suppliers, constantly improving the operation.
* A focus on preventing mistakes.

STRATEGIC QUALITY PLANNING

This category relates to how the company integrates quality into business planning. Also, the existence of both long- and short-range goals is a major factor. Key elements include:

* The existence of quality strategic planning for at least five years.
* Strategic plan includes benchmarking, comparing the performance of the company with the best in the world.
* Existence of quality priorities for both the short and long term. Short-term is less than two years. Long-term is two to five years.

INFORMATION AND ANALYSIS

This component considers the usefulness and management of data that supports the quality system. Major factors are:

* Existence of a database and its use in information systems.
* Analysis of quality data and information.

More information is included in the application guidelines for the Malcolm Baldrige Quality Award. This is available from the National Institute of Standards and Technology, Gaithersburg, MD 20899. The guidelines provide an excellent list of activities needed for a company to achieve continuous quality improvement. For some companies, this may be helpful in getting a vision of what they would like to be. For others, it may be helpful in fine-tuning their quality improvement efforts.

APPROACH FOR IMPROVEMENT

There are many approaches to making improvements. Some are elaborate. Others are very simple. Almost all approaches are tailored to the company using them. Often, these approaches center on the following steps:

* Find the problem to be solved.
* Study the conditions or environment around the problem.
* Develop several solutions to solve the problem.
* Evaluate the solutions to find the best one.
* Implement the best solution and performance measures to evaluate the solution.
* Compare the actual results against the expected results.
* Make adjustments for further improvement.

The steps need not be in order. Certain steps may be done simultaneously. Many popular improvement approaches are based on what is called the Shewhart Cycle shown in Figure 4-8. It is also called the "Plan-Do-Check-Act" cycle after its four stages. This approach is well suited for use by cross-functional improvement teams.

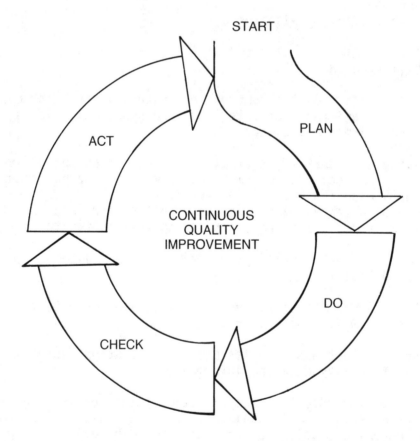

Figure 4-8. One approach to improving quality using the Shewhart Cycle.

STAGE 1 - PLAN. Planning is the first step in achieving improvement. Team members discuss the various opportunities for improvement in a process. Brainstorming techniques are good for identifying potential improvements. A consensus can be reached on what may be the most likely process changes; this may involve modifying the major sources of variation. Data may be collected to increase knowledge about the process and place facts before the team. The questions that must be answered for the team will identify the types of data that are collected.

STAGE 2 - DO. This step starts when the plan for getting the data has been finished. Data is collected. The data should be reviewed by the team when it is available. Often, the original plans are adjusted based upon the preliminary reviews of data. The data are analyzed using graphical and statistical methods to answer the questions raised by the team in Stage 1. The next chapter discusses various methods of analyzing the data. Sometimes help from a statistician or other expert may be needed.

STAGE 3 - CHECK. The results of the analysis in Stage 2 are tested against the knowledge of the team members about the process. Theories about what is happening may be changed so that they are based upon factual observations. Consensus is reached about the theories so that action can be based upon them.

STAGE 4 - ACT. In this phase, team members use the theories to find what changes are supported, then changes are made. The cycle begins again at Stage 1 to check what improvements were caused by the changes. The confirmation is made through data collection and analysis.

The Plan-Do-Check-Act cycle is repeated by the team often, until the process acts in the way it should. Hopefully, each repeat of the cycle will result in continuously improving quality. If setbacks occur, they will be found in the next cycle. Action can be taken quickly to bring the improvement efforts back on track.

The next chapter describes tools that may be used by teams to analyze data to find needed improvements.

BIBLIOGRAPHY

Application Guidelines, Malcolm Baldrige National Quality Award. Washington, DC: National Institute of Standards and Technology, 1990.

Brache, Alan, W. and Rummler, Geary A., "The Three Levels of Quality." Quality Progress, October 1988, p. 46.

General Motors Statistical Process Control Manual. Detroit: General Motors Corp.

Godfrey, Blanton, A., "Strategic Quality Management." Quality Progress.

Harwood, Charles C. and Pieters, Gerald R., "How to Manage Quality Improvement." Quality Progress, March 1990, p. 45.

Jaehn, A.H., "Using the Malcolm Baldrige National Quality Award Criteria to Assess a Company's Quality Program." Tappi Journal, May 1990.

Juran, J.M., Editor, Quality Control Handbook, 4th ed. New York: McGraw Hill, 1988.

Juran, J.M., "The Quality Trilogy." Quality Progress, August 1986, p. 19.

Linkow, Peter, "Is Your Culture Ready for Total Quality?" Quality Progress, November 1989, p. 69.

Main, Jeremy, "How to Win The Baldrige Award." Fortune, April 23, 1990, p. 101.

Moen, Ronald D. and Nolan, Thomas W., "Process Improvement." Transactions. Milwaukee: American Society for Quality Control, 1987.

Sullivan, L.P., "The Seven Stages of Company Wide Quality Control." Quality Progress, May 1986.

TESQA, Tooling and Equipment Quality Assurance. Detroit: Chrysler Corp., January 1989.

Total Quality Management, 1st ed. Dearborn, MI: American Supplier Institute, 1989.

CHAPTER 5

TOOLS FOR CONTINUOUS QUALITY IMPROVEMENT

In this chapter. . .

TOOLS FOR ANALYSIS DURING DESIGN

BENCHMARKING

QUALITY FUNCTION DEPLOYMENT

DESIGN FOR MANUFACTURING

DESIGN OF EXPERIMENTS

FAILURE MODE AND EFFECTS ANALYSIS

VALUE ANALYSIS

TOOLS FOR ANALYSIS DURING PRODUCTION
1. Natural or Random Variation
2. Not Natural or Not Random Variation

PROCESS FLOW CHART

PARETO CHARTS

CHECK SHEETS
1. Attribute Check Sheet
2. Location Check Sheet
3. Variable Check Sheet

CAUSE AND EFFECT DIAGRAMS
1. Environment
2. Organization
3. Measurements

STRATIFICATION CHARTS

SCATTER DIAGRAMS

HISTOGRAMS

CONTROL CHARTS

OTHER TOOLS

Appendix information

Pareto diagram (Courtesy of Charney & Associates, Inc. A-20--A-22

Variable control chart (Courtesy of Ford Motor Company) A-23--A-24

Attribute control chart (Courtesy of Ford Motor Company) A-25--A-26

Force field analysis worksheet
(Courtesy of Charney& Associates, Inc.) A-27

Criteria analysis worksheet
(Courtesy of Charney & Associates) A-28

5

Tools For Continuous
Quality Improvement

This chapter discusses the tools used in continuous quality improvement.
These are the tools that manufacturing professionals should know for
analysis. Not all the tools will be needed each time. The key to their
effective use is the ability to select the proper one for the occasion.
Proper selection means that the time spent will be more productive.

Some tools are useful for analysis in the design phase. In reality, the
design of the product is the first manufacturing step. There is an integral
relationship between design of the product and design of the process. A
company cannot meet quality objectives with isolated design and
manufacturing operations. Product design and process planning must be
integrated in one common activity, usually a product development team.

Just what is a good design is a fair question at this point. A study of
many successful designs revealed that there are two basic concepts that
embody a good design. The first relates to functions needed by customers.
In a good design, each function is satisfied by some aspect, feature, or
component within the design. The second concept concerns simplicity. It
was found that good designs provide the required functions without undue
complexity.

Use of a team helps make sure that decisions are based upon a wide
foundation of knowledge and experience. To avoid being trapped into bad
designs, decisions that cannot be changed easily are not made by the team
until absolutely required. The objective of the team is to match the
process to the product design so that all needs and requirements are met in
the best way. From a processing outlook, a major goal is to have a product
that is easy to make.

There are many issues to be dealt with by the team. They include how to
translate customer needs into the design of the product. This must be
matched with how the product will be made. Also dealt with are the
organization structure and many administrative procedures. This is a
complex undertaking for the members of the team. Obviously, how it is
handled differs among companies, but concepts are likely to be similar.
Typical concepts are shown in Figure 5-1. This illustrates the iterative
nature of the team approach to design. This is a big change from the step
by-step approach used in the past by isolated functions in a company.

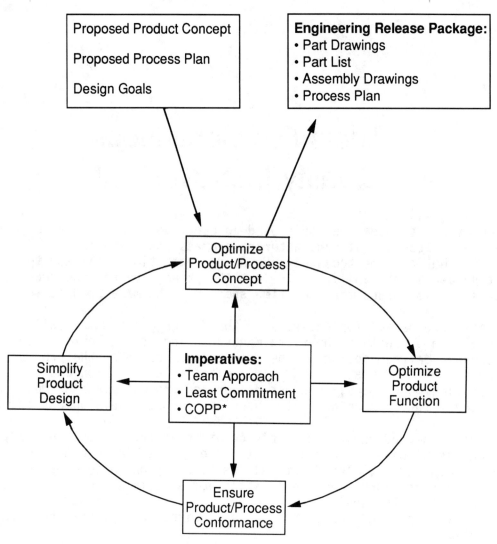

Figure 5-1. Typical DFM process. *(Copyright 1988. Industrial Technology Institute)*

* Continuous Optimization of Product and Process

The team design approach likely starts with developing a concept of the product and the process to make it. Also, a set of design goals for the product and the process is developed at this time. Four major activities, iterative in nature, critique the concepts and design goals:

1. The first activity is directed toward optimizing the product and process concepts. The objective is to make processing easier by matching the needs of both concepts.
2. A second activity simplifies the design of the components for ease of assembly and handling.

3. The third activity deals with matching the design to process needs. A simple example would be providing locating holes for welding brackets to another part.
4. The fourth activity concerns the selection of the right materials to optimize the functions required by the customer.

The deliverable result of this approach is a complete package for the engineering release of the design of the product and the process. This approach has an immense advantage--it minimizes surprises when the product goes into production. Another important byproduct is that all parties share equally in ownership and commitment to the final plans.

The design phase is the best place to plan improvements. Solving problems at this stage prevents costly "firefighting" when production starts. Designs on paper can be changed and justified easily. There is no expensive remachining of tools and equipment required. The savings from the improvement start on the first day of production. Of course, the major benefit of doing it here is that customers likely will be more satisfied. They will soon learn they do not need to be suspicious of the first products off the line.

If time for getting designs done is short, there may be a reluctance to use these tools for needed analysis. There is plenty of time to fix problems after they happen. So, why shouldn't there be time to get problems solved before they occur? This is a powerful argument for taking the time during the design phase.

Other tools are chiefly used for analyzing problems in production. These are for improving customer satisfaction and reducing failure costs. Many concern ways of studying data to focus efforts. The integrity of the data must be sufficient so as not to mislead those using it. Data helps put a reason behind a decision. Where teams are involved, data aids in reaching a consensus among the members. Some say reasonable people given the same facts reach almost the same conclusions.

TOOLS FOR ANALYSIS DURING DESIGN

In the past, product design engineers did not work closely with manufacturing, but this has since changed in most companies. Now, those in manufacturing are at least involved in design reviews. This is done regularly so changes can be made before production starts. Changes may be in both the product and the process.

Many companies do simultaneous engineering, where the product and process are developed together. Product development teams have members from each discipline involved. It is likely that manufacturing will play a big part on these teams. Members will suggest ways in which the consumer will receive more value. This will include changes in the way the product is designed and processed.

For the most part, basic designs are final before production starts, but changes do occur after production. Often, they are disruptive. Some are applied like bandages--they attempt to adjust for mistakes in judgment. Some changes are successful. A few are followed by a series of other changes with no real resolution. The mistakes show up as rework and scrap inside the plant or at the supplier. Those not caught and corrected show up as warranty problems and unhappy customers.

Sometimes, failures in production are due to features of the parts or assembly. The parts may be too difficult to make. For example, radii may be too small to process a part in a draw die without cracking. Also, tolerances may be too tight for the variability of the process being used.

Assemblies also may be too hard to make. Parts may not be self-aligning with mating parts. Symmetrical parts could be inserted in the reverse direction. Another example is that joining methods may be such that the integrity of mating surfaces is in doubt. Not allowing for adverse conditions in the design during assembly also can cause failure. For example, it may not be possible to wash out soldering flux trapped in a crimped joint.

Other problems arise when the assembly is too complex. Designs that must be adjusted during or after assembly increase the chance of errors. Also, there may be more parts than necessary to do the job for the customer. Many parts will increase the chances of an assembly error. The errors could range from the wrong parts used to missing parts. Also, a high number of parts can cause scheduling problems. The chance of part shortages will be increased; inventories will be higher than necessary. For those using Just-in-Time (JIT) inventory concepts, the concepts will be harder to apply.

Other causes of scrap and rework are due to problems in handling or storage. The design may be very frail and easily damaged. Perhaps costly storage containers may be needed. Without proper treatment of materials, corrosion or other contaminants also could be a big problem during storage.

The following general design guidelines for quality improvement can be a big help in dealing with the problems just reviewed:

1. Design should provide only functions needed by the customer.
2. Design of product and process should be done simultaneously.
3. Assemblies should have the least possible number of parts.
4. Versions of similar parts should be at a minimum.
5. Adjustment provisions in designs should be avoided.
6. Assembly procedure should be easy.
7. Parts can only be assembled correctly.
8. Well-understood, reliable processes should be used where possible.
9. Tolerances should match inherent process capability.
10. Design should allow function and performance tests.
11. Design should be sturdy to survive handling and shipping.
12. Goal for design changes after release should be zero.

The problems just discussed can be reduced by the involvement of manufacturing at the very beginning. The best way to accomplish this is by being a member on a product development team. The team must meet regularly. By this close and intense relationship, the inherent manufacturability of the product will be greatly improved. The tools discussed in the chapter can help the team and the manufacturing members. The tools help identify the changes needed in basic design. If changes in the design are not possible, then perhaps processing can be changed. By this approach, time is available to plan ways to get around obstacles.

The more complex tools for improvement require specialized training for most people. This may be from someone else in the company who is trained in using the tool, or it may require attending courses offered outside the company. Alternately, some may find enough information in specialized books and papers on the subject. Other tools may be obvious to some people and require little or no additional training. Some tools that may be useful to a product development team, and particularly those in manufacturing, are:

BENCHMARKING. Through benchmarking, a company observes the traits of another company and its products. Where possible, traits are expressed in numerical terms. As an example, a company may have 95% satisfied customers with a certain product. The strengths of the other company and its products often become the baseline for goals of the observing company. If the other company or product is a competitor, its weaknesses become targets to gain a competitive advantage.

Normally, the company observed is a competitor, but a company looked on as the best in performing a certain task also may be of interest. For example, a manufacturing company may want to improve shipping. It may visit a mail order firm to get ideas and help in setting goals.

A major advantage of benchmarking is that the baseline for the goals to be set is realistic. It is realistic because other companies are doing it now. Another big advantage is that what it takes to be competitive is defined in numerical terms. Being numerical, it is easy to gage progress.

A company can shoot for beating or just meeting its competition. Just meeting the competition poses a danger. The competitor is likely improving too. Goals should be set at least high enough to allow for the projected improvement of competition.

Benchmarking is useful for all activities of a company. For the product development team, it can be used to establish design goals and fine-tune concepts for both the product and process. Some ways that this information can be obtained are:

1. Customer clinics where proposed new products and competitive products are critiqued by customers.
2. Mail and telephone surveys of users of products similar to that proposed. This would include critique of products from the company and the competition.
3. Independent testing agencies asked to evaluate a proposed product against products from competitors.
4. In-house teardown and testing of products from competitors for comparison against the proposed product.
5. Questioning the distributors and retail sales agents of similar products.
6. Public information from magazines, government publications, and trade shows.
7. Visits and discussions with other companies.

In seeking this information, legal and ethical implications should be carefully thought out. Through asking the right questions and thoroughly evaluating the results, much insight will be gained. Numerical goals based upon realism can be used for planning the product and process.

QUALITY FUNCTION DEPLOYMENT (QFD). This technique is a way of allowing customer needs and views to be entrenched throughout a company. These are translated into the product design and manufacturing operations. Use of the approach starts with the development of the product. Information from benchmarking about customer needs and desires can help in the initial stage of the approach. If benchmarking is not done, needs of customers found by other means can be used.

First developed in Japan, quality function deployment was introduced to the United States in the mid-1980s. Many approaches to QFD exist. This is due to the unique way that each company applies it. Yet, the concepts are the same though the details differ.

QFD helps a company focus on being customer-driven instead of perhaps technology-driven. The approach improves teamwork among the various activities in a company. Through QFD, activities work together on a new product, often in product development teams. By working together, there is a common understanding of customer needs.

QFD allows each activity to bring expertise into the planning. It also helps obtain consensus on the plans. Sorting large amounts of data for analysis is easier because of the matrix approach used by QFD. After finishing a QFD analysis, what was considered is clearly documented for review by others. Also, the tasks that must be carried out are specific and assigned to entities in the company.

A typical approach for a QFD study is shown in Figure 5-2. The general steps are:

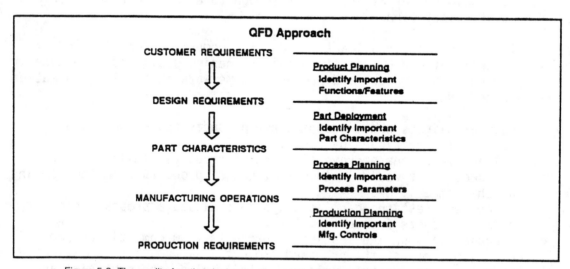

Figure 5-2. The quality function deployment approach. *(Copyright 1989. American Supplier Institute)*

1. Translating customer needs into design requirements such as important functions and features.
2. Changing the design requirements into critical characteristics and specific parts required.
3. Finding the manufacturing operations and critical process traits for the critical characteristics and specific parts.
4. Developing production requirements like manufacturing controls for the manufacturing operations.

An example of the approach is in Figure 5-3. Matrixes placed in series are at the heart of this approach. The first matrix is used for step 1, above. It is commonly called the "House of Quality." The first matrix is where the needs of the customers are entered. This is "what" customers need. Also "how" this will be achieved is entered. "How" is a key feature of the design.

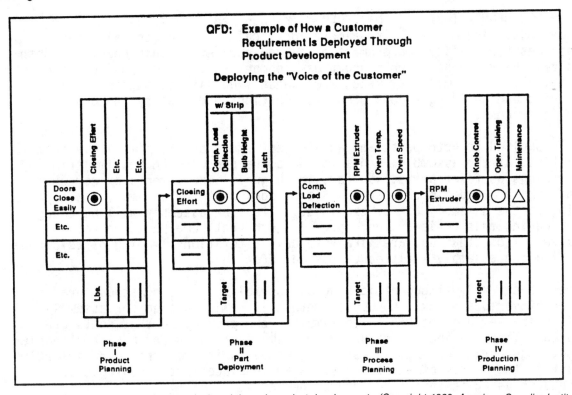

Figure 5-3. QFD: Customer requirement deployed through product development. *(Copyright 1989. American Supplier Institute)*

For the example, "what" is that "doors close easily." This is entered in the left side of the first matrix. The upper side of this matrix is where "how" to provide this is listed. "Closing effort" is "how" it will be done. "Closing effort" is a key feature for the design.

Each matrix in the series has both "what" is needed and "how" it will be done. The "how" of a matrix becomes the "what" of the next matrix. Step 2 in Figure 5-3 starts with copying "closing effort" from the "how" part of the first matrix to the "what" part of the second matrix. "How" to do it is listed on the top side of the second matrix. In this matrix, "how" will be a critical characteristic or specific part. For the example, "how" is compressive load deflection, bulb height and the design of the latch.

The symbols within the matrix denote importance. This is a judgment by the team. Because the latter two items are not very important, only the first "how" is copied to the third matrix as a "what." This starts step 3 in Figure 5-3. The "how" of the third matrix specifies critical process traits. These are the RPM extruder, oven temperature, and oven speed. The team does not think oven temperature is very important. Only the first and last process traits are copied to the "what" part of the fourth and last matrix (only RPM extruder is illustrated). This starts step 4 in Figure 5-3.

In the fourth matrix, controls are specified for the process traits. The "how" section of the example lists knob control, operator training and maintenance for the RPM extruder. Note that the bottom side of the matrixes lists the targets or nominal values for the parameters listed in the "how" section. The Taguchi Method, mentioned later in this chapter, may be useful for finding the right nominal values.

DESIGN FOR MANUFACTURING (DFM). DFM is recognized chiefly as a tool to reduce cost. The concepts are almost identical with the general design guidelines for quality improvement discussed earlier in this chapter. Both involve a heavy emphasis on product development to improve manufacturing. Intuitively, the similarity makes much sense. Quality is obtained by designing and building a good product. Getting good quality is consistent with lower cost.

DFM is applied to both parts and assemblies. Most of the time it is best to look first at the assembly: this is where the product can be simplified by such things as fewer parts. So far, the biggest improvements by companies using DFM were made in this area. After looking at the assembly, each part making up the assembly can be examined. Often, an assembly will be changed a lot during this review. The change is such that some parts do not survive. Those that do, are likely to have alterations. Doing parts after handling the assembly will reduce wasted effort.

There are several methods of looking at assemblies. These methods are called by various names. A popular method is called design for assembly (DFA). The key goal of DFA is to simplify the product so that costs are reduced. This may include reducing the number of parts and making it easier to put together. For example, stacking of parts is preferred over inserting a part in the bottom of an assembly. Snap-in-place parts are suggested instead of using fasteners to secure the parts.

The changes may affect more than cost. They also have a positive effect on quality. With fewer parts, there is less possibility of things going wrong. If the product is easier to put together, chances are that human errors will be reduced. Another advantage is that inventory needs are also significantly reduced, making JIT easier to use. Just-in-Time also has its own positive effect on quality. Defects come to the surface quickly with little inventory. Also, they can be corrected quickly and have less effect on production because there is less inventory.

DFA can be approached manually, or by using PC based software. It has two basic steps:

1. Criteria are applied to find whether parts can be combined or eliminated. This is where the largest contribution is usually made. Simplification can lead to significant improvement. The deliverable from this step is that fewer parts could be needed to give desired functions. Also, this step provides a basis for measuring the quality of design.
2. Costs to put each part into the assembly are estimated for different methods. These include manual, robotic, and automatic assembly. Costs are developed to judge whether changes will make enough savings to be justified. This is a considerable advantage, since this information is often hard to obtain quickly during product development.

Figure 5-4 shows a spindle/housing assembly before DFA was used. It has 10 separate parts. The assembly efficiency was calculated to be 7%. Figure 5-5 shows the deliverable from using DFA. The alternate spindle/housing assembly has only two parts and its assembly efficiency is up to 93%.

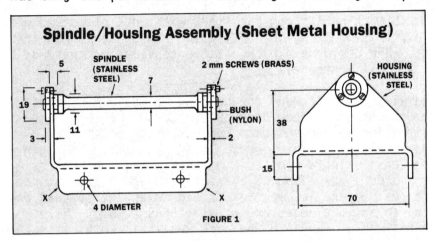

Figure 5-4. This spindle/housing assembly has 10 separate parts and an assembly efficiency rating of 10%.

(Used by permission of Boothroyd Dewhurst, Inc.)

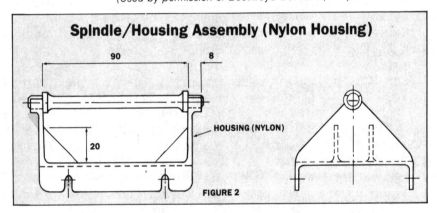

Figure 5-5. The two-part design, utilizing an injection molded nylon housing has an assembly efficiency rating of 93%.
(Used by permission of Boothroyd Dewhurst, Inc.)

For analyzing a part, DFM is often not a rigid procedure. It is highly flexible in nature. The approach is largely based upon the skill and experience of the person or team doing it. Often, checks against established design practices are made. Examples of published design practices are those about forging, casting and forming. These practices may help point out features to be changed to avoid cost. Following these practices also could improve quality by avoiding defects when processing parts. Examples of opportunities for improvement that may be found during DFM of parts are:

1. Surfaces that are called out on designs to be smoother than necessary requiring additional finishing operations.
2. A radius in a formed part too small to be made without cracking.
3. A plastic part with too large a variation in wall thickness inhibiting material flow in injection molding.
4. Holes in a sheet metal part, located too close to a bend line to be made without distortion.

Another use of DFM on a part is to lower material costs through selecting alternatives. A complex task for the DFM of a part concerns matching alternate processes and designs for the best combination. One option for a stepped shaft is to machine it from bar stock with lots of wasted material turned into chips. A second option is to cold head one end and finish machine the rest. DFM could help pick out the best option that may be neither of the two just mentioned.

In the past several years, software for helping in the DFM of parts in the product development phase has been developed. Currently, PC programs are available for injection molded and machined parts. Programs for other types of parts are reportedly being developed. These programs select and compare alternative approaches using a limited amount of detail on the design. They are useful in the product development phase to compare different conceptual approaches where designs are incomplete. A big advantage is that complete details of the parts are not necessary to use the software. More information on this can be found in the book Realistic Cost Estimating for Manufacturing, 2nd Edition, available from SME.

DESIGN OF EXPERIMENTS (DOE). In the product development phase, DOE concepts can be used in many ways. They can, for example, be used to plan experiments for the least number of test runs. Any statistical book will provide details on this and other uses of DOE.

One important use of DOE in product development is to find the nominal values and tolerances that will achieve design goals. The Taguchi Method (TM) is a popular technique for this. Finding the nominal value is called Parameter Design. This is where the performance is made as insensitive as possible to variations of parameters that cannot be controlled easily. Allowance design is where tolerances are found for each parameter. Tolerances are larger where variation has little affect on performance. Tighter tolerances, which are costly, are specified for parameters having variation that greatly effects performance. The premise behind TM is that the amount of variation in the performance of a design is affected much more by some parameters than by others. Also, the amount of variation in performance may possibly be changed by choosing different nominal values.

Tolerances can be relaxed on those parameters without affecting the performance a great deal. See Figure 5-6 for an illustration of this. Some parameters must not vary from the nominal value too much. If they do, there will be a large variation in the performance. For this, the design is said to be very sensitive to the parameter. Such a parameter is labeled "WIDTH" in the illustration. On the other hand, some parameters can vary a great deal from the nominal and have little effect on performance. For this, the design is said to be not sensitive to the parameter. This is shown by "HEIGHT" in the illustration. Tolerances will be tight for the parameter labeled as "WIDTH," but for "HEIGHT," the tolerances can be looser.

In nonlinear relationships, the choice of nominal values has a great effect on how sensitive the design is to a parameter. This is shown in Figure 5-7.

If the nominal value chosen is 0.6 mm, the design performance is not very sensitive to moderate changes in clearance. For that situation, tolerances can be looser. Now, consider what happens if 0.2 mm is now chosen for the nominal. The design performance is now very sensitive to even small changes in clearance. For the new nominal, tolerances will need to be tight.

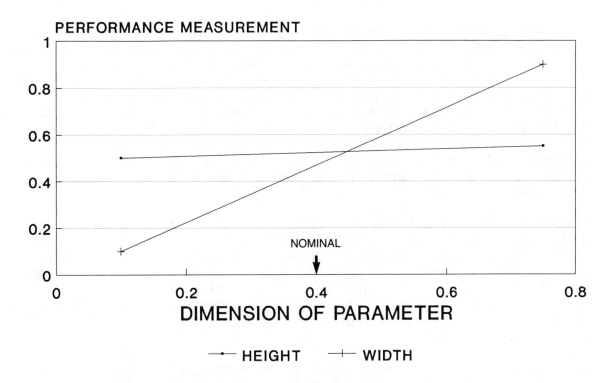

Figure 5-6. Sensitivity of design to parameter: relation of dimension to performance.

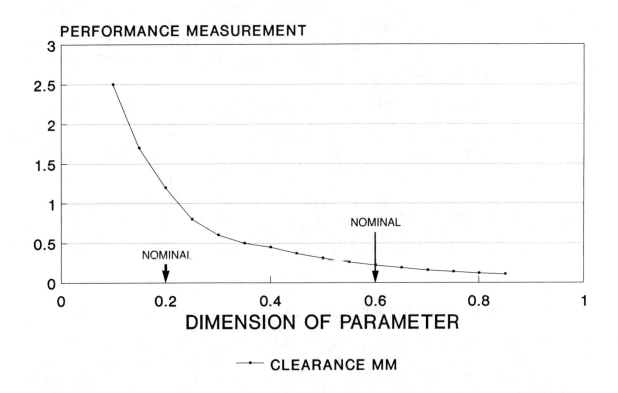

Figure 5-7. Sensitivity of design to parameter: nonlinear effect.

It is important to understand that the tolerances identified by TM are what the design needs. Also important is that the tolerances can be changed, for example, by selecting new nominal values. These tolerances are not necessarily what can be provided by manufacturing. What can be provided by manufacturing is an outcome of process capability studies that were discussed in Chapter 2. TM provides a way of matching the tolerances that the design needs with the tolerances that can be met on the factory floor. Performance on the factory floor also can be improved by a similar TM approach called process parameter design. This approach finds the optimum nominal values and tolerances for each process parameter, such as the temperature of an oven.

FAILURE MODE AND EFFECTS ANALYSIS. This technique provides a way for the product development team to study the causes and effects of failures before designs are completed. Design failure mode and effects analysis (DFMEA) is used for product design. For manufacturing processes, process failure mode and effects analysis (PFMEA) is used. All potential failures are identified. For each failure, the effect is determined. Corrective actions are identified to prevent the failures from occurring. Both DFMEA and PFMEA are discussed in Chapter 3.

VALUE ANALYSIS (VA). A renewed interest in VA occurred in the late 1980s. This is because VA addresses the functions wanted by the customer. Addressing customer needs was recognized as very important during this period. Generally, the product design is methodically examined for providing functions needed by the customer. Functions not wanted by the customer and features not needed are removed from the design. The approach simplifies the product, reducing cost. But besides cost, VA also improves quality. Customer needs are better addressed. The product is more simple and easier to build with fewer failures.

VA focuses on function. Function is described by using a verb and a noun. For example, the function of a cup is to hold liquid. This breaks a problem into simple parts that are more easily handled by a team. Creative ways are used to eliminate unnecessary features and functions. Also looked at are ways to get the necessary functions at a lower cost.

Value of a product is seen as two types: use value and prestige value. Use value describes properties that do the work. Prestige value describes properties that make ownership of the product attractive. Both are important to compete in the marketplace. VA attempts to optimize the value of a product in relation to its cost.

TOOLS FOR ANALYSIS DURING PRODUCTION

There is much data that could be collected during production. Only a fraction that could be collected is gathered, however. Most would agree that even the small amount that is collected is often not useful for making improvements. Computer printouts litter many desks; reporting data that is not used. One reason for this is that it is hard to see the meaning behind the numbers. To understand the meaning, the data needs to be changed to information. This means summarizing and placing in a format that does show meaning.

Regular reports with a fixed format usually do not meet the needs of improvement teams. Teams need narrowly focused information to get started in the right direction. Often, the team collects their data from processes they seek to improve. The tools discussed in this section are for turning the data collected into information useful to the team. For continuous improvement, the data that is collected is driven by the improvement desired. The type and nature of the data changes for each particular situation.

Data can be viewed as either being numerical or not numerical. For this book, data that is numerical is obtained by a measurement. It may be the height in inches of a workpiece, or the hardness expressed in Rockwell C scale. This data is also called "variable data" and is usually used in quality improvement efforts.

Data that is not numerical is thought of as facts. This may be based upon the perception of the person observing the situation. For example, a go-no-go gage either fits the workpiece or it does not fit. The answer is that the workpiece is either good or bad. Note that this does not address how good or how bad, which is possible with numerical data. Data that is not numerical is often called "attribute data."

Variable data is normally the best choice for improvement efforts. It can be used to see how far away actual dimensions are from the desired value. To do this, an understanding of variation is necessary. It is important to realize that there is variation in everything. Some variation is natural. Under the conditions present, natural variation will always occur. Another term for the natural variation is "random variation." The other type of variation is not natural; it is caused by something that may be present. It is not random in nature.

Fundamental for studying and improving processes is understanding that variation has two types of causes:

1. Natural or random variation. The causes of this type of variation are called "common causes." This is due to the conditions present in the process and will occur all the time unless the process is changed. Reducing the variation due to these causes is normally costly. It may include new equipment, dies, or controlling temperature. Once fixed, the variation normally stays reduced.
2. Not natural or not random variation. The causes of this type of variation are called "special causes." These causes are not always present. They generally occur when something does not go right. Examples may be a new operator not trained, wearing or breaking of tools, or adjustments not made when they should be. These causes can usually be eliminated relatively easily. When they are eliminated, only natural or random variation remains. This process is called "stable." "Special causes" may occur again with little warning, so constant vigilance is required.

This concept of variation and its causes questions the traditional notion of a process being either good or bad. With "common causes" the process may be as good as it can be until costly changes are made. "Special causes" can be controlled, stopping chaotic quality problems. The concept focuses on the causes of variation and can provide a basis for improving it.

When "special causes" are removed, the process becomes "stable." When measurements are plotted, they often resemble a normal, or bell-shaped, curve as in Figure 5-8. A "stable" process has the following advantages:

1. It has a predictable performance.
2. Costs and quality are predictable.
3. Productivity is greatest, and costs lowest, unless the process is changed, removing "common causes."
4. Effect of changes in process can be measured more easily, since "special causes" do not confound the results.

In Figure 5-8, the measurements have a central value, called the average or mean value of the measurement. The measurements vary around the average or

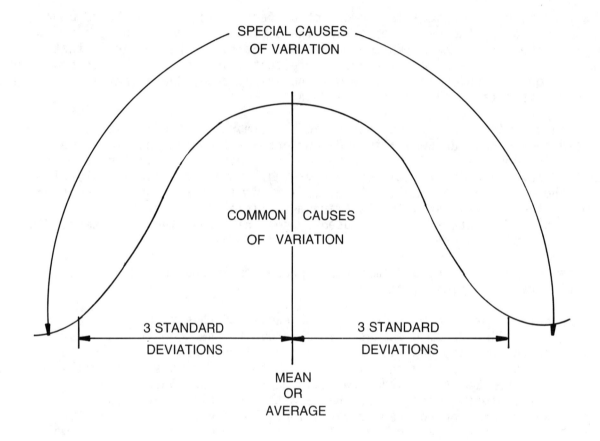

Figure 5-8. A stable process usually has a normal distribution of measurements.

mean value. This spread in the data is called variability. The measures of variability can be range, variance or standard deviation. Range is the difference between the highest and lowest readings. Variance is calculated by the following formula:

$$S^2 = \frac{\Sigma (X - \overline{X})^2}{n - 1}$$

X = individual measurement
$\overline{X}$ = mean value
n = no. of measurements

Standard deviation is the square root of the variance. Often range is used because of its ease in calculation. Range is easily converted by a factor into variance or standard deviation. These factors are discussed under control charts in this chapter.

In a stable process, measurements within plus or minus three standard deviations of the mean or average are considered to be caused by "common causes." To reduce the spread of data in a stable system, the "common causes" must be removed. If there are measurements beyond these limits, the process is not stable. These measurements probably have "special causes." The "special causes" must be removed to make the process stable. This takes constant attention.

Measurements are hardly ever taken on an entire run of the process. More often, a small part of the run is measured. This small part is called a "sample." Usually more than one sample is taken. The sample data is used to make estimates about the entire run of the process. In taking samples, some things must be taken into consideration. Since the sample represents the entire run of the process, it must be picked so that no bias occurs. Also, the sample must be large enough to be meaningful. For SPC charts, at least 12 samples of four to five measurements each are needed to calculate control limits. For single samples, often 30 measurements are needed to estimate the mean and standard deviation.

PROCESS FLOW CHARTS. A simple process flow chart is shown in Figure 5-9. It shows the various steps in a process. This is usually the first step in

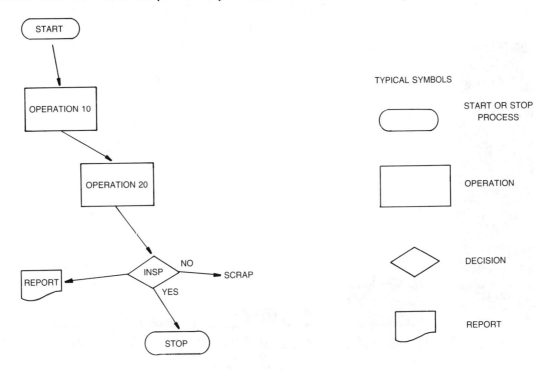

Figure 5-9. Process Flow Chart.

approaching an improvement, and helps a team understand a process. It also helps them decide what they are going to try to improve. The flow chart can help define the extent of the process that will be studied. It also helps define where the starting and stopping points of the process are, and helps the team find the factors that influence the process. Through a detailed process flow chart, such things can be specified as:

1. Where materials and parts come from.
2. The sequence in which the materials and parts are used.
3. The operations and sequence that make up the process.
4. The inspection and testing that is done.
5. Where completed material goes.
6. How scrap and rework are handled.

PARETO CHARTS. Normally, the second step in approaching an improvement is making a Pareto chart. The data for this chart is usually available in the company. The Pareto chart is a bar chart with the bars arranged in decreasing order of magnitude. It provides direction to the improvement team on where to work for the greatest return. A simple Pareto Chart is shown in Figure 5-10. This chart is named after an Italian who in the late 1800s found that all the wealth in his country was owned by just a few people. This concept applies to problems in a company. It is often called the 20-80 rule. This rule states that 20% of the categories will typically account for 80% of the observations. In a plant, for example, 20% of the products are typically found to cause 80% of the problems. A similar relationship is found for many other things. A format for a Pareto Chart is located in Appendix A for the reader's use.

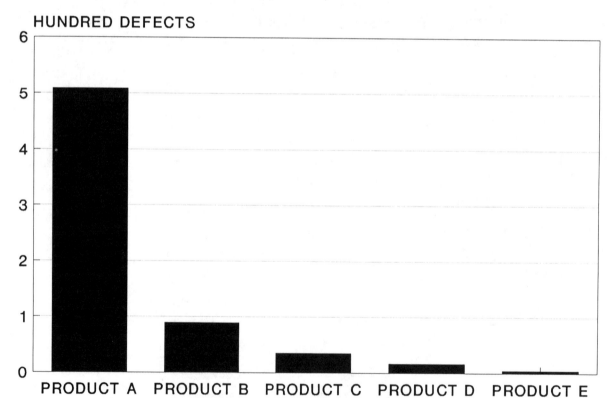

Figure 5-10. Pareto Chart recognizes 20%–80% rule.

In Figure 5-10, product "A" does cause approximately 80% of the problems. Yet, it is only one out of five products, or 20% of the products. This would lead the improvement team to concentrate on product "A" first. By concentrating on only 20% of the products, 80% of the problems are being addressed. Some refer to the 20% of the products as the "vital few" and the remaining 80% of the products as the "trivial many." The "vital few" are the few parts that make up the largest part of the total problems. The "trivial many" are the many parts that account for the small remainder of the problems.

CHECK SHEETS. The next step for an improvement team is to collect data to further define the opportunity for improvement. Check sheets may be used throughout the improvement effort whenever data needs to be collected. Check sheets are made to record the data. Before the check sheets are designed, the following two issues should be thought out:

1. What possibly will be learned from the data?
2. Given the possible results, what action will likely be taken? This will help design the best format for getting the best use out of the data that is collected. Check sheets are custom made for individual problems.

Three general types are:

1. Attribute Check Sheet. This may be used for such things as determining the reasons for defects and the proportion of each. Figure 5-11 is an example of an attribute chart. It was designed to

SHIFT *1* WEEK STARTING 7/9/90

TYPE OF DEFECT	MON	TUE	WED	THUR	FRI
BUCKLING	/	//	/	/	//
METAL FIN	//	///	//	/	/
PAINT					
CRACKS	ЦНТ ЦНТ /	ЦНТ ///	ЦНТ ////	ЦНТ /	ЦНТ ЦНТ //
WIDTH					
METAL TK		/			
DEPTH	/	/		/	
NO HOLES			/		
CONTOUR	//	/	/		/
OTHER DIM		/		/	
OTHER					
TOTAL	17	17	14	10	16

Figure 5-11. Attribute check sheet.

find what are the major reasons for problems in product "A." If the reasons can be determined, a solution will be sought by the improvement team. Figure 5-11 shows that cracks are the major reason for defects in product "A."

2. Location Check Sheet. This is used to find where a failure is occurring on a part. The check sheet is usually a sketch of a part on which a person indicates the location of a defect. Figure 5-12

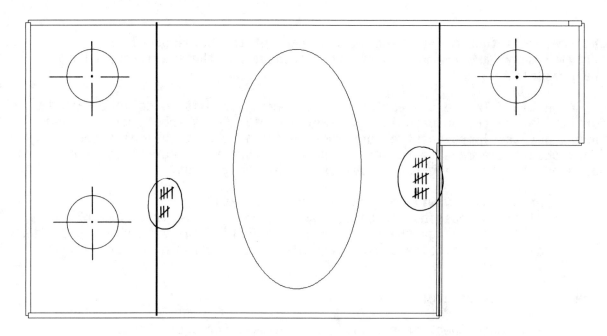

Figure 5-12. Location check sheet.

is a location check sheet that shows where cracks are occurring on product "A." Knowing the location of the defect could lead the improvement team to a better focus on the solution.

3. Variable Check Sheet. This is used to collect information about the effect of certain variables. One use is to find out how the occurrence of a defect changes when a variable is adjusted. Figure 5-13 illustrates how the occurrence of cracks change on product "A" by adjusting set height. From the results, it appears that set height "D" may eliminate cracks.

CRACKING	SHIFT *1* WEEK STARTING *7/16/90*					
	MON	TUE	WED	THUR	FRI	TOTAL
SET HEIGHT						
A	ЖНТ ЖНТ					*10*
B		ЖНТ *11*				*7*
C		*111*				*3*
D						*0*
E		*1111*				*4*
TOTAL						

Figure 5-13. Variable check sheet.

CAUSE AND EFFECT DIAGRAMS. The cause and effect diagram is also called a fishbone diagram. It originated in Japan with Professor Ishikawa in the 1960s. It is a visual sketch using lines and symbols to show the linkage between an effect and the potential causes of that effect. The diagram is drawn backward. First the effect is stated. Then the causes of this effect are determined. The purpose is to help people identify many factors that influence a process. The idea of the concept is that this knowledge could lead to the root cause of a problem and then to its solution. The development of the diagram produces many potential causes. Perhaps only one cause is really producing the problem.

A cause and effect diagram was the next step after cracks were identified as the major problem by an attribute checksheet on product "A." Figure 5-14 shows a simplified cause and effect diagram that was made up for the cracking problem. The "effect" is the part cracks. In general, it is seen that this could be caused by four major factors. These major "causes" are the method, the material, the person, and the machine. Other major causes that could be considered are:

1. Environment, such as temperature and humidity.
2. Organization, such as policies and procedures.
3. Measurements.

Each of the major causes is broken down into more specific factors. One of these factors in Figure 5-14 was set height. Identification of this cause led to the Variable Check Sheet that was discussed previously.

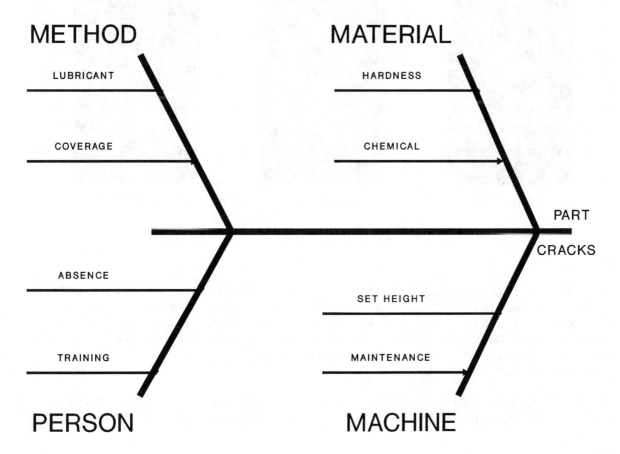

Figure 5-14. Cause and effect diagram.

There are two ways of developing the diagram. One is by directly drawing the diagram in an informal session. The second is by brainstorming. Both ways use people, each having a different perspective. Brainstorming will be discussed in Chapter 13 of this book.

STRATIFICATION CHARTS. This is a way to break down a problem to aid in focusing on the cause. Instead of looking at the total number of defects, the chart breaks down the defects by similar contributors. It "stratifies" the data according to like contributors. The contributors may be such things as shifts, plants, machines, or operators. It is a bar chart. The stratification chart compares like contributors against frequency of occurrence of, for example, defects. Figure 5-15 is an example that

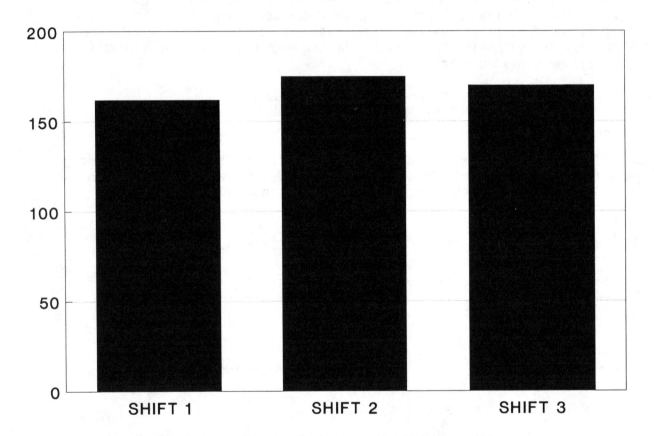

Figure 5-15. Stratification Chart showing break down defects in product A by shift.

compares the defects caused by each shift for product "A." From this chart, results are the same for each shift. Therefore, shift differences can be ruled out as a cause. Figure 5-16 compares the defects of product "A" caused by each machine. Machine "D" produces far more defects than the other four machines. For the improvement team, this is a key finding in their search for improvement.

SCATTER DIAGRAMS. The diagrams are used to study how one factor relates to another. An example is shown in Figure 5-17. The diagram illustrates the

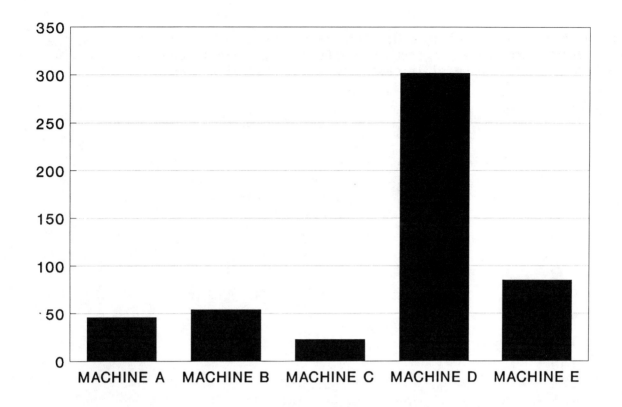

Figure 5-16. Stratification Chart showing break down defects in product A by machine.

relationship between temperature and a dimension. Data points representing the dimension at various temperatures are plotted. The more it resembles a straight line or a curve, the stronger the relationship. On Figure 5-17,

DIMENSION

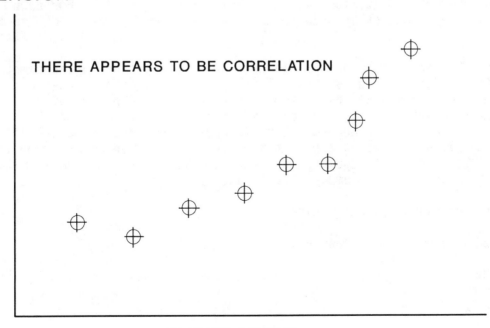

THERE APPEARS TO BE CORRELATION

TEMPERATURE

Figure 5-17. Data points resembling a straight line or a curve indicate a strong relationship between factors.

there is a strong relationship. This is not true for Figure 5-18 where the data points are scattered throughout the chart. This information is useful to lead the team to possible cause and effect relationships.

DIMENSION

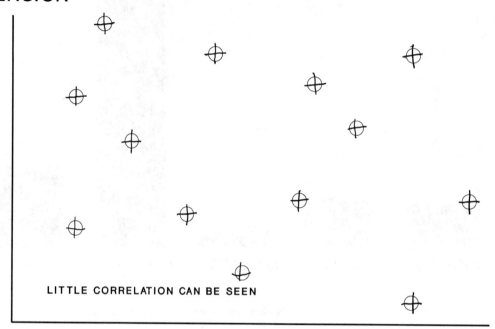

TEMPERATURE

Figure 5-18. Scattered data points indicate factors are not related.

HISTOGRAMS. These charts present data in a visual format. The type of distribution and variability is readily apparent. Some histograms are based on attribute data. An example is shown in Figure 5-19. This presents the data collected by the attribute check sheet for product "A." For each condition, the frequency of occurrence is represented by the height of the bar.

A variable histogram is shown in Figure 5-20. It shows how often something occurs for different temperatures. This is grouped by class interval. In this case, the class interval is two degrees wide. The number of class intervals in a set of data is determined arbitrarily. A rule of thumb states that there should between 10 to 15 class intervals for a set of data. The cell midpoint is set at the center of the class interval as shown in Figure 5-20. The cell midpoint represents the value of occurrences within the class interval. An example of this is:

For the following observations:

Temperature	Frequency
149.5	1
150.1	1
150.61	1
149.8	1
TOTAL	4

CRACKS FOR EACH SET HEIGHT

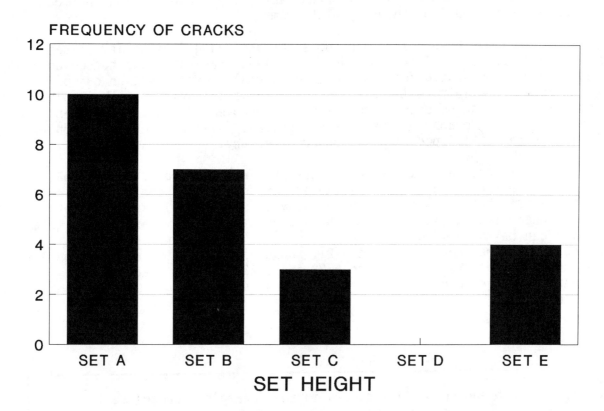

Figure 5-19. A histogram based on attribute data.

These would be in the class interval from 149 to 151 having a cell midpoint of 150. The height of the bar will be 4. See Figure 5-20.

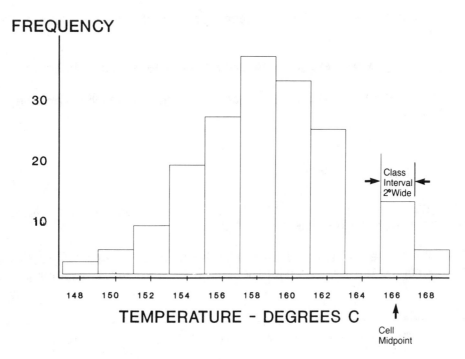

Figure 5-20. A variable histogram.

Standard SPC textbooks contain important information how to find the meaning of various distributions shown by histograms.

CONTROL CHARTS. These charts are tools for analyzing variability to see what should be done. They avoid over reaction. Variation due to common causes can be separated from that due to special causes. Action can be taken more directly to eliminate the real causes of variation. Variable control charts can be used where needed by improvement teams. They can direct the team to appropriate causes. Progress will be seen on the charts. Their use can be stopped when no longer necessary.

Before the study, obvious special causes of variation should be eliminated. Examples are the use of a qualified operator and using incoming material from the same batch. Data should normally be collected in subgroups of five consecutive parts. At least 25 subgroups should be considered. Trial limits can be found with 12 subgroups as well. The control chart calculations are shown in Figure 5-21. Results are plotted as shown on the variable control chart in Figures 5-22 and 5-23. Various factors for converting range into standard deviation and establishing limits are in Figure 5-24.

---

1. For each subgroup (five pieces in this example), calculate the average $(\overline{X})$ and range (R):

$$\overline{X} = \frac{\text{Sum of the 5 measurements}}{5}$$

$$R = \text{Largest value} - \text{Smallest Value}$$

The data and results for the 25 subgroups are shown in Figure 5-22 and Figure 5-23.

2. Plot the subgroup averages and ranges on the $\overline{X}$ and R chart.

3. Calculate the grand average $(\overline{\overline{X}})$ and average range $(\overline{R})$ for the set of data:

$$\overline{\overline{X}} = (\overline{X}_1 + \overline{X}_2 \ldots \overline{X}_{25}) \div 25 = 111.2 \div 25 = 4.448$$

$$(\overline{R}) = (R_1 + R_2 \ldots R_{25}) \div 25 = 44 \div 25 = 1.76$$

Plot the grand average ( ) as the centerline on the average chart and the average range $(\overline{R})$ on the range chart.

4. Refer to Figure 5-24 and determine the proper D_3 and D_4 values for the subgroup size (D_3 is undefined, D_4 = 2.115, for a subgroup size of 5).

Figure 5-21. Control chart calculations. *(Courtesy of General Motors Corporation)*

5. Calculate the upper and lower control limits for the sample ranges. Draw the limits on the range chart.

$$UCL = D_4 \times \overline{R} = 2.115 \times 1.76 = 3.7$$
$$LCL = \text{no lower control limit for subgroup size}$$
$$\text{less than 7}$$

6. Analyze the chart for statistical control. For the process to be in control, there must not be any points outside of the control limit or any patterns within the control limits.

7. Refer to Figure 5-24 and select the proper A_2 value for the subgroup size ($A_2 = 0.577$ for a subgroup size of 5).

8. Calculate the upper and lower control limits for the sample averages. Draw the limits on the average chart using dashed lines.

$$UCL = \overline{\overline{X}} + (A_2 \times \overline{R})$$
$$= 4.448 + (0.577 \times 1.76 = 5.47$$
$$LCL = \overline{\overline{X}} - (A_2 \times \overline{R})$$
$$= 4.448 - (0.577 \times 1.76) = 3.43$$

9. Analyze the chart for statistical control. For the process to be in control, there must not be any points outside of the control limits or any patterns within the control limits.

Figure 5-21. Control chart calculations (continued).

The control chart in Figure 5-22 has all points within control limits. This usually means that "common causes" must be eliminated to reduce the variation shown. Figure 5-25 shows another situation where a point is below the lower control limit. Where one or more points are outside control limits, the process may not be considered "stable." This situation is assumed to be due to "special causes."

Sometimes, a trend toward a control limit occurs as shown in Figure 5-26. This also shows that there may not be a "stable" process. It may be caused by "special causes" like tool wear or other factors listed in Figure 5-26.

Normally, a trend is recognized by seven consecutive points that continue to either increase or decrease from the centerline.

A "run" may also show that the process may not be "stable." This is illustrated in Figure 5-27. A common run pattern is when seven successive points are all on one side of the centerline. Variable Chart and Attribute Chart forms, may be found in Appendix A.

OTHER TOOLS. There are other more elaborate tools that can be used in improvement efforts like design of experiments and Taguchi on-line quality control. However, many feel that the simpler tools described will handle most improvement efforts in an effective and understandable manner. A force

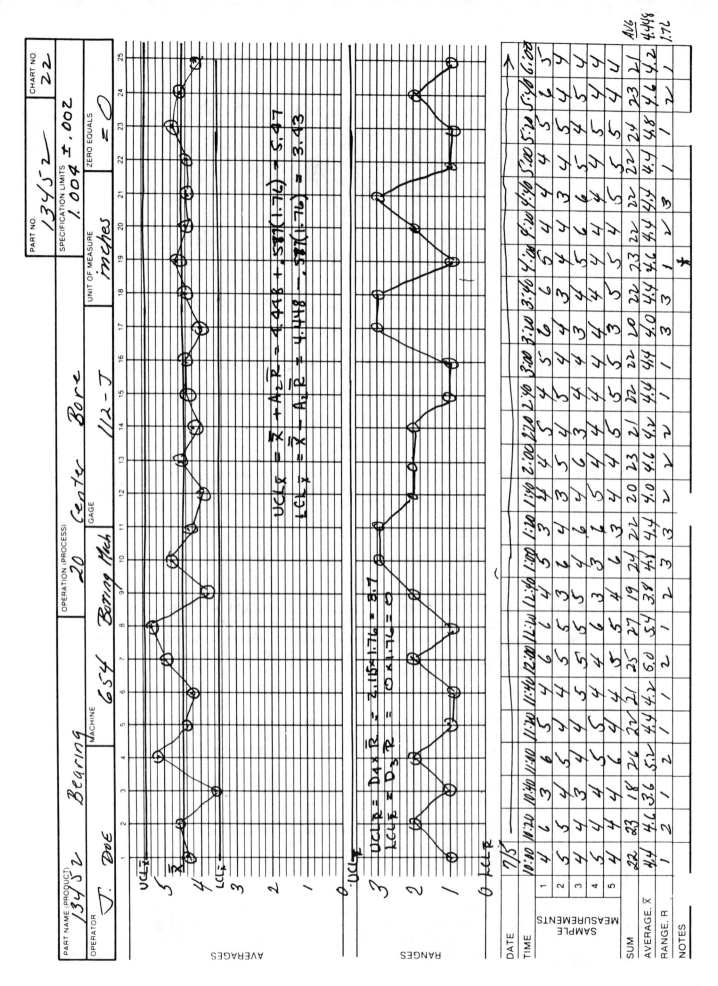

Figure 5-22. Variables control chart ($\bar{X}$ & R). (Courtesy of Ford Motor Company)

PROCESS LOG SHEET

ANY **CHANGE** IN PEOPLE, MATERIALS, ENVIRONMENT, METHODS OR MACHINES SHOULD BE NOTED. THESE NOTES WILL HELP YOU TO TAKE CORRECTIVE ACTION WHEN SIGNALED BY THE CONTROL CHART.

DATE	TIME	COMMENTS	DATE	TIME	COMMENTS
✱ 7/5/90	4:00	CHANGE IN OPERATORS NEW OPERATOR R 911 C			

Figure 5-23. Control chart process log. *(Courtesy of Ford Motor Company)*

Number of Observations In Subgroup	Factor for S' Estimate from $\bar{R}$	Factor for $\bar{X}$ Chart	Factors for R Chart	
			Lower Control Limit	Upper Control Limit
	$d_2 = \bar{R}/S'$	A_2	D_3	D_4
2	1.128	1.880	—	3.267
3	1.693	1.023	—	2.575
4	2.059	0.729	—	2.282
5	2.326	0.577	—	2.115
6	2.534	0.483	—	2.004
7	2.704	0.419	0.076	1.924
8	2.847	0.373	0.136	1.864
9	2.970	0.337	0.184	1.816
10	3.078	0.308	0.223	1.777

Figure 5-24. Control chart constants.   *(Courtesy of General Motors Corporation)*

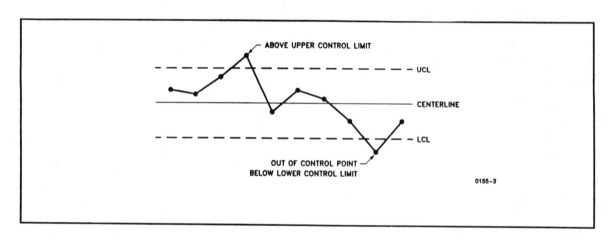

Figure 5-25. Points outside control limits.   *(Courtesy of General Motors Corporation)*

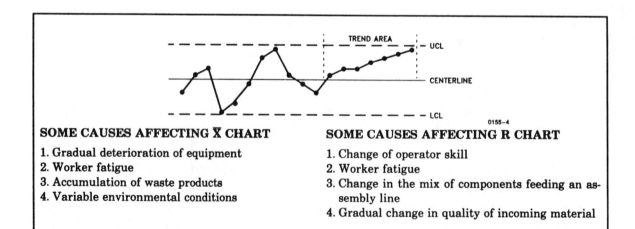

SOME CAUSES AFFECTING $\bar{X}$ CHART

1. Gradual deterioration of equipment
2. Worker fatigue
3. Accumulation of waste products
4. Variable environmental conditions

SOME CAUSES AFFECTING R CHART

1. Change of operator skill
2. Worker fatigue
3. Change in the mix of components feeding an assembly line
4. Gradual change in quality of incoming material

Figure 5-26. Trends affecting $\bar{X}$ and R charts. *(Courtesy of General Motors Corporation)*

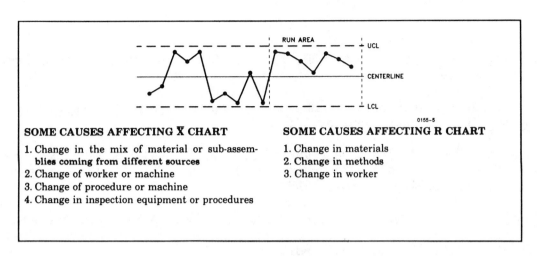

Figure 5-27. Runs affecting $\overline{X}$ and R charts. *(Courtesy of General Motors Corporation)*

field analysis worksheet and a criteria analysis worksheet can be found in Appendix A.

BIBLIOGRAPHY

Boothroyd, G. and Dewhurst, P., "Product Design for Manufacture for Assembly." Manufacturing Engineering, April 1988, p. 42.

Boothroyd, G. and Dewhurst, P., Product Design for Manufacture for Assembly, 1st ed. Wakefield, RI: Boothroyd Dewhurst Inc., 1987.

Brown, John E., Statistical Methods in Engineering and Manufacturing, 1st ed. Milwaukee: Quality Press, 1990.

Burr, John T., SPC Tools for Operators. 1st ed. Milwaukee: Quality Press, 1989.

Daetz, Douglas, "The Effect of Product Design on Product Quality and Product Cost." Quality Progress, June 1987, p. 63.

Ford Corporate Quality Office. Advanced Quality Planning Manual. 1st ed. Dearborn, MI: Ford Motor Company.

General Motors Statistical Process Control Manual. Detroit: General Motors Corp.

Gitlow, Howard; Gitlow, Shelley; Oppenheim, Alan, and Oppenheim, Rosa, Tools and Methods for the Improvement of Quality. 1st ed. Irwin, 1989.

Gunter, Berton, "A Perspective on Taguchi Methods." Quality Progress, June 1987, p. 44.

Miles, L.D., Techniques for VA and VE, 2nd ed. The Miles Value Foundation, 1972.

Moran, John W.; Talbot, Richard P. and Benson, Russell M., Guide to Graphical Problem Solving Processes, 1st ed. Milwaukee: Quality Press, 1990.

Nolan, Thomas W. and Provost, Lloyd P., "Understanding Variation." Quality Progress, May 1990, p. 70.

Quality Function Deployment QFD, 1st ed. Dearborn, MI: American Supplier Institute, 1988.

Stoll, Henry, "Tech Report: Design for Manufacture." Manufacturing Engineering, January 1988, p. 67.

Syverson, Roger J. and Dale, Everett D., "Value Analysis Makes SPC Even More Powerful." Quality Congress Transactions. Milwaukee: American Society for Quality Control, 1987.

Thompson, Diane M.M. and Fallah, M. Hosein, "QFD--A Systematic Approach to Product Definition." Quality Congress Transactions. Milwaukee: American Society for Quality Control, 1989.

Total Quality Management, 1st ed. Dearborn, MI: American Supplier Institute, 1989.

Winchell, William, Realistic Cost Estimating for Manufacturing, 2nd ed. Dearborn, MI: Society of Manufacturing Engineers, 1989.

CHAPTER 6

THE NEED FOR BUY-IN

In this chapter. . .

IDEAL TRAITS OF A COMPANY
1. Goal Setting
2. Holism
3. Hierarcies
4. Inputs and Outputs
5. Transformation
6. Energy
7. Entropy
8. Equifinality

EXTERNAL FORCES ON A COMPANY
1. Constituent Groups
2. Groups Served
3. Industry Customs and Tradition
4. Technology
5. Economy
6. Values, Mores and Ethos
7. Public Opinion
8. Political Trends
9. Legal Climate
10. Markets

STAGES IN A COMPANY'S LIFE
1. Formative Stage
2. Mature Stage
3. Aging Stage
4. Demise Stage

STRATEGIC PLANNING BY TOP MANAGEMENT

STEPS IN DEVELOPING A STRATEGIC PLAN
1. Setting the Stage
2. Develop a Mission
3. Find Issues
4. Develop Strategy
5. Long-term Objectives
6. Integrate Objectives
7. Financial Projections
8. Summarize and Present

SPECIFIC ACTION PLANS FOR DRIVERS OF THE BUSINESS
1. Product Development Plan
2. Marketing Plan
3. Manufacturing Plan
4. Financial Plan

CASCADING INTO FUNCTIONAL AREAS AND DEPARTMENTS

Appendix information

Organizational culture self-assessment profile. (From Management Vitality: The Team Approach) A-29--A-31

Questionnaire assessing culture at different levels of the organization From Time to Market: Reducing Product Lead Time) A-32--A-34

6

The Need For Buy-In

Buy-in by everyone in a company is a central issue in creating a climate of continuous improvement. Each person in a company must understand the need for change and be dedicated to making it happen.

The first step is to address the question: "Why change?"

Many answers can be offered, but the best is that a company cannot survive without it. For companies making cars in the past decade, competition from foreign manufacturers was fierce. Domestic producers needed to change to survive. The bottom line of this change was two-fold: they needed better quality and lower costs. There were many successes in making these changes; there were also some failures. The failures included plant closings and the capture of the small-car market by foreign producers. Individuals were hurt in the process through layoffs.

To need change does not mean the company must be on the verge of going out of business. It does mean, however, that everyone in the company must realize that changes are necessary to maintain a competitive advantage. Status quo must be seen as a sure way to weaken the company.

There is no magic formula for making changes. Starting at the top of the organization is the best way. Top management must have a vision. Each company must develop its own vision. This must be translated into strategy and tactics. Measurable goals and objectives must be developed. Support and commitment must be gained from everyone in the company to achieve the vision. As time goes on, the vision will be adjusted to meet new challenges. This will cause further changes. Changes will never stop.

Making the vision come true is not easy. It is much easier to talk about change than to do it. Shared visions are difficult in view of company politics and empire-building. Turf battles between activities still occur. Yet, for the vision to be realized, all activities in a company must act in unison. Overcoming these barriers and others is a challenge for top management. Without the active involvement of top management, removing the barriers would be an immense task. There have been efforts to change from the bottom up in an organization, but without a strategy for dealing with change at the top, the risk of failure is high.

Through a conceptual model, the traits of a company can be better understood. What an organization is and what factors influence it will help in understanding how changes are made.

Individuals create an organization to do what they cannot do themselves. An organization may be thought of as a system. Some general views about a system are:

1. The whole is more than the sum of its parts.
2. The whole determines the nature of its parts.
3. The parts can only be understood by their relation with the whole.
4. The parts are related and dependent upon each other. The relations do not stay the same but change constantly in a dynamic way.

Generally, this is the ideal company. It is important because it shows that a company must be looked at in its entirety. Top management must look at the big picture and constantly guide the company towards its purpose. The activities in a company are not important for themselves. The value of the activities lies in how they help the company be what it wants to be. The activities must act in unison, but they must change to meet different conditions. Leaders of each functional area must meet the global needs of the company and do away with self-serving actions. Teamwork is the key.

IDEAL TRAITS OF A COMPANY

There are traits of a system that can be useful in a company (Figure 6-1).

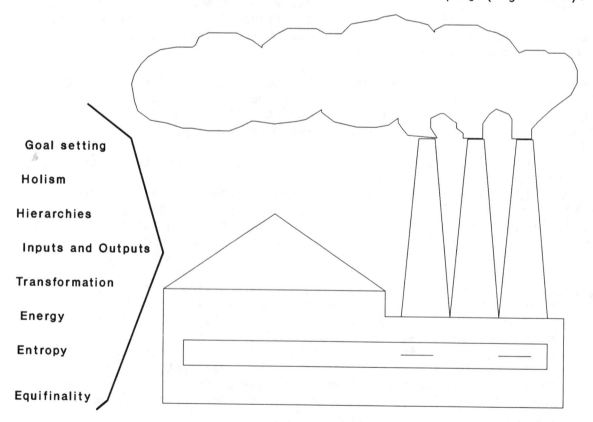

Goal setting

Holism

Hierarchies

Inputs and Outputs

Transformation

Energy

Entropy

Equifinality

Figure 6-1. Conceptual traits of a company.

An organization having the traits of a system can better deal with needed change. The major traits are:

1. Goal Setting. A system and a company should have a central purpose which is supported by goals. The goals are of two general types. One is for the internal operations; the other is to deal with the forces outside the system or company.

2. Holism. The parts of a system or activities in a company should be cohesive and act in unison. They should support each other in pursuing a central purpose. When forces from outside the system or company pose a threat, the parts should tend to be even more cohesive. The activities cannot act alone; they depend on each other for support.

3. Hierarchies. Subsystems are nested in a framework or structured in such a priority to support the central purpose of the system. For a company, for example, this may refer to the ranking of individuals by authority. Those with a higher accountability have a higher ranking in the hierarchy.

4. Inputs and Outputs. An open system has input from outside the system. It also has output. For a company, the input involves such things as people, money, and machines. The output is the goods that are made.

5. Transformation. In an open system, inputs are transformed into outputs. A company changes material into a product by using people and machines. The output, or product, is much different from the inputs. In a profit-making company, there is economic value added by the transformation. The revenues from the output exceed the cost of input, making a profit. Another term for transformation in a company is "conversion."

6. Energy. All systems use energy to keep going. A system might also generate energy from within using the inputs. Companies use conventional forms of energy like utilities. In a way, companies also may generate "power" by the influence of their people on the forces outside the company. This may be important in dealing with external forces that play a major role in the performance of a company.

7. Entropy. This is a term borrowed from thermodynamics to indicate that any system is gradually wearing out. An open system or company uses inputs in two ways. One is to produce output. The other is to maintain itself. As a system or company ages, there is more spent for maintenance. There is also a tendency to create staffs that may not add value to the product. The productivity of a company constantly erodes if changes are not made wisely.

8. Equifinality. This term means that there are many ways in which an open system or company can reach its goals. Inputs can be changed. Also, goals can be adjusted to conform to changed conditions. An open system or company does not have to wear out. To avoid this, the company must constantly change the way things are done.

The key to all this is that companies have control over their destiny. A company can be successful over the long-term. Top management must lead the way in providing the vision for the central purpose of the company. Company vision and goals must be adjusted regularly as conditions change. Everyone must work together to achieve the vision and goals of the company. Flexibility must be practiced and changes made wisely.

EXTERNAL FORCES ON A COMPANY

External forces (Figure 6-2) which affect a company include:

* consitituent groups;
* groups served;
* industry customs and traditions;
* technology;
* the national economy;
* values, mores, and ethos of society;
* public opinion;
* political trends and legal climate;
* markets.

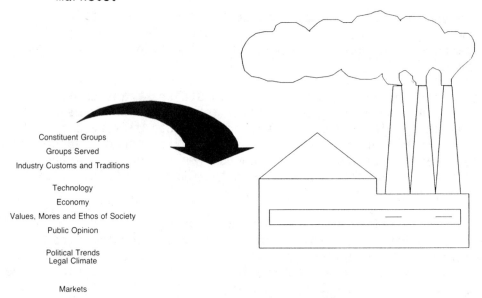

Figure 6-2. External forces affecting a company.

The elements previously discussed show why a company is very difficult to run. There are other elements that further complicate running a company. They concern the company's operating environment. In a sense, the environment can be affected by forces that act on a company (listed in the previous paragraph). The company has little control over these forces.

A real danger is that they could divert the company from its vision; the company must be sensitive to this. Goals must be developed to deal with these forces. The company also must be flexible enough to adapt; this may require changing things inside the company. It also may mean attempting to modify the external force by making the effort to clear up confusion, for example. Also, it may require modifying the vision of a company. The forces that can impact a company dramatically are as follows:

1. Constituent Groups. These people provide support to the company. They may be shareholders. Some of the shareholders may be on the board of directors. The group also may include bankers and other holders of the debt of a company. In a sense, the community in which the company resides may be looked at as providing support. It is important that these groups understand and support the direction of the company. Changes that are not understood can be mistrusted and cause controversy. Lately, shareholders have been extremely effective in influencing the direction of companies regarding social issues.

2. Groups Served. These are the groups who benefit from the products and services provided by a company. For the most part, they are customers. This force is particularly powerful. Customers decide the revenue that a company collects. If their perception of the product is not good, revenue may go down. With shrinking revenue, company visions are harder to reach. Some companies are placing ads in newspapers describing their progress toward better quality over the years. This is intended to create a more positive image for the company and its products. The customer is expected to feel reassured by the clearing up of any confusion that may have existed about quality. It is hoped that this will help regain lost market share. A big factor in how customers feel about the company and its products is what the competition is doing. A thorough understanding of what may be available in the marketplace from other companies can be very helpful. Without this knowledge, a company cannot develop a viable strategy for the future.

3. Industry Customs and Traditions. Companies in the same industry generally act in a like manner. Each type of industry has certain customs and traditions. Historically, companies in each industry were expected to observe these customs and traditions. For example, car styling changes occurred on a fairly regular schedule. Those that did not change, lost the interest of some customers. Another example is the electronics industry. Leading companies are expected to offer "state-of-the art" products. If they do not, customers go elsewhere. Today, certain traditions are being questioned and companies sometimes gain a market niche by not conforming to what happened in the past. For example, the largest industrial computer manufacturer now makes PCs for the home market.

4. Technology. It is critical for a company to stay abreast of the latest technology in both products and manufacturing. When competitors reach new levels of technology, the pressure becomes intense. In fact, the cost of playing catch-up may put the future of a company in jeopardy. Only the largest companies can afford sizable in-house research activities. For the vast majority of companies, the technology must come from outside sources. Many innovations have come from the government, such as through the NASA program. Others came from universities and independent research laboratories. It is a challenge to a company to seek and choose the right technology to pursue. Timing may be critical so as not to miss the opportunity. For some, the investment required almost means betting the future of the company on the change. Companies must be sensitive to available technology to foster continuous improvement.

5. Economy. Some companies must react quickly to the economy to stay in business. With profit margins in many companies less than 5%, swings in the economy have a widespread effect. The reaction may be quite complex, especially for companies that also have plants offshore. The progress of many companies toward a vision is often slowed by the economy. The cost of capital might cause the rethinking of immediate expansion plans. Policies regarding currency exchange may favor investment in one country over another. Product plans might be changed because of expected high inflation rates in certain commodities. Of course, markets expand and contract based upon the health of the economy. Much effort is spent trying to predict the economy so companies can plan actions instead of reacting. This prediction is done by both the government and private organizations.

6. Values, Mores, and Ethos of Society. These are the factors that form the foundation for human behavior. This behavior often influences what products are bought. Abrupt changes in values are quite disturbing to a company that must adapt to the new conditions. These changes are often not accounted for in the vision for the company. One example occurred in the mid-1970s. An oil embargo forced up the price of gasoline. The public's values shifted from large cars to small cars that could get better gas mileage. Domestic auto producers could not react quickly to the change and lost market share to offshore producers. Companies making products for several countries sometimes find they must have different features. Marketing studies are often done to predict shifting values, allowing companies to plan for changes.

7. Public Opinion. Companies often sway to the pressure of public opinion. This opinion might be expressed as either strong support or rejection regarding issues. Public opinion is usually emotional in nature and hard to deal with. Often, it requires the altering of the vision of the company. Examples of intense public opinion reaction occur in many plant relocations due to the loss of jobs in the affected communities. Other examples concern the making of war materials considered objectionable by certain groups. Often, public opinion polarizes in court actions and political pressures. Unfortunately, the image of a company and its products can be tarnished through adverse public opinion. On the other hand, the image of many companies is helped by being respected as good corporate citizens.

8. Political Trends. Politics always change. A company may have to adjust its vision and plans to match what is politically possible. On a national level, certain administrations are much more favorable to business. For example, mergers are looked upon with favor by some administrations while in others they may not have been possible. Antitrust laws may get more liberal interpretations. The government may work closer with business in bringing about foreign trade. Conversely, other influences such as environmental laws are constantly being tightened due to interest groups. On a global basis, certain markets never before open are presenting tremendous opportunities and risks. Locally, tax incentives are given to get industry into communities. Public funds are made available for training employees. Political trends are likely to change in the

future. A company must be sensitive to these trends and take full advantage of the benefits. The potential benefits may be very influential in the shaping of the vision for the company. They also may help in achieving goals. Conversely, politics could be adverse to a company. If so, a company needs to work at making a more favorable political climate.

9. Legal Climate. A company must, like any citizen, obey the laws of the land. These laws are interpreted differently as the needs of the society change. Many years ago, laws concerning selling products were based upon letting the buyer beware. Laws now have evolved to a point where a company is responsible for any harm done because of a defect in the product. Many product liability actions have multimillion-dollar awards. For a company, legal penalties further stress the need for continuous improvement of quality. Other laws are made to assure the safety of products, such as passive restraints in cars. There are laws to protect the environment. Still other laws, such as those related to OSHA, are intended to make workplaces safe. It is important that the vision of a company and its goals take into consideration the laws that apply. For those competing internationally, the laws of other lands may be different but must be obeyed in the same manner.

10. Markets. A company needs resources to function. These include people, capital, land, equipment, and materials. Each resource is supplied through a market for that resource. The availability and cost of the resource is determined by the factors in that market. Take, for example, a company seeking to hire a manufacturing engineer. If the market has few manufacturing engineers, it may be difficult to find the right one. Then, after finding the right one, a high salary may be required to attract the person. The same situation exists with capital. In times of gloomy economics, a higher interest rate may be charged or the money may not be available. Land may be available for a low price in a rural setting. However, it may not have the utilities and ready transportation that are found on more expensive land in an urban setting. In brisk economic times, equipment may have to be back-ordered and take a long time to receive; this may not be true in slower times and the price also may be lower. The cost of materials varies widely and often may have little to do with general economic conditions. It seems that when there is a major oil spill or a crisis in the Mideast, the price of gasoline rises abruptly well before any change in supply can be noticed. The vision of the company and goals must consider the timing for adding resources. Cost and availability may cause adjustments to be made in plans to have decisions that are best for the company.

A company does not have much control over the forces just discussed. They are external to the company, but goals must be developed to deal with them. Through well thought-out actions, some influence may be obtained. This should be attempted, but cannot be counted on. These forces are certainly important to the vision and goals of the company. Understanding how these forces work helps to make adjustments to deal with them. It also helps to have an idea of what the forces may be in the future, so that better planning can be done.

STAGES IN A COMPANY'S LIFE

Understanding what stage of development a company may be in could be helpful to those making changes. A company could conceptually be in one of the four stages shown in Figure 6-3. These stages are similar to what a human being

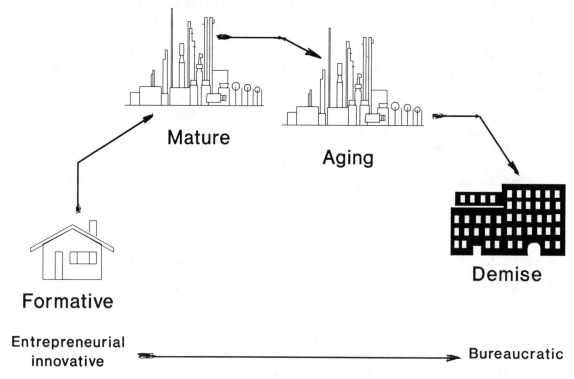

Figure 6-3. Stages in the life cycle of a company.

experiences in proceeding through life. Unlike human beings, however, a company can adapt itself and have a perpetual existence. The stages are as follows:

1. Formative Stage. When a company begins, an entrepreneur is usually involved. This person sees the company as a way of achieving a personal goal. Basically, the company secures inputs, converts the inputs, and sells the outputs. There is little in the way of procedures and protocol. The few people involved work closely together, constantly adapting to make things happen. Motivation is high. The teamwork and spirit of things offset the inefficiency of the operation. Priority is on short-range goals. Often, it is hard to see beyond the immediate problems. This stage is ideal for developing a vision and purpose for what the company is desired to be.

2. Mature Stage. Surviving the formative stage, a company gets organized. Activities are created and people hired to staff them. There are now product engineering, marketing, and finance departments to support production. Systems for cost accounting, scheduling, and inventory are developed. Time is spent making procedures. With this, top management loses touch with day-to-day problems. They delegate authority to those closer to the problems.

Lower-level managers should be responsible for inputs, conversion, and outputs. Top management should take this opportunity to concentrate on the future--what the company should be like five and 10 years from now. They should also actively pursue installing the culture that is needed to succeed. Changes should be carefully made to support the vision for the company.

3. Aging Stage. Things get formal during this stage. Top management rarely visits the factory floor. Flexibility and adapting seem a thing of the past. Communications flow up the chain of command. Talking to other activities may be discouraged. Even more communication comes from the top down. How things are done appears to be more important than what is achieved. Procedures are more exacting and specific. Staff is added to act as watchdogs on the operations and report problems. Innovating appears not to be rewarded. People are afraid to make mistakes and be honest about situations. Professional managers are hired to further organize efforts. Some of the activities are centralized. Reviews of performance are regularly done. The time taken to prepare for the reviews sometimes feels awesome. Planning is now a formal procedure requiring more reviews. Bureaucracy is rampant, replacing innovativeness, the spirit that was once so much a part of the formative stage. This stage is a challenge for top management. Big changes must be made quickly for the survival of the company. A shared vision among those in the company is top priority. The culture of the company must be molded to support continuous improvement.

4. Demise Stage. This stage can best be described as rigor mortis setting in. The company is dying and can only be revived through instant action by top management. Typically, too much is being spent on maintaining the company. This includes the traditional fixing of equipment. Even more serious is the number of professional managers and staff, added over the years, who do not directly contribute to the product. Procedures and the red tape involved make changes almost impossible in this stage. No one is happy. Workers blame managers. The managers feel that the workers let them down. Customers have lost much respect for the products made by the company. Top management must quickly rid the company of bureaucracy and instill a new culture. In many respects, this may be the most favorable stage for change. No one is satisfied with the way things are. Everyone knows that changes must be made quickly to survive. The changes must not only cause an abrupt improvement, but set the cornerstone for continuous improvement.

STRATEGIC PLANNING BY TOP MANAGEMENT

Change is always difficult. The type of change called for in continuous improvement is especially difficult because it is fundamental. It reaches through the entire organization. Perhaps the hardest change is the change in the culture of the organization--the way in which it does things. Premises and the principles on which the company is organized must be revised. Activities must adapt to what is required to achieve the vision of what the company wants to be. All this must be orchestrated by the top person so the transition is smooth. In a sense, this may take more stamina and commitment than companies or individuals have ever had before.

It may take altering the company to facilitate change. Some larger companies have reorganized into many separate business units. Each business unit is a company within itself. The business units are smaller and easier to deal with when it comes to instituting change. Other companies have reduced staffs, placing people into positions directly affecting the product. Many companies are now actively pursuing strategic planning to find changes that are needed.

There are many roadblocks in the way of progress. Strategic planning efforts may be seen by individuals as just another in a series of programs. There have been many programs--quality improvement, inventory reduction, the list goes on--but the effort will fail if it is only given half-hearted attention. Another roadblock is that achieving full results will take time. With the pressures of day-to-day deadlines, it is often hard to maintain a constant focus on the long term.

A third roadblock is that most people in the company don't have the experience or skills to cause the type of change required. Intensive training is needed. The time taken to provide this training may be seen as taking away from getting products to the customer. Recognizing the roadblocks in the path of continuous improvement is critical. If the roadblocks can be brought out in the open, they can be dealt with positively.

For many companies, planning starts with the strategic plan. This is based upon the vision of what the company should be like in the future. The focus may be five or 10 years from now. This depends on the intensity of the competition and how fast markets are changing. The strategic plan is developed in a team effort by the top management of the company. Usually, this requires a series of intense discussions. Consensus is sought from the leaders of the major functional areas. Often, input is sought from known opinion leaders both inside and outside the company. Some companies involve union leaders, suppliers, and customers in the discussions. Adjustments in the strategic plan are made constantly through regular reviews.

Figure 6-4 shows an approach that can be used for strategic planning. Specific details and the sequence of the approach differ among the companies that use strategic planning. Generally, it starts with setting the stage for what is to come. It includes visionary thinking to decide the mission of the company. The effort continues to address the nature of the business and the strategy to achieve long-range objectives. Integration of operational and financial objectives are key ingredients. When the company strategic planning is completed by top management, much more specific plans are developed. These include action plans for manufacturing, marketing, financial, and product development. Quality is normally dealt with as an integral part of these plans. When done effectively, planning for action continues its cascade down the organization into departments and activities.

STEPS IN DEVELOPING A STRATEGIC PLAN

SET THE STAGE. Top management personnel must do the job themselves. They cannot delegate the details to a staff person or activity. The top officer

Set the stage

Develop mission

Find issues

Develop strategy

Long term objectives

Integrate objectives

Financial projections

Summarize
and present

MANUFACTURING PLAN   MARKETING PLAN   FINANCIAL PLAN   PRODUCT DEVELOPMENT PLAN

QUALITY PORTION

Figure 6-4. Strategic planning.

and the heads of the various functions must be focused and committed. It is important that sessions be open and not dominated by anyone. At the beginning, it should be made clear that everyone is an equal partner. The sessions will be intense and must occur regularly. There should be a consensus that strategic planning needs to be done quickly for the survival of the company. To get to this point requires an understanding of the rationale for the change. It must be in terms that are in the language of top management. This includes such things as expected downturns in return on investment, market share, and capital availability. If things are working now, getting agreement will be more difficult. But it must be done. Top management must be committed to active involvement for the long haul to first develop and then regularly fine-tune strategy.

There is much information and insight to be gained from the start. This will be a learning experience for most of those involved. Often, the help of a trained facilitator proves valuable in making the sessions worthwhile. The facilitator probably should be from outside the company. Not having an interest in the outcome increases the effectiveness of the facilitator. Meetings should be held off-site to avoid distractions. Normally, approaches like those in Figure 6-4 are discussed first, and consensus reached on the path to follow for developing the strategic plan.

The first step in planning could be finding out what each employee thinks. Top management opinions are then merged, and consensus reached on the outcome. Figure 6-5 shows how this may be summarized in a sample company.

HYDROCLEAN CASE

Description of Company
* $200 million annual sales
* Manufacturer of washers and driers
* Located in Midwest
* Markets products to department store chains

Description of Product
* Three models of each
* Four color schemes for each—baked on
* Retailer's label glued on when requested

Physical Facility
* Two assembly lines, each capable of handling both products
* Warehouse for storage of finished product
* 40-hour work week
* Manufacture of frames, drums and finish panels
* Purchase of hardware, motors and electronic controls
* Subassembly of control panels and heating units

Product Change
* Major change each model year
* Only safety or emergency change within model year
* Part number change if a changed part is not interchangeable with the old part
* Change part number of an assembly if a changed component changes the fitup or performance of the assembly as a whole

Scheduling
* Product is built to stock
* Product is sold from the warehouse

Figure 6-5. How top managers feel about the company is an important element in strategic planning.

After agreeing what the company is like now, current traits of the company may be compared to the ideal traits discussed earlier in this chapter. External forces, mentioned previously, may be evaluated as to how they influence the company as it exists now. Time also may be spent reaching agreement about the present stage of development of the company. This is important because if the company is dwindling rapidly, drastic short measures and added cash flow may be required to survive. This must be a priority.

This step also should define the culture of the company. Different viewpoints will likely be raised for discussion. Some may be biased and hinge on the management style of the person. Often, persons succeeded in the past because they were good at "firefighting" or solving problems. Preventing or avoiding problems clearly doesn't address their strengths or the past value system. This takes a big change. "Time out" may have to be taken to go to outside training to help in the re-tuning of "mindsets."

An organizational culture self-assessment profile appears in the Appendix. This type of questionnaire may help focus on what is good and bad in the culture of the company. Similar questionnaires may be used to assess perceptions of the culture in different departments and levels of the organization. Results can be summarized to give a good picture of where the company stands regarding culture.

Benchmarking of competition also can provide help in strategic planning. Other pertinent information should be sought that will help in understanding the company. Discussions are likely to be lively and filled with disagreement, but by going through this exercise, top management will learn to work together as a team. They will also learn a great deal about themselves and the company. Different perspectives and getting consensus among the managers are key factors in gaining this insight. As the top managers work together, they become more committed and motivated to get results. With this, the foundation is laid for getting a vision of what the company should be like five years from now.

At this point, there should be a deep and broad understanding about what the company is really like. It is very important that there is agreement among the top managers on this. Also there should be agreement on what the company is not. An image of what has to be done should be forming in the mind of each manager. There also should be a vision forming of what the company should be like in the future. A vision statement helps promote "ownership" by those doing strategic planning. It also focuses the effort that is still required. The vision should address the following elements:

1. Who are we?
2. What should the culture be?
3. What are our purpose and our ultimate goals?
4. How should we be perceived by our customers, suppliers, employees, competitors and the public?

The different visions from each manager should be shared and discussed. What conditions will be five years in the future needs to be projected. Expected changes in external forces should be covered at this time. What the competition will be like in the future also should be considered. The way the company wants to do its business in the future will mold the cultural change required. By testing the possible visions against these factors, consensus should be reached on what is the best foundation for completing the effort. Much knowledge has been gained about the present business and how it should be in the future. Consensus and ownership in the outcome so far has been reached by top management, making a strong base for further progress.

DEVELOP A MISSION. The cornerstone for strategic planning is developing a mission statement. The purpose of the business is in the statement. The statement is short, usually a paragraph. In a concise form, it could provide guidance to such things as the following:

1. What is the business of the company now?
2. What is provided by the products?
3. What business should the company seek or what business will the company be forced to undertake in the future?
4. Who are the customers, now and in the future?
5. How much growth does the company want?
6. What market share does the company seek?

The value of a mission statement is that it focuses the ideas and energies of the company in one direction. Its strength lies in the fact top management developed the statement by consensus. To make the statement requires the different perspectives of the top management team. Usually, there is controversy and intense discussion before consensus is reached.

Quite important is that those developing the mission statement have a sense of ownership in what it says and means. This feeling will continue and build as strategic planning proceeds. A typical mission statement might read:

> The mission of the company is to market company built gardening equipment for the family home market.

Sometimes a company addresses its quality policy in the mission statement. More often, a separate quality policy is issued under the signature of the top manager. This is covered in Chapter 3 and includes an example of a typical quality policy statement.

FIND ISSUES. This step deals with finding the critical issues facing the company and ranking them according to seriousness. This is important because chaos can result from trying to do everything at once. By selecting the most critical issues, efforts can be focused and are likely to be more successful. The critical issues can be developed first. Examples of issues are:

1. Culture of company does not promote teamwork and being responsible for decisions at lower levels in the organization. This causes many errors in judgment by those not familiar with circumstances.

2. Costs of maintaining inventory take up funds that could improve operations. High inventory is caused by backup due to erratic quality. Erratic quality is caused by processes not being capable.

3. Sales projections require expansion of manufacturing within two years. But 40% of current plant is taken up by inventory that is in-process and rework operations.

4. Cost of products is higher than prices of offshore competitors. Failure costs for scrap and rework account for more than the difference.

Like the mission statement, consensus must be reached by top management on what the critical issues are. Often, people both inside and outside the company are consulted to find the factors affecting these issues. Critical issues are evaluated in light of possible trends in external factors and company traits. Discussed are steps to resolve the issues within the time frame of the strategic plan. The output from this step is a database for developing the strategy and long-term objectives.

DEVELOP STRATEGY. From the viewpoint of top management, this is the global direction in which the company should be going. It directly follows from and supports the mission statement. Some elements include the following:

1. Products to be offered in the future.
2. Needs that customers will have in the future.
3. Infusion of technology in products and business or manufacturing processes.
4. Future capability of the business and production processes.
5. Availability of natural resources in the future.
6. Future means of distributing and selling products.

7. Growth of the company and by what means--acquisition, joint venture, or expansion?
8. Development of suppliers as partners.
9. Development of culture of company.
10. Return on investment thresholds anticipated.

Some companies list these elements by priority. The highest-priority element may have the greatest influence on the future direction of the company. Once consensus is reached by the top managers, a short strategy statement is finalized.

LONG-TERM OBJECTIVES. Developing objectives by top management should be a natural flow from the previous steps. These steps should have focused the energies of top management and identified the future challenges. A long "laundry list" of objectives is not suggested; there should be only a few, to increase the likelihood of achieving them. It is important that the objectives have a high potential for success and that they are expressed in quantified terms. Often, performance measures also are developed for each step of the ladder toward the objective.

During this step, the objectives should be tested against some criteria to assure that they will work. For example, each objective should be looked at to see if it really can be measured to determine progress. Also, each objective should be analyzed to see how sensitive it is to changes in the external forces on the company. If it has a high sensitivity, it may not be under the control of those in the company. Examples of long-term objectives are:

1. Reduce inventory levels by going from 4 turns to 27 turns annually by 1992.
2. Improve quality by reducing defects to one part per million by 1993.
3. Expand market by plant in Common Market area by 1994 providing 10% of revenue and profit for the company.
4. Use cross-discipline product development teams for all development by 1992.

INTEGRATE OBJECTIVES. This step may be the toughest part of the strategic planning process. Objectives are tested to see if they support each other. Another question is, with the perceived support, will the specific objective still work as intended? Much fine-tuning is usually required by top management. Thought must also be given to the availability of resources, including people and money. Conflicts must be worked out and consensus reached by top management. Sometimes, new approaches are suggested in these intense discussions that may be better for the company.

FINANCIAL PROJECTIONS. In this step, the chief financial officer prepares the financial projections for the duration of the strategic plan. It usually has income statements, balance sheets, and projected capital investments. By this approach, the strategic plan drives the addition of new equipment and other resources. This minimizes the danger of a short-term focus on making capital investments. Key financial issues and major implications of the strategic plan are addressed in the report. Also included are trends that may occur in prices, volumes, and cost over the period that the plan covers. This report is presented to top management, who arrive at a consensus concerning the results. If the plans appear not to result in a favorable financial picture, they are altered.

SUMMARIZE AND PRESENT. The executive summary is written by the top
management team. It is presented by the top officer to the management of
the company. The purpose is to cascade the planning through the
organization. The future of the company is now closely linked to the
strategic plan. Bound copies are given out for reference in developing
action plans for each functional area. Figure 6-6 shows the payoff of
strategic planning.

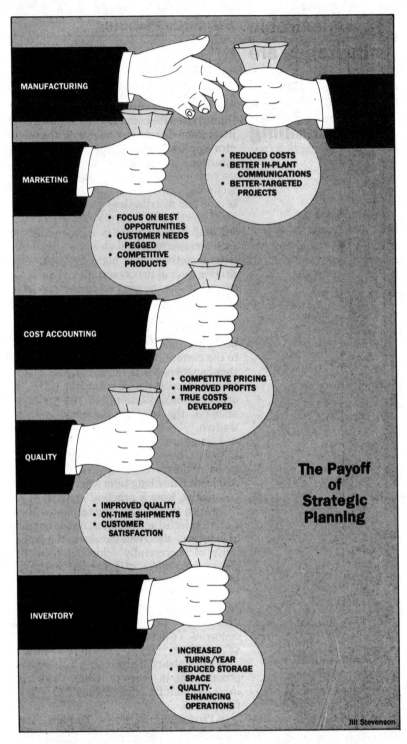

Figure 6-6. Strategic planning pays off in different ways for each functional group

(Courtesy of Manufacturing Engineering Magazine.)

SPECIFIC ACTION PLANS FOR DRIVERS OF THE BUSINESS

When the global strategic plan is completed by top management, more specific plans are developed for the drivers of the business. These include action plans for manufacturing, marketing, finance, and product development. It is important to realize that these are not plans for individual departments. They relate to the major drivers of a company for which the responsibility is shared among several departments or functional areas. These drivers are aligned with the global strategic planning by a company's top management shown in Figure 6-4.

The plans for the drivers must mesh with the global strategic plan. They also must mesh with each other. The interaction is iterative in that information from one plan changes another. If they don't mesh with each other, chaos will result. For example, an increase in marketing activity may not be matched with production being able to meet order deadlines. Time will be wasted making temporary fixes that will drain the resources of a company. Quality considerations are normally embedded in each specific plan.

All plans are done in unison to make sure there is no conflict. Membership on the planning team includes the top person of each functional area that has an interest in the action plan. This makes possible an integrated approach. The product development plan would probably involve, as a minimum, the heads of product engineering, marketing, and manufacturing.

PRODUCT DEVELOPMENT PLAN. This action plan addresses how the product line will change during the period of the strategic plan. New products will be added. Others will be modified. Those that are obsolete or no longer of value will be dropped. A timing chart is usually made summarizing the expected changes. All this requires close coordination among product engineering, marketing, and production.

The action plan may be a reaction to an effort to boost market share or return on investment. Some change may be needed to get products that are easier to make and improve quality. Laying out this plan will enable production to project when resources need to be added. This will allow the timely recruitment of people and the scheduling of necessary training for the skills required. Expansion also can be projected and new equipment can be added. Regarding product development teams, this can help determine what people are needed from the various disciplines and when they must be available. For product engineering, the timing for new purchases of laboratory equipment can be established and justified. Through this, planning can be done with a long-range focus.

MARKETING PLAN. The marketing action plan addresses the price strategy and quality issues in the marketplace. These issues have a direct effect on the future profits of a company. Because of this plan, for example, an activity to identify customer needs may be started. The market focus is also specified in this plan. Whether the focus is broad or narrow, it will be of great importance. Different markets, especially offshore, require distinct products to be developed. The expected time that a product may be viable is also of interest. Timing of new products to replace obsolete ones is vital for achieving the objectives of strategic planning. The way sales in the future will be handled is also part of this plan. Sales could be direct or to a distributor. The sales may be handled internally or left up to a

119

manufacturer's representative. These factors affect such things as warehouse requirements and inventory. The outcome of this plan directly concerns the future actions of the product engineering and production functions. Particularly important to manufacturing is the forecast of sales of each future product. This is used to get the right quantity of resources.

MANUFACTURING PLAN. This concerns the resources of a company. These could be people or equipment and buildings. It also includes suppliers and the availability of sufficient materials.

Necessary inventory levels need to be projected. The actual plan may be a timing chart for procuring and adding the various resources. This plan needs inputs from the other action plans to be successful. The issue is timing. Resources must be in place when needed. The timing must be precise. If they are added too early for a new product, the expense will cause profits to decline. This also will happen if they are added too late, with the compounded problem of unhappy customers not receiving deliveries.

Accurate predictions of sales also are critical. The prediction is developed from the marketing action plan. Low-volume production is different from high-volume. The variety of models is also important. Different equipment may be used for the various scenarios. Once equipment is bought, jumping from one scenario to another could be a disaster. It must be recognized that any plan may be wrong to an extent. Allowing tolerance for an unknown change in the manufacturing plan is a challenge.

FINANCIAL PLAN. Most companies need to borrow money to make changes especially for the long term. The timing of borrowing and the type of financing could affect the bottom line of a company for some time. Input from the other plans is needed to forecast the amount and timing of borrowing. Predictions of inventory levels and capital investments affect the amount of money that needs to be invested in the business. The cost of the money must not exceed the benefits to be gained. For the manufacturing plan, monies may not be available to provide the needed resources. If so, other ways must be sought. This may be by such things as outsourcing or increasing the number of shifts to gain capacity. Reduction of inventory and improving quality are other ways of gaining funds.

CASCADING INTO FUNCTIONAL AREAS AND DEPARTMENTS

Much detail is available from the global strategic plan and the action plans for product development, marketing, production, and finance. The direction is clear where the company is now going. Objectives have been established by top management. The heads of the functional areas agreed on the scenario for the company regarding products to be offered and resources provided. Now it takes someone to act. The plans and results so far have to be cascaded to the functional areas and departments. The need is for everyone in the company to direct action toward achieving the long-range objectives.

The planning that takes place on the lower rungs of the organization is similar to that of the top managers, only the focus is narrower. It is driven by the objectives of the company, but it needs to be placed into the narrower perspective of each employee. It is a team effort. Those in each department must reach a consensus regarding their plans. Usually, a department mission is developed first. Such a mission statement might be:

> The mission of the Design Engineering Department is to provide production drawings representing the product to be manufactured.

Next, personnel in the department reach consensus on several long-range objectives. These objectives must flow from the global business objectives, and they must help to achieve a global objective. Some may be in terms of the quality of product or service. Others may involve the cost of the product or service. Still others may concern the promptness of providing the service. Many companies are benchmarking what other companies are doing on a department level. This could be helpful in making attainable goals and providing improvement ideas.

As in the case of global objectives, a long laundry list of objectives is not suggested. There should be only a few, to increase the likelihood of achieving them. It is also important that the objectives have a possibility of success and that they are expressed in quantified terms. Often, performance measures also are developed for each step of the ladder toward the objective.

Examples of department objectives are:

1. Reduce changes in drawings from 10 to 0 each month by 1992.
2. Implement integrated CAD system to reduce lead time for a drawing from three months to one week by 1993.
3. Reduce cost of a drawing by 50% by 1993.

Like the global objectives, the department objectives should be tested against some criteria to assure that they will work. For example, each objective should be looked at to see if it really can be measured to determine progress and how sensitive it is to changes in the external forces on the department. If it has a high sensitivity, it may not be under the control of those in the department.

The department objectives are tested to see if they support each other. This is usually done through review with the department managers. They, in turn, take it up the line to their management for review. Also to be discussed with management is what resources are required. This includes people and budget.

Methods for strategic planning differ widely in companies. It helps to get people in the company to focus on what is needed for continuous improvement. There is a buy-in because there was participation and consensus in finding the best approach for the company.

The next chapter will discuss ways to plan for improvement.

BIBLIOGRAPHY

Gilreath, Arthur, "Participative Long-Range Planning: Planning by Alignment." Industrial Management, January-February 1990.

Hayes, Roger H., Wheelwright, Steven C. and Clarke, Kim B., "Dynamic Manufacturing." The Free Press, 1988.

Lawler, Edward E. III, "High Involvement Management." Jossey-Bash, 1988.

Nadish, Norman L., "Are You Planning in the Dark?" Manufacturing
Engineering, July 1988, p. 58.

Spartz, Donald A., Management Vitality--A Team Approach, 1st ed. Dearborn,
MI: Society of Manufacturing Engineers, 1984.

Wittry, Eugene J., Managing Information Systems, 1st ed. Dearborn, MI:
Society of Manufacturing Engineers, 1987.

Wright, Robert G., Systems Thinking: A Guide to Managing in a Changing
Environment, 1st ed. Dearborn, MI: Society of Manufacturing Engineers,
1989.

CHAPTER 7

PLANNING
FOR IMPROVEMENT

In this chapter. . .

ROADBLOCKS
1. Overloaded Resources
2. Changing Project Scope
3. Project Roles Unclear

PROJECT PLANNING AND MANAGEMENT
1. Planning
2. Organizing
3. Staffing

CONFLICT

TOOLS FOR PLANNING AND MANAGING PROJECTS
1. Gantt Chart
2. CPM or PERT Charts
3. Network
4. Activities
5. Work Breakdown
6. Precedence Diagram
7. Predecessor Activity
8. Successor Activity
9. Critical Path
10. Scheduling

RESOURCE PLANNING

CRASHING PROJECTS

REPORTS

Appendix information

Project planning process chart
(Courtesy of Charney & Associates, Inc.) A-35

Steps in designing a PERT network
(Courtesy of Charney & Associates, Inc.) A-36--A-38

7
Planning For Improvement

This chapter concerns planning for improvement by teams. As discussed in the previous chapter, goals and objectives from strategic planning cascade down into the organization. Making it happen is often left up to a team. This team includes members of the various disciplines concerned with establishing and achieving the goal or objective. Often, team members are not managers but are usually at the working level of an organization. Most, if not all, are directly affected by the impending change. Because of this, decisions regarding issues are usually better made by a team.

Planning takes more time at the start of a project. One could ask where this time comes from. A good answer would be that there always seems to be enough time to correct problems after they happen, but never any time to plan for eliminating the problems before they occur. Time taken for planning reduces time required for firefighting problems. Often, problems are complete surprises that could have been prevented. Using an old cliche, "an ounce of prevention is worth a pound of cure."

Planning is needed for many reasons. First, it reduces uncertainty. Discussions can clarify situations that otherwise would be questionable. Planning fine-tunes objectives of the project and agreement is reached among parties. Through developing measures concerning performance, a basis is formed for evaluating progress as the project progresses. These measures concern the cost, timing, and quality of the effort. Another important benefit of planning is that participants learn immediately what they must do and when it has to be completed. This allows the company and outside sources of supply to organize their efforts.

Managing a project goes hand-in-hand with planning it. Competitive pressures force a company to have projects that are well-managed. This minimizes the risk of failure. Some factors that make it mandatory for a company to have good management of projects are:

1. In today's world, the length of time in which results must be obtained is decreasing. Any wasted effort is unacceptable.
2. Companies often invest much money and resources initially in a project. Some companies risk their future survival on the outcome of key projects.
3. Market competition is more intense than ever before. Higher costs

for projects could affect pricing decisions. High prices could limit sales for a company.

4. Projects not done when needed could affect the availability of new products, giving a competitor the edge.

5. Advancements in technology are more complex to put into production. Also, the technology requires the involvement of more functions in a company. The likelihood of cost overruns with new technology also is great.

Typically, any team effort required is imposed on top of each team member's regular job. This is not easy, but the challenge of making a real improvement may make it worthwhile. Though the members may not be managers, they must plan and manage the project. Without this, wasted effort and extra work would result. This would dilute the progress of the team and erode time available for the regular job of each team member.

The key to continuous improvement is completing projects by the teams. Solutions to problems in production must be put in place. Prevention of problems must occur before going into production. For products now being made, seeking the permanent elimination of the source of problems is most important; so is improving the stability of a process. New processes must assure that products will conform to standards specified by product engineering, to ensure customers will be satisfied.

ROADBLOCKS

Often, the teams face roadblocks that are seemingly beyond their control. If they can be recognized, talks with management are often fruitful and solutions can be sought that are workable. Examples of these are:

1. Overloaded Resources. In this scenario, teams are constantly being added to address new issues. Sometimes, the mentality of management is to create a new team when each new issue surfaces. This means people are on more teams as time goes on. For individuals, priorities become unclear. Each team is just as important as another, but there is a finite number of projects that they can handle effectively.

   To correct this, management must set priorities. Projects with lower priorities must be set on the "back burner" for a while. A periodic, critical review of projects also may reveal projects that are no longer viable. These projects could be dropped and resources given to projects still to be undertaken.

2. Changing Project Scope. For this, project deliverables are unclear. Neither management or the teams have a clear understanding of what is needed. Typically, the project is constantly being modified. When this occurs, much of the prior work is wasted. Starting over causes the project to be even longer. The team is frustrated and management is unsure of the benefits.

   The cause of a change in project scope could be several things. One is that the user of the deliverable is not a team member and valuable input is missing. Another is that the project is too long in duration. Projects should be short. Long-term projects should be divided into deliverables from several short projects that are in series. Often, things that are far into the future are unclear by nature. A dynamic society changes rapidly, and much of this change cannot be predicted accurately.

3. Project Roles Unclear. Sometimes, team members do not understand their roles. This can be taken care of by good project planning, which would specify who is responsible for carrying out each task. More critical, is that resources outside the team may not understand the support needed. Perhaps the toolroom lacks capacity to make needed gages. Again, a good project plan can justify management action to create needed priorities. A plan communicated early would give support groups time to allocate resources when needed.

PROJECT PLANNING AND MANAGEMENT

Management of a project involves several major factors, like people, systems, procedures and technology. Orchestrating these factors is necessary to complete a project. By success, it is meant that the project is completed on time, within budget and performance constraints. Timing may be critical. Looking at the extreme, a late project may be no longer needed. A project that is too costly perhaps should not have been started in the first place. Again, looking at the extreme, the realized benefits of the project may no longer justify the cost. Performance relates to the quality of the completed project. It concerns how well it accomplishes the objective for launching the project. If the result is too unwieldy, it may work over the short term but be quickly discarded by those using it.

In the past, projects were managed by one department in an organization. Some companies continue this practice today. Most projects cross department lines. Usually, the department that had the most to gain was assigned the job. This department first planned what was to be done and then attempted to do it.

Working with other departments was often difficult. Each department had a different agenda and priorities. Much time was put in on issues that did not really contribute to getting the project done. Much conflict and emotion concerned "second guessing" how a project should be done. This was because of the lack of involvement of departments in the planning process. By joint planning, ownership of the project is naturally shared. A lack of ownership by all departments involved was the major reason for projects not being successful in the past. It became difficult for the management of any one department to complete a project successfully.

With the use of teams, a different situation arises. The management of a project can now be done by the team responsible for the project. Members on a team are from each department involved. For the project, team members have a common objective. Discussions can lead to agreement on the approach. Commitment can be obtained regarding needed resources and timing.

By having a common objective, a project can be done with a minimum of wasted motion. Each department "buys-in" and, in a sense, owns a piece of the project. There is a unified approach to getting the job done. Agreement is reached at the beginning of the project. This way, efforts during the project can be focused on the work at hand.

First on the agenda for any team is understanding what is expected. Priority for any team must be to examine critically the objective given by management. Unclear objectives must be clarified. Sometimes this can be done by communicating with management. More often, it can be cleared up through discussions in team meetings.

Developing the mission of the team is one technique used for this. The mission concerns specifically what the team must do. By all members taking part in developing this, a clear understanding is had by everyone. It is important that the job is clear to everyone. The team must know when it starts, and more importantly, when the job is done.

The team should produce a deliverable or series of deliverables. It may be, for example, an analysis or a piece of hardware. The nature of the deliverable must be understood. Also important is just where it will be delivered. This identifies who is the customer of the team. As an example, it may be a manufacturing department. It is important that the customer, in this case, the manufacturing department, fully supports and really needs the team effort. Many feel that the responsiveness of the customer of the team is the key factor in whether a project is successful.

Another factor is the length of the team effort. This should be kept as short as possible. Shorter projects are easier to handle and more effective. The end is easier to see and planning the project is a lot easier. Also, the environment within and outside a company is constantly changing. A short project is easier to deal with in changing environments. In a short span, the environment will change less and not have as big an effect on the project. Shorter projects tend to be less complex. As complexity increases, the tools needed to manage the project become increasingly sophisticated. The danger is that the time taken to use the more sophisticated tools takes away time needed to do the project.

When a company uses teams, the team has to manage the project. This has to do with the allocating and the timing of resources to reach an objective in the best way. It cannot be left up to a manager who is not directly involved with the team. Sometimes, this is a shared responsibility among the members of the team. Consensus is reached regarding details concerning direction. In other cases, a person on the team is designated the project manager. The choice may be made by management or by the members of the team. In either case, the person selected must have strong interpersonal relationships and the support of the other team members.

The activities of managing concern planning, organizing, staffing, directing, and controlling:

1. Planning. This involves finding steps necessary to reach the objective. The best planning involves making up different scenarios and selecting the best one. Each department in an organization has a unique view of the objective and the steps needed. The team framework provides a means of sharing these views and reaching a consensus of what is best for the company. This process brings potential problems to the surface and increases the likelihood of success. A Project Planning Process Chart is in the Appendix.

   After the steps are defined, the timing of each step is determined, along with who is going to do it. By consulting with the person

128

performing a step, agreement and "buy-in" is obtained. Additional information also can be found through talking with this person. This may include projections about the cost of needed resources such as the costs of designing gages.

Also, the results expected by the team can be tested against the feelings of someone who has to do the work. This can be used to develop performance measures. These are the minimum expectations for each step in the plan. The performance measures can be used to evaluate the actual results for each step. Steps having marginal results may have to be repeated to assure the success of the project.

Through planning, the team develops several measures for deciding how well a project is progressing. First, the necessary steps are identified. Steps that are not done could signal efforts that are superficial. Second, the team knows the expected cost and timing of each step. Not achieving cost targets could place the justification of the project in question. Also, not completing steps on time defers the ultimate benefits farther into the future. Lastly, performance measures help a team to identify steps that are poorly done. These steps, although completed, could weaken the entire effort. The measures collectively provide a foundation for the team to manage the project. Areas of weakness can be recognized and needed corrections made before damage is done.

2. Organizing. The next step is organizing to do the project. Mostly this means tailoring activities in view of other things going on in the company. In all companies, resources are limited. There are many things to do and some may never get done. By seeking commitments well ahead of time, the risk of being let down is minimized. The protocol and the right procedure for doing this differ among companies.

   First, the team must be organized. Time commitments for each member must be projected. Agreement must be reached with the management for this investment of time. Usually, this requires individual agreements with each functional area having a member. A room for holding team meetings may need to be booked in advance. Effort might be required to find secretarial and clerical support. Management reviews may need to be scheduled well in advance. Timing of the management reviews may be critical. The days that people are available may be scarce due to out-of-town commitments and vacations.

   Other resources in the company need to be organized. This includes money and people. Decisions are required as to whether services inside the company will be used. If not, qualified suppliers must be sought. Priorities need to be established in view of other work that is expected simultaneously. Commitment and support from management for these resources is vital to the success of the project.

3. Staffing. Providing team members is part of staffing. First, the talent required to do the different tasks must be determined. Then the people in the company must be reviewed to see who matches the

needs. It may be difficult to get the right people. They may be in high demand, but having the right people is critical to getting the job done. Where there is no right match, the answer may lie in providing training through outside seminars and workshops. Training is now done on a wide scale to gain certain skills that a company needs.

Sometimes outside consultants may be necessary to provide specialized knowledge. The job requiring a consultant should be specifically defined. A consultant should be sought who can do this job. Establishing informal contacts and sources of information outside the team is also necessary. Such contacts and sources are often critical to the success of a team.

Some companies do not use the same members on the team for the entire project. As needs appear and disappear, different people assume membership roles. For example, marketing professionals may be valuable when planning an improvement. They may not be necessary, however, when the machinery required for the improvement is being installed. This way the availability of talent for other projects can be maximized. On the other hand, the solidarity of the team is threatened with constant changing of members. Perhaps the most difficult aspect of staffing is replacing someone when they leave the team unexpectedly. Be careful to select a replacement who is compatible with the others. Training may be necessary to bring talents up to the level required.

4. Directing. This deals with the guidance and supervision of the project. Agreements regarding resources make this job much easier. Conflicts will be minimized since priorities for the resources already have been established. Project management tools can be used effectively here; these will be discussed later in this chapter. It is important that some leeway be given to those who must do the work. People do best when they can exercise some degree of self direction. Empathy is also needed at times. The important thing here is attempting to understand the needs, feelings and motives of those doing the work. Much skill in interpersonal relationships is necessary. This will aid greatly in getting a slipping schedule back on track.

5. Controlling. This means regulating the project so that the plan is achieved. Most projects tend to slip while they are being done. The important thing is to recognize quickly when this happens and fix any problems right away. Control often means the difference between a project succeeding or not. Measures for deciding how well a project is doing are derived during planning. One measure concerns the steps that are required to complete the project. If steps are skipped, a strong signal is given to the team that the project may be in trouble.

During planning, the team also estimates the expected cost and timing of each step. If cost targets and completion dates are not met, a strong signal is also given to the team. Many teams also define performance measures. Not meeting these performance measures signals that certain steps may be poorly done.

The measures provide a way for the team to compare actual progress against expected progress. By paying attention to this, areas that need shoring up can be quickly recognized and fixed before it is too late. This may mean providing additional resources. An example may be getting outside help to complete an installation that unexpected absences caused to fall behind. Sometimes, plans must be rethought and other approaches used. For example, a planned activity may no longer be necessary. Much flexibility must be exercised to be responsive to what is needed as the project is being executed.

In most planning efforts, there are trade-offs among cost, timing and the risk that objectives will not be obtained. Frequently, altering one of these directly affects the others. Dropping one step in the plan may save some cost and reduce the time required. This may increase the risk that the performance of the end item will not be adequate. Another example is that timing may be shortened by spending more money like paying overtime. These trade-offs are an important part of planning a project. Many trade-offs concern cost and timing.

For continuous improvement, these factors also are important. Conceptually, continuous improvement depends upon many projects in series. As one project is completed, the need for another project is identified. Improvement occurs incrementally as each succeeding project is completed. This is shown in Figure 7-1. When each project is completed, the quality level rises. Similarly, the failure cost, for example, decreases.

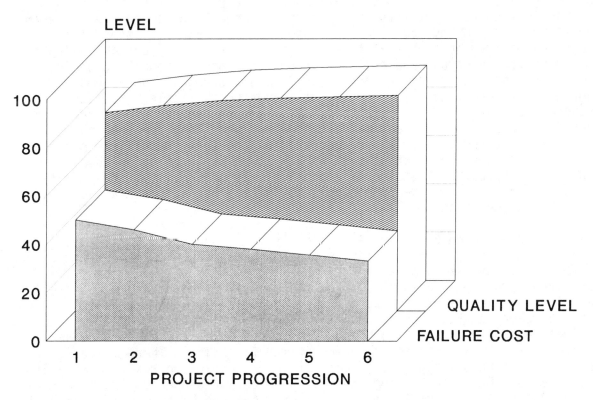

Figure 7-1. The relation of projects to quality and costs.

In a sense, perfection gets closer as each project is done. If a project drags out, the expected improvement in quality level becomes more distant. There also is a cumulative effect. The results expected from each succeeding project are delayed. Conceptually, results from all projects become more distant in the future. Also, the reduction in cost becomes less each year for the company. The proper planning and management of projects is a crucial factor in fulfilling hopes for continuous improvement.

CONFLICT

Conflict exists on all projects. If not dealt with, it could destroy a project. Schedules could slip badly while members on the team argue. This is a natural occurrence on a team because of strong opinions of team members. If dealt with, conflict is a positive force and can contribute greatly to improved performance of the team and the project.

In the past, companies saw conflict as negative. Production was repetitive and highly organized through work simplification concepts. Organizations were run from the top down. If you had a problem, you worked with your supervisor and not your peers. Roles and relationships were well developed. They were based on goals made by those at the top of the organization. Usually, direction was not openly questioned. "Don't rock the boat" was the motto of many in the past. Conflict tended to destroy this status quo and was dealt with severely. Often, it was blamed on personality conflicts. The fix was to separate the parties physically. In the extreme, employees who could not get along with others were discharged. Managers in the past either ignored conflict or did everything they could to stop it.

Now things are different. Organizations have to be more flexible to react quickly to changes in markets. The need for cooperation among the different functions in a company has to be understood and accepted. Competition is tough and management sees that they need all the help they can get. Input is sought from everyone and conflict is brought into the open. Conflict that is controlled is recognized as positive and strongly encouraged. Managers now see it as a way of getting issues on the table. By recognizing issues, they can be solved. In this way, projects can be strengthened. Conflict can act to bond team members together when they see that their concerns are taken seriously and addressed by the team. Conflict is in reality a healthy byproduct of team work. It helps in bringing about innovative approaches that increase productivity and quality. Many ways of doing something often come from conflict. With alternatives available, the best one can be chosen.

There are times when functions in a company view other functions as having opposing viewpoints. In the past, product engineering was seen by the factory floor as making hard-to-build designs. There was no empathy perceived toward manufacturing. From the opposite view point, manufacturing was viewed as unwilling to take a risk in building something. These feelings over the years created an artificial wall between product engineering and manufacturing. Product designs were often described as "thrown over the wall" into the hands of manufacturing. There may have been some truth in each viewpoint. Teams with both parties represented made it possible for these conflicting viewpoints to be aired openly. Both parties realized through this conflict that designs that can be made easily benefit everyone.

But conflict on teams must be controlled. Disruptive conflict must be avoided. This type of conflict occurs in situations in which one party must

win and the other has to lose. Also, it occurs where a good solution is
viewed negatively only because it is not invented here. Often, this is
caused by team members taking a narrow view of the situation. A broader
perspective can turn conflict into something constructive. This can be
brought about by each member trying to understand other viewpoints.
Constructive conflict occurs where there is a combination of open debate and
an effort to share meanings. Its value lies in being a source of many good,
diverse ideas that could be useful in solving problems that are relevant.

Constructive conflict will occur when members on the team know that it
arises through a sincere desire to make the team successful. The best
solutions probably come through a combination of opposing viewpoints.
Through conflict, solutions can be intensively tested, increasing the
likelihood of success.

TOOLS FOR PLANNING AND MANAGING PROJECTS

There are many tools for planning and managing projects. They range from a
simple calendar to sophisticated computer programs. The choice of which to
use depends upon the complexity of the project and the level of detail
required. For a simple project of several days' duration, making a list of
what needs to be done on a calendar may be adequate. The most popular tool
used in project planning is a simple Gantt Chart. Sometimes, a tool is
chosen that is more complicated than necessary. In this situation, using
the tool may become more time consuming than the project.

Success of a project depends upon how carefully the objective is translated
into resources and the timing of those resources. The tools for planning
and managing projects help in doing this. All factors have to be considered
collectively. They cannot be pursued independently or failure is likely.
First, the objective must be clarified and an idea of the general timing
obtained.

Resources that could be planned for include people, money, tools, equipment,
facilities, products and technology. But project management usually only
considers resources that are used, such as people and money. It normally
does not consider things that are consumed like construction material. This
limits the focus to something that can be controlled through scheduling of
activities.

Some resources, such as technology, may not be available and may need
development. Most of the planning for a project is iterative: it starts
with a rough plan that is honed using the tools discussed in this chapter.
Good planners are aware of roadblocks and restraints that may occur. By
proper planning and proper use of the tools discussed here, the effect of
such obstacles can be minimized.

Gantt Chart

The first technique to be used in project planning probably was the Gantt
Chart. It is still very popular today. It is easy to make. Also, it is
readily understood when discussing project details with others. A simple
Gantt Chart is shown in Figure 7-2. The horizontal axis has a time scale
representing the expected duration of the project. Horizontal bars are used
to portray the expected start and finish times of each major activity in the

project. The bars are organized to show which activity must be completed
before another starts. For example, in Figure 7-2, the "Bids" must be
completed before the "Order" activity can be started. On the other hand,
the "Test" activity can be done at the same time as the "Alter" activity.

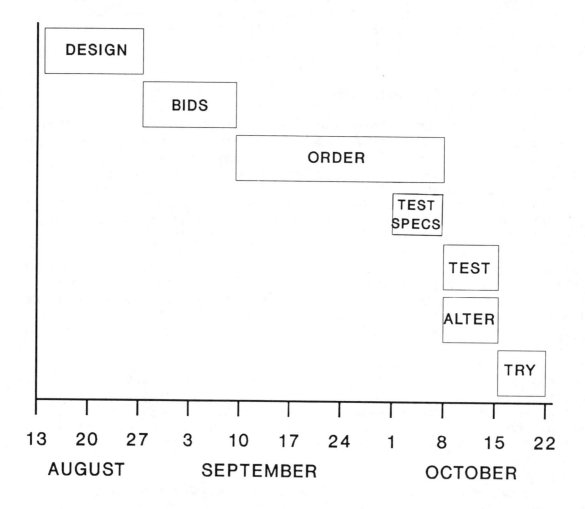

Figure 7-2. A simple Gantt Chart.

Regarding the management of the project, the bars can be shaded in to show
progress. The degree of completion can be shown by how much of the bar is
shaded. A vertical line drawn from the current date will show how the
actual progress compares to what was planned. An example of this is shown
in Figure 7-3. For this example, it appears that the actual "Order" is
lagging behind that expected and the finish date of the project is in
jeopardy. Note also that the "Test Specs" activity should be just starting.

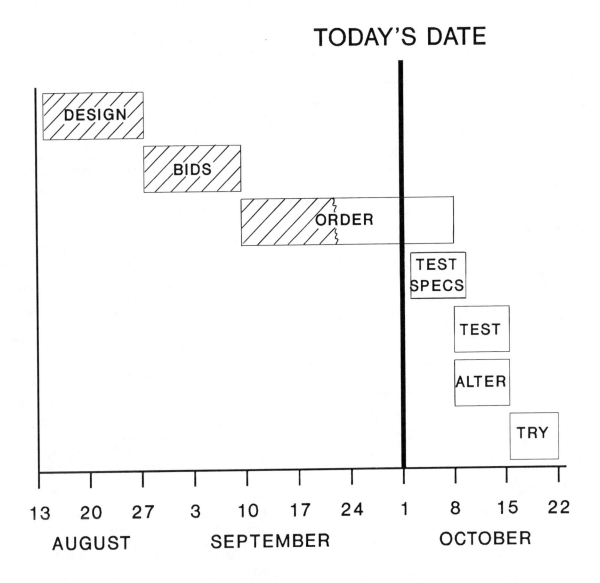

TODAY'S DATE

Figure 7-3. A simple Gantt Chart showing progress.

A more sophisticated Gantt Chart is shown in Figure 7-4. This was done using a computer software package. Note that the duration of each activity is broken down into time required to do the activity and slack time. For example, "cn existing" requires five days to do. It can be started after "design specs" is done. But it doesn't have to be finished until "tryout" over six weeks later.

It can be done at any point during that span of time without delaying the project. The slack time is the excess time available to do the activity. There is slack time in the "test specs" activity also. No slack time exists for doing the activities of "design specs," "bids," "order," "bench test," and "tryout." If any of these activities take longer than projected, the project likely will not be finished on time.

Gantt Charts are considered a useful tool to plan and manage simpler projects. The plan is made as a Gantt Chart is constructed. Comparing

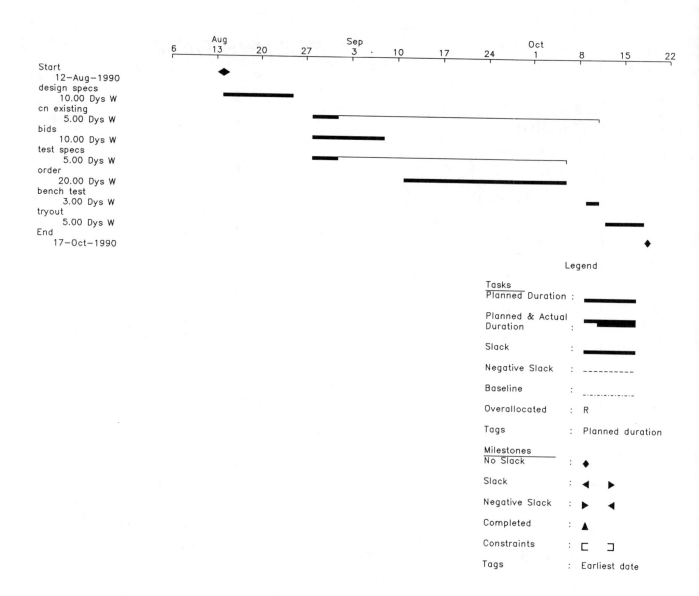

Figure 7-4. A computer-generated Gantt Chart.

actual progress against expected results is easy to do. It is also an
effective way to talk to others regarding the project. However, it cannot
be effectively used for more complex projects that have interactions among
the activities. CPM or PERT Charts are more useful in these situations. An
example of a PERT Chart may be found in Appendix A.

CPM or PERT Charts

CPM (Critical Path Method) and PERT (Project Evaluation and Review
Technique) charts had different origins about the same time. CPM started in
the construction industry. The Polaris missile program, a research and
development project, is where PERT started. Each is credited with saving
much time in doing projects. But today, both have evolved to where they are
very similar. This similarity is so strong that the names are often used
interchangeably.

Conceptually, the major difference is that CPM uses one number for the duration of an activity. PERT allows for uncertainty by using a range of numbers for the duration of an activity. Three time periods are specified for each activity. They are times from the optimistic, most likely, and pessimistic viewpoints. Many feel that estimating a range of times is too difficult with the information that is usually available.

NETWORK. In both CPM and PERT, the activities to do the project are shown by a network. This shows in what order the activities probably should be done. The network is made up of nodes and arrowed lines connecting the nodes. Figure 7-5 shows two approaches for doing this. For the "activity on node approach," (AON) each node represents an activity. The arrowed lines between the nodes only show the relationship among the nodes.

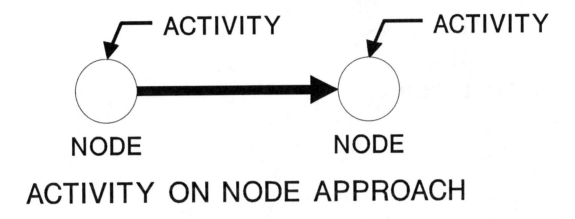

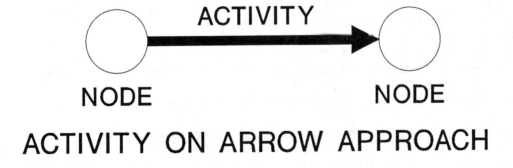

Figure 7-5. A network showing two ways to approach project activities.

In the "activity on arrow approach," (AOA) the activities are shown by the arrowed lines between the nodes. The nodes are called events and show the start and finish of the activities. For AOA, dummy activities are often needed. A dummy activity is the dashed arrowed line in Figure 7-6. The dummy activity takes no resources or cost to do. It is only there to specify what activity is next.

ACTIVITY ON ARROW APPROACH

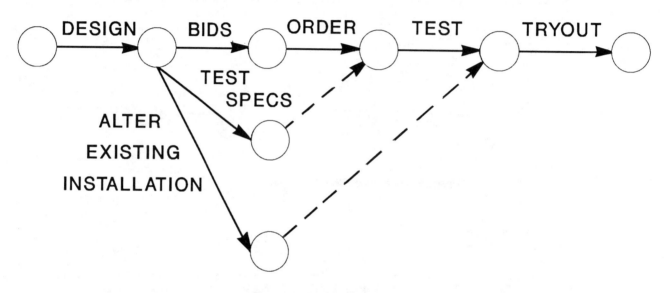

Figure 7-6. A CPM Chart.

There are several rules that should usually be followed when making networks. They are:

1. A network can only have one start and one end node. These are the first and last nodes in Figure 7-6. To assure this, all arrows must point toward the end. There can be no doubling back or closed loops.
2. No activity can start until all activities feeding into it are finished. In the network shown in Figure 7-6, "Test" cannot start until "Test Specs" and "Order" are finished.
3. Each activity must have a recognizable start and end.
4. All nodes, except the end node, must have a following node separated by an arrowed line.
5. Every arrowed line must have a starting node and ending node.

It must be remembered that the network is only a plan. No plans are followed exactly. Things come up that make it wise to change what was planned to be done. The network is only a best estimate of the steps that should be followed.

ACTIVITIES. Deciding how large an activity should be is a matter of judgment. An activity could be as small as motions in work measurements. This would result in an awesome number of activities for most projects. Obviously, this size activity would not be acceptable. At the other extreme, an activity could be as large as the entire project. This activity would be too big, since no details of the project are revealed. In essence, the size depends upon what is suitable to track while the project proceeds. The important thing is that an activity must:

1. Be required in the project.
2. Consume resources.
3. Have a beginning and end that can be easily recognized.

WORK BREAKDOWN. A tool that can be used by a team to decide upon what and how large activities should be is the work breakdown technique. This technique partitions the project into activities of work for which costs, budgets and schedules can be done. Using this technique, a work breakdown structure (WBS) is developed as shown in Figure 7-7. It looks like an inverted tree. The project is broken into more detail as the levels descend. This approach is almost mandatory to find the activities of a complex project. Otherwise, activities would be missed. Doing a work break-down enables a team to look at the project in a broader light. First, the major activities are decided and then more detail is sought. It avoids getting immediately lost in detail.

As shown in Figure 7-7, the effort starts with defining the goal or objective of the project. The next level specifies the major activities that are required to obtain the goal. In the example, the goal is to put a new electronic gage in a machining center. To achieve this requires the major activities of design, build, test and install the new gage. Blocks for each major activity are placed on the first level down from the goal. Then, each major activity is further broken down on the next level down. For example, the major activity of build was seen as done by a supplier. This was broken into get bids and order. The test was seen as developing test specs and bench testing. These, too, were placed on the next level down.

This process is continued until the lowest level activity to be dealt with is reached. The work content of each newly defined activity decreases as a level descends. The number of activities on the lower level increases. In this way, the possibility of not recognizing an important activity in the project is small. When the number and size of activities seem reasonable, the process can be stopped. The activities can be used to prepare networks as well as other timing and resource charts.

In reality, there is no right way to prepare a WBS. Neither is there a wrong way. If two groups prepare a WBS on a project, they will be different. But there are some guiding principles. They are:

1. The team should have members from various functional areas.
2. Effort must be extended to do a complete job so all required activities are found.
3. Partitioning by functional area or organization must be avoided.
4. Activities should be partitioned into two or more activities in the next lower level.
5. An activity cannot be connected to more than one activity in an upper level.

PRECEDENCE DIAGRAM. A precedence diagram is used to display in a graphical format the activities for the project. This is a specialized network

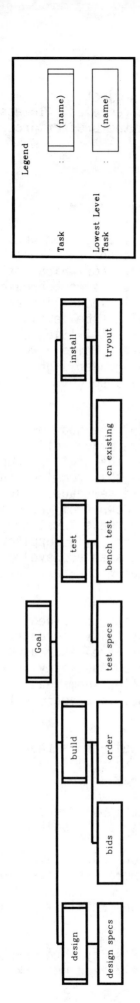

Figure 7-7. Work breakdown Chart.

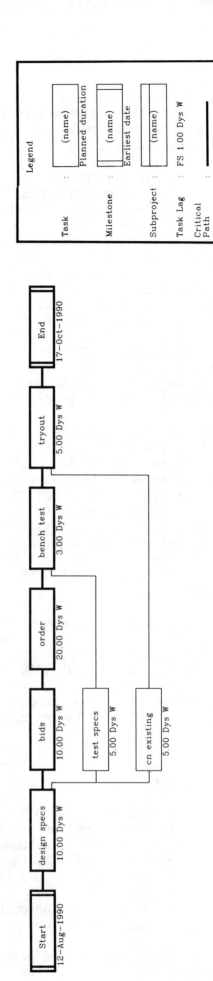

Figure 7-8. A computer-generated CPM Chart.

diagram. It is specialized because it shows the order in which each
activity must be completed. For this diagram, activities are often
classified as follows:

Predecessor activity. This type of activity immediately precedes the
one under consideration. It must be completed before the activity under
consideration can be started. In Figure 7-6, "Bids" is a predecessor to
"Order."

Successor activity. This activity immediately follows the one being
considered. Referring again to Figure 7-6, "Test" is a successor to
"Order."

The order in which activities must be completed is dictated by certain
constraints that must be met. These constraints are recognized as either
technological, procedural, or imposed. Sometimes, constraints can be
neutralized by increasing the amount of resources being used, such as by
overtime.

The first type of constraint, however, cannot be avoided despite the level
of resources. Technological constraints must be met. For example, in
Figure 7-6, "Bids" cannot proceed until "Design" is done. The problem, in
this case, is you cannot find out how much something will cost until you
have an idea of what it is.

Procedural constraints can be neutralized. They are usually evolve from
company policies. Referring again to Figure 7-6, management could relax the
requirement that bids must be obtained before ordering something. If they
do, the "Bids" activity is no longer required before "Order" can proceed.

Imposed constraints happen because of the way the project has been planned.
Often, they are due to a perceived limit on resources. These constraints
usually can be neutralized by either changing plans or providing more
resources. As an example, "Test" occurs before "Tryout" in Figure 7-6. A
bench test is planned to validate the performance of a new electronic gage
before its installation. In this way, debugging can be done off-line before
it is in place. This will reduce the risk of downtime of the production
facility. If demand for the product is high, this is very desirable.
However, if production schedules are light, the possibility of more downtime
may not be critical. If so, "Test" can be dropped as part of the project.
By doing so, management accepts the risk of additional downtime if the gage
is faulty after it is in place.

Figure 7-6 is really more than a network diagram. It is a precedence
diagram since the required order of the activities is shown. It also
recognizes the constraints in the project.

CRITICAL PATH. The primary goal of a network analysis is to find the
critical path. The critical path is a sequence of activities that if taken,
will result in the least time to complete the project. The project cannot
be done any quicker with the existing activities and constraints. Also, if
any activities on the critical path are not done when planned, the project
will be delayed.

The critical path is shown in Figure 7-8. It is the heavy line between the
tasks. Note that this chart has a different format than that in Figure 7-6.

It is based on an "activity on node" (AON) approach instead of AOA. Also it was done using a computer software program. The approach to find the critical path manually is to find first all the possible paths and then to select the longest one. There are three possibilities in Figure 7-8. They are:

Path 1: design specs-bids-order-bench test-tryout.

Path 2: design specs-test specs-bench test-tryout.

Path 3: design specs-cn existing-tryout.

In more complex projects, there could hundreds of possible paths. A computer software program could be of immense assistance.

Below each node in Figure 7-6 there is the time that each activity takes to do. Using this information, the length of each path is calculated by adding up the individual times for each activity. For Figure 7-8, they are:

Path 1: 10 days + 10 days + 20 days + 3 days + 5 days = 48 days.

Path 2: 10 days + 5 days + 3 days + 5 days = 23 days.

Path 3: 10 days + 5 days + 5 days = 20 days.

The longest path is the critical path, which is Path 1. This verifies what is indicated in Figure 7-8. Under the conditions planned, the project will take 48 days to complete. Also, if an activity that is not on the critical path is done faster or eliminated, the project will still take the same time to complete.

To shorten project time, the following could be considered for activities on the critical path:

1. Starting an activity sooner. By integrating two or more activities, time can be saved, allowing for a quicker start.
2. Breaking a longer activity into two parts so that each can be done simultaneously. This way, the time duration required for the task is shorter.
3. Using different technology to shorten the time to do an activity.
4. Increasing the number of people assigned to an activity.

In doing this, often there is a choice as to which activity can be changed. The following may be helpful when making this choice:

1. Select activities that are earlier in the project. After the project starts, the later activities can be looked at for improvements.
2. Look at longer duration activities first. They usually have more potential than the shorter activities.
3. Avoid activities where change could present technical problems.
4. Change activities that are directly controlled rather than those controlled by others. This increases the likelihood of success.
5. Select activities that use fewer resources over those that are more intense.

142

6. Transfer resources from activities that are not critical to those that are.

SCHEDULING. The next step is to find when the various activities must be done. Usually, this is specified by dates. For activities not on the critical path, there is some leeway. Starting these activities after they could be started will not slow the project down. The amount of leeway is called the slack time.

To find the starting and finishing dates for activities, the paths on the precedence diagram are reviewed. The difference between the starting and finishing dates is the duration of the activity. Both the earliest and latest dates must be found for starting and finishing an activity. For the earliest dates, this review proceeds from the start of the project. This will fix the project finish date. To find the latest dates, the review is reversed starting from the end of the project.

A listing of dates for the project being used as an example is shown in Figure 7-9. This listing assumes that the company works five days a week and there are no holidays during the project. If the project starts on August 13, 1990, it will finish at the earliest on October 17, 1990. The activities on the critical path have no leeway or slack time. They must be started when specified or the project will be delayed. The earliest and latest times for start and finish of an activity are the same for each.

ACTIVITY	PLANNED DURATION DAYS	EARLIEST START	LATEST START	EARLIEST FINISH	LATEST FINISH	SLACK DAYS
DESIGN SPECS	10	8/13/90	8/13/90	8/24/90	8/24/90	0
BIDS	10	8/27/90	8/27/90	9/7/90	9/7/90	0
CN EXISTING	5	8/27/90	10/4/90	8/31/90	10/10/90	28
TEST SPECS	5	8/27/90	10/1/90	8/31/90	10/5/90	25
ORDER	20	9/10/90	9/10/90	10/5/90	10/5/90	0
BENCH TEST	3	10/8/90	10/8/90	10/10/90	10/10/90	0
TRYOUT	5	10/11/90	10/11/90	10/17/90	10/17/90	0

Figure 7-9. Schedule Chart.

The activities of "cn existing" and "test specs" are not on the critical path. There is some leeway, as to when they must be started or completed. The leeway or slack times are 28 and 25 days, respectively. Therefore, the earliest and latest dates for starting and finishing these activities need not be the same.

Many projects, as they proceed, will vary from the original plan. Making a good project plan is just a start. As soon as the project starts, surprises happen. Constraints occur that were not apparent. Activities are not completed on time. When this happens, a new critical path may exist. Properly managing a project requires updating plans regularly. For more complex projects, a computer software program can update the project plan with a minimum of effort.

RESOURCE PLANNING

Some companies do resource planning as part of project management. From a project management viewpoint, resources like people, for example, are something you use to accomplish a project. It does not usually include something that is used up like construction material. By this restriction, the focus of managing is narrowed to the tailoring and scheduling of activities. This is what project management is all about.

Through resource planning, management can be aware of the level of resources required and the expected cost before a project is started. Also, actual expenditures can be compared to those originally planned. For a company that has many projects, resource leveling is often done. By this technique, the activities of the many projects are sequenced so there is a more uniform demand for the resources of the company. Peak demands are minimized and there is less need for seeking resources outside the company.

The first step of resource planning is determining the cost of each of the resources. Figure 7-10, prepared using a computer software program, is a list of resources that can be used on the example project. For each of the resources which are people, the cost per hour is listed. In a typical project, this cost includes wages or salary, fringe benefits and maybe variable overhead.

16-Aug-1990

Resource name	Quantity	Time units	Cost/unit	Resource calendar	Responsible
plant eng	1.000	Hrs	25.00		plant eng
purchasing	1.000	Hrs	20.00		purchasing
quality	1.000	Hrs	20.00		quality
tool eng	1.000	Hrs	32.00		tool eng

Figure 7-10. Resource list.

The next step is estimating how much of each resource is needed for each activity. This is listed in Figure 7-11. A computer software program was also used to help prepare this. Note that for the activity "Bids" two resources are required - tool engineering and purchasing. For most of the activities, the needed work time is the same as the duration of the activity. Exceptions are "Bids" and "Order" where no resources are required while replies are being prepared by outside suppliers. Note that the format of this report allows for comparing actual work against the planned work for each activity. Since this was printed before the project was started, there are no actual costs listed.

When using a computer software program, required calculations are automatic. Figure 7-12 is a listing of the cost of resources for each activity. The biggest cost is that of "design specs." As in the last form discussed, provision is allowed for displaying actual costs for each activity after the project starts, so a comparison can be made.

In planning some projects, the available resources may be less than needed. For example, the only available maintenance person may have to work on two activities that are scheduled simultaneously. Something has to be changed

144

ALLOCATION BY TASK

Allocations by Task

16-Aug-1990

Task name	Task start date	Task finish date	Resource name	Resource quantity	Planned work	Actual work	Remaining work
bench test	8-Oct-1990	10-Oct-1990	quality	1.000	24.00 Hrs W	0.00 Dys W	0.00 Dys W
bids	27-Aug-1990	7-Sep-1990	tool eng	1.000	20.00 Hrs W	0.00 Dys W	0.00 Dys W
bids	27-Aug-1990	7-Sep-1990	purchasing	1.000	20.00 Hrs W	0.00 Dys W	0.00 Dys W
cn existing	27-Aug-1990	31-Aug-1990	plant eng	1.000	40.00 Hrs W	0.00 Dys W	0.00 Dys W
design specs	13-Aug-1990	24-Aug-1990	tool eng	1.000	10.00 Dys W	0.00 Dys W	0.00 Dys W
order	10-Sep-1990	5-Oct-1990	purchasing	1.000	8.00 Hrs W	0.00 Dys W	0.00 Dys W
test specs	27-Aug-1990	31-Aug-1990	quality	1.000	40.00 Hrs W	0.00 Dys W	0.00 Dys W
tryout	11-Oct-1990	17-Oct-1990	plant eng	1.000	40.00 Hrs W	0.00 Dys W	0.00 Dys W

Figure 7-11. Allocation by task.

TASK AND MILESTONE LIST

Task & Milestone List

16-Aug-1990

Task name	Start date	Finish date	Planned duration	Pln total cost	Actual duration	Act total cost
bench test	8-Oct-1990	10-Oct-1990	3.00 Dys W	480.00	0.00 Dys W	0.00
bids	27-Aug-1990	7-Sep-1990	10.00 Dys W	1040.00	0.00 Dys W	0.00
cn existing	27-Aug-1990	31-Aug-1990	5.00 Dys W	1000.00	0.00 Dys W	0.00
design specs	13-Aug-1990	24-Aug-1990	10.00 Dys W	2560.00	0.00 Dys W	0.00
End	17-Oct-1990	17-Oct-1990				
order	10-Sep-1990	5-Oct-1990	20.00 Dys W	160.00	0.00 Dys W	0.00
Start	12-Aug-1990	13-Aug-1990				
test specs	27-Aug-1990	31-Aug-1990	5.00 Dys W	800.00	0.00 Dys W	0.00
tryout	11-Oct-1990	17-Oct-1990	5.00 Dys W	1000.00	0.00 Dys W	0.00

Figure 7-12. Task and milestone list.

because this person cannot be in two places simultaneously. The following may be helpful when conflicts arise in the scheduling of resources:

1. Assign priorities to the resources so that the highest priority resource is resolved first. This priority can relate to the scarcity of the resource. For example, usually there are many more inspectors than maintenance people. For this example, the maintenance person would have the higher priority. In this way, the situation that has the least flexibility is resolved first.
2. Assign higher priority resources to activities with slack, if possible. These activities are easier to reschedule.
3. For activities with the same slack, assign the higher priority resource to the longest duration activity. This is the activity that needs the resource the longest. Other, shorter activities may be rescheduled more easily.
4. Assign the higher priority resource to the activity that uses that resource the most.
5. Schedule the starting dates of activities with slack, so they do not conflict with other activities using the same resource.
6. Schedule a different but equivalent resource if available.
7. Use overtime to expand the time a resource has available.
8. Allow a resource to work part time on two competing activities and lengthen the duration of each activity.

CRASHING PROJECTS

Sometimes, after completing plans, it is found that a project must be done sooner. Revising the plans to achieve this objective is called "crashing" the project. One thing that could be done is to increase the number of people assigned to the activities. This could have diminishing returns. Adding too many people, for example, may result in much wasted time and could stretch out the project even longer. Overtime also can be a solution. Another example involves having to wait until some new design software can be obtained. A solution then may be to source the design outside instead of waiting.

The methods for "crashing" differ for each project. Often, they depend on the creativity of those involved in the planning. In general, the following guidelines should be used:

1. Look at activities that are on the critical path. Changing activities not on the critical path will not shorten the project.

2. Develop alternative solutions and consider the option that has the most favorable cost implications. This is the option that shortens the project most for a given cost. There are, of course, other considerations besides cost in making this choice. For example, an option may be the most favorable regarding cost, but may not shorten the project enough. An option that does shorten the project enough would be selected instead.

A popular measure for evaluating cost implications is detailed as follows:

$$\text{Crash Ratio} = \frac{\text{Added Cost}}{\text{Days shortened}}$$

If one scenario takes $3,000 in overtime to shorten a project by three days, the Crash Ratio would be:

$$\frac{\$3,000}{3 \text{ days}} = \$1,000/\text{day}$$

This would be favored over another scenario that has a Crash Ratio of $1,500/day. Often, changing activities when "crashing" projects creates a different critical path. Each time a new critical path occurs, a new analysis may be necessary.

REPORTS

There are a variety of reports that can be issued to reinforce planning and project management in a company. The actual formats used depend upon the needs of those involved. Several possible report formats that have been discussed previously are:

1. Gantt Charts.
2. CPM Charts.
3. Work Breakdown Chart.
4. Schedule Chart.
5. Task and Milestone List.

Another format useful for giving detailed information to a department regarding a specific activity is shown in Figure 7-13. This also may be given to the person who will be doing the job. It tells when the activity must be started and how long it should take and cost. Other pertinent

```
                                                16-Aug-1990

    Task: design specs

                Name  design specs                   Code
            Duration  10.00 Dys W         Responsible  tool eng
           Pln start  ASAP               Pln other cost          0.00
           Act start                     Act other cost          0.00
          Act finish                     % Complete  0

    Description

                    Start           Finish         Duration       Res work
    Planned  13-Aug-1990         24-Aug-1990        10.00 Dys W   10.00 Dys W
     Actual                                          0.00 Dys W    0.00 Dys W
    Baseline                                         0.00 Dys W    0.00 Dys W
    Earliest  13-Aug-1990        24-Aug-1990
      Latest  13-Aug-1990        24-Aug-1990         Slack    0.00 Dys W

                    Resource        Other        Total cost
    Planned         2560.00         0.00           2560.00
     Actual            0.00         0.00              0.00
    Projected       2560.00         0.00           2560.00

    Predecessors      Lag           Lag           Successors
    Start                                         bids
                                                  test specs
                                                  cn existing
```

Figure 7-13. Task and milestone forms.

ALLOCATION BY RESOURCE

16-Aug-1990

Allocations by Resource

Resource name	Task name	Task start date	Quantity	Planned work	Actual work	Remaining work	Projected cost
quality	bench test	8-Oct-1990	1.000	24.00 Hrs	0.00 Dys	0.00 Dys	480.00
purchasing	bids	27-Aug-1990	1.000	20.00 Hrs	0.00 Dys	0.00 Dys	400.00
tool eng	bids	27-Aug-1990	1.000	20.00 Hrs	0.00 Dys	0.00 Dys	640.00
plant eng	cn existing	27-Aug-1990	1.000	40.00 Hrs	0.00 Dys	0.00 Dys	1000.00
tool eng	design specs	13-Aug-1990	1.000	10.00 Dys	0.00 Dys	0.00 Dys	2560.00
purchasing	order	10-Sep-1990	1.000	8.00 Hrs	0.00 Dys	0.00 Dys	160.00
quality	test specs	27-Aug-1990	1.000	40.00 Hrs	0.00 Dys	0.00 Dys	800.00
plant eng	tryout	11-Oct-1990	1.000	40.00 Hrs	0.00 Dys	0.00 Dys	1000.00

Figure 7-14. Allocation by resource.

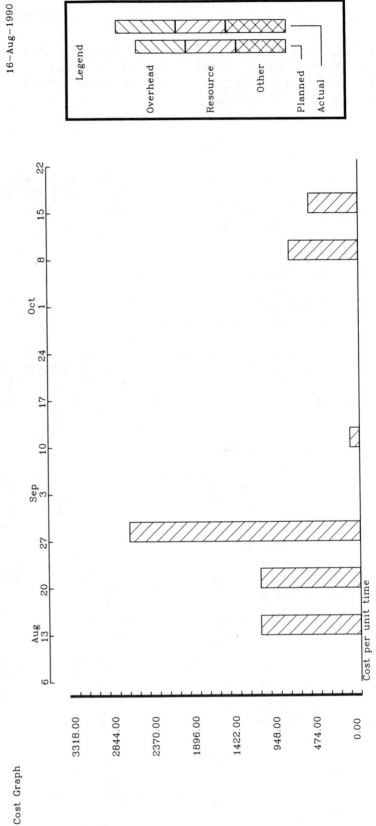

Figure 7-15. Cost graph.

information is also included. For example, it contains provisions for including what the activity actually costs and for feedback after it is completed.

Figure 7-14 is a format that summarizes cost data for all the activities ongoing in the project. It may be useful to those orchestrating the project. Note that this format also has provisions for keeping track of the hours put in for each activity.

Cost breakdowns can be graphically displayed. Figure 7-15 shows planned cost expenditures for each week. As the project proceeds, the actual costs can be displayed for comparison. Figure 7-16 is also a cost breakdown. In this format, the planned cumulative costs for resources can be compared to actual costs as the project proceeds.

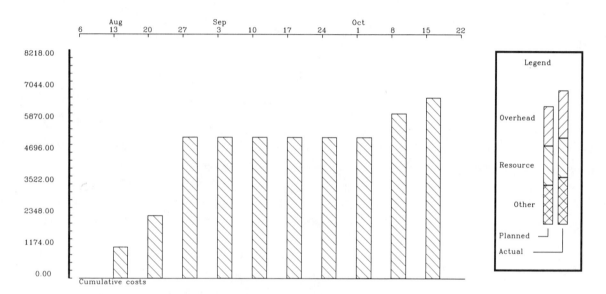

Figure 7-16. Cumulative cost graph.

Computer software makes the preparation of these reports almost effortless. They can be updated frequently and reissued as needed. On the other hand, the use of standard formats supplied by computer programs may not suit the needs of those using the reports. If so, custom reports may have to be programmed or done by hand. Some computer programs do allow generating custom formats.

The next chapter discusses how to organize for improvement.

BIBLIOGRAPHY

Badiru, Adedeji B., Project Management in Manufacturing and High Technology Operations, 1st ed. New York: John Wiley and Sons, Inc., 1988.

Harvard Project Manager 3.0, Software Publishing Corporation, 1988.

Huber, Laurence E., "Using Project Management Techniques in Manufacturing Systems." Industrial Management, March-April 1988.

Kezsbom, Deborah S.; Shilling, Donald L., and Edward, Katherine A., Dynamic Project Management, 1st ed. New York: John Wiley and Sons, Inc., 1989.

Lyons, James, Establishing Critical Attributes for Successful Implementation, Alfred NY: Alfred University, April 1990.

Salvendy, Gabriel, Editor, The Handbook of Industrial Engineering, 1st ed. New York: John Wiley and Sons, 1982.

Schonberger, Richard J., "Operations Management." Business Publications, Inc., 1981.

CHAPTER 8

ORGANIZING FOR IMPROVEMENT

In this chapter. . .

PEOPLE
1. Theory X
2. Theory Y
3. Maslow
4. Herzberg

ORGANIZATIONS
1. Policy Making
2. Administration
3. Natural
4. Functional Organization
5. Matrix Organization
6. Project Organization
7. Small Business Units

INDICATORS OF SUCCESSFUL CHANGE IN AN ORGANIZATION
1. Customer Focus
2. Management Commitment
3. Change
4. Management Philosophy
5. Risk Taking
6. Information
7. Roles
8. Team Work
9. Strategy
10 Tasks
11. Decision making
12. Stability
13. Innovation
14. Trust
15. Problem Solving

QUALITY COUNCIL
1. Problem solving
2. Organization Change
3. Team Development
4. Continuous Improvement
5. Tools for Improvement
6. Cost Monitoring
7. Focus Team Effort
8. Control of Resources
9. Facilitate Progress

TEAMS

SUMMARY

8
Organizing For Improvement

This chapter describes how a company can organize for improvement. It would be great if there were a perfect way of accomplishing this organization. But, this is not possible. Instead, only general guidelines can be offered and issues explored. Each company is unique and in a different stage of development. The blend of personalities in a company creates a diverse culture distinct from other companies. External factors also vary widely among companies and are constantly changing.

Methods that work for one company may not work for another. As an example, many companies tried using quality circles in the past decade. It seemed like a good way to introduce continuous improvement. The success rate was high in Japan. But, most companies in the U.S. found that they could not make it work. Many reasons are given for the lack of success. Clearly it was not the right tool at the time for many companies. By the same token, something that did not work in the past may work for a company now.

One study found most companies have organizations that are unstable and are modified regularly. This was felt to be due to management constantly searching for a better way of organizing resources. The search was never finished because the optimum organization was never reached. An optimum organization is an elusive goal. This is because people, resources and markets are always changing. When a new organization is in place, conditions are different making results less than expected. Once this is realized, the search continues.

A change in an organization is sometimes a response to symptoms that were around for a while. Often these symptoms grow, as time goes on, and become very disruptive. There is a time lag in reacting to these symptoms and taking action. This lag really aggravates the situation. A big shake-up may be seen as the only solution to correct the problems. If the symptoms were recognized when they first occurred, minor adjustments could have been made to correct the situation. The best way is to have an evolutionary approach where fine-tuning takes place regularly.

PEOPLE

An organization must focus on the person. It is people that make up a company. Decisions and plans are made by people. Work is done by people.

In reality, continuous improvement will be achieved only through people. An organization can be described as a way of structuring the relationship of people to accomplish certain goals. The structuring of an organization is intertwined with motivation of the people. It must support the management philosophy being used. For example, a bureaucratic "tops-down" organization may not allow participation of workers in decisions.

Motivation is what managing is all about. It is directing or influencing human behavior to get desired goals. Currently, influencing is the main thrust rather than directing. Many believe that this is more an art than a science. Conceptually, there are the following popular motivation models:

1. Theory X. This theory was very popular in the past. Now, it is felt that there is no appropriate application for this belief. The foundation of Theory X is that the worker does not really want to work. The worker must be constantly driven by supervision to do the job. This required the following:

   * Many rules that must be followed precisely.

   * Rewards and punishments must be used to make the worker do better.

   * Rewards must be given to recognize better efforts.

   * Firing from the job is not a remote punishment.

2. Theory Y. This is the opposite of Theory X. Variations of Theory Y are in the management philosophy of many companies today. The theory supports the participation of workers in the management of companies. In this theory, the worker wants to work. In addition, the worker wants to plan and control the actions required to achieve the goals of the company. Supervision is challenged with how to merge the needs of the organization with those of the individual. Often, supervision takes on a role of supporting the worker. Characteristic of this theory is:

   * The worker is involved in making decisions.

   * The worker is involved in developing how the work is to be done.

   * There is a good relationship among the workers and supervision.

3. Maslow. This is often called hierarchy of needs. Needs are arranged by levels. Once a level of needs is achieved, it is felt that it is no longer important as a motivator. The next higher level then becomes the motivator. The levels from the lowest to the highest are:

   * Physiological needs. These are basic needs. It includes such things as food, water, housing and clothing. Money is very important to get these things.

   * Safety needs. These include the needs of security, stability in life and freedom from physical harm.

* Social needs. These include the needs of social approval, friends, love, affection and being part of a group.

* Esteem needs. This level includes needs of accomplishment, respect, recognition, attention and appreciation.

* Self-actualization needs. This is the recognition in an individual that they have arrived where they want to be in life.

As the life of a person becomes more accomplished, it takes different things to motivate that person. For example, if social needs are satisfied then esteem needs will be the key motivation for a person. According to Maslow, money is not important at the upper levels of needs. Perhaps, that is why nonmonetary incentives that appeal to esteem are so popular now.

4. Herzberg. The ideas of Herzberg are integrated in many management philosophies. Two types of motivators are found in this theory. The first type is made up of hygiene factors. A person that perceives a hygiene factor to be inadequate likely will be unhappy and not be motivated. Strangely, the person will not necessarily be happy and motivated if hygiene factors are perceived to be adequate. In essence, hygiene factors are expected to be adequate. The hygiene factors are:

* Management policies.

* Supervision.

* Working conditions.

* Salaries or wages.

* Personal life.

* Peer, superior and subordinate relationships.

* Status in job and life.

* Security and safety of the environment.

The second type is made up of what is called motivators. These motivators must be ingrained in the work to be effective. They are:

* Achievement. Each job should allow the worker to achieve both personally and through the job.

* Recognition. Jobs should be designed so that outstanding performance is readily seen.

* Work content. Work should be interesting and challenging.

* Responsibility. The worker should be personally responsible for how the job is done.

       * Professional Growth. The work should allow the worker to
        continue to aspire for advancement.

The motivators form the backbone of many job enrichment programs. These
factors help make the job more interesting. In a sense, the worker can have
more control over destiny and be motivated to do so. Attention to these
factors can help directly motivate workers to superior performance.

Different approaches to organizing and managing cannot be classified as
either good or bad. The effectiveness of any approach depends on how it
meshes with the conditions that are present. Theory X, in different
degrees, combined with work simplification helped the United States be a
leader in manufacturing. But, conditions that existed in the past have
changed. Practice of Theory X today will likely result in a non-competitive
company. It is crucial to develop a style that fits conditions that exist
today. This style must be supported by an organization designed to help
promote the relationships among people that are necessary.

The combination of interesting work, participating in decisions about their
work, and feedback has a positive effect in many companies. People feel
responsible for how well work is done. They become highly motivated to do
their work well. Rewards are related to self-esteem and personal
fulfillment. Through this, people become motivated to do high quality work.
People need to be part of high quality work to satisfy self-esteem. This is
a major factor in the pursuit of continuous improvement.

Teams also act to support meeting the needs of the workers. They allow
workers to meet social needs by being part of a group. Teams also allow a
worker to participate in decisions regarding the company and work. Workers
who plan jobs feel personally responsible for how a job is done. In
addition, work should be much more challenging and interesting through being
on a team. Solving a major problem has to result in a feeling of
achievement.

ORGANIZATIONS

There are both formal and informal organizations in any company. The formal
organization is what is shown on organization charts. The informal
organization is how the company really works. Not everyone in the company
is aware of its existence or extent. Sometime when an official change in
reporting relationships is made, nothing different occurs. This is because
it is "business as usual" in the informal organization.

A company can be looked at as having three superimposed structures. They
are:

   1. Policy Making. This structure handles the general direction of the
      company. It is involved in policies, strategy and tactics.
      Formally, it consists of the managers at the very top of the
      organization chart. Although not formally recognized, it could
      include "opinion leaders" thinly scattered throughout the company.

      Opinions are often sought by top management before making policy
      decisions. In other cases, opinions may be spontaneously offered
      by influential people in the lower levels of a company that have

access to top management. This might occur, for example, by the union leaders in a company that has a union. The informal policy organization is, perhaps chaotic and much more complex than on the organization chart.

2. Administration. Formally, administration is recognized as the level of management between the workers and top management. The position on the organization chart implies that these managers translate general direction into specific action plans. These plans are then executed by the workers. Although management serves an important purpose, it is the workers that largely control the flow of products.

   In reality, most of the business is run by informal agreements among the workers. Workers handle most of the administration in a company among themselves. This is being more recognized as teams use these strong relationships. The role of middle management is changing to supporting the needs of the various teams.

   In a sense, information systems are part of administration. They tie the various parts of the company together by passing information from one group of workers to another. These relationships do not show up on the formal organization chart. Neither do the union relationships that are in some companies.

3. Natural. The natural organization does not show on the formal organization chart. It is the way a company really works. It is often developed over the years and is largely the result of personal relationships. Departments are not important except the function they do. It is the relation among people. Characteristic of this is the flow of information among people.

   For example, a part being processed is sent from one machine to another and then to shipping. People make sure this happens by talking to each other. An information system may help the people make this happen. Another example is a review of a new idea for a product by a manufacturing engineer. This review may be just a favor to the product designer.

   These relationships happen all the time. Often, management is not aware of this. These relationships are what make a company tick. Describing the natural organization on paper would be almost hopeless. It would be a maze of lines that would not be understandable.

It is unlikely that the formal organizations of any two companies are identical. They differ because the conditions within each company are different. Also, organizations are often designed to take advantage of strong personalities within management. Conceptually, the different structures can be broadly classified as follows:

1. Functional Organization. This is used by most companies in various forms. It is most often used in companies where manufacturing is the major thrust. People are placed in various groups that do specialized functions. Pools of experts are created whose

knowledge and expertise can be shared. Often the products are standard and the groups do many repetitive and highly structured tasks. Because of this characteristic, it is somewhat easy to establish policies, procedures and standards.

A functional organization is shown in Figure 8-1. In this organization, major functions report to the top officer. For simplicity, marketing and the comptroller are not included in this chart. A functional organization is often called a pyramid because of its broad base at the lower levels reaching toward a point at the top. In larger companies, the specialized functions often develop into power bases resembling "fiefdoms." Each power base has its own objectives and finds great difficulty cooperating with others where conflicting objectives exist. As a result, changes are hard to implement. Also, support for company goals is often difficult to gain. Its strengths lie in the technical competence of each specialized function. Attempts at modifying the functional organization in larger companies to capitalize on its strengths and increase cooperation have been tried.

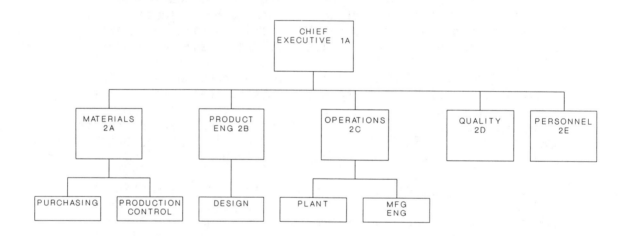

Figure 8-1. Functional organization found in most companies.

The advantages for a smaller company of a functional organization are:

* provides clearly defined duties and channels of communication.

* provides pools of specialists that can be readily accessed.

* maximizes potential for developing technical leadership in products that company sells.

* allows continuity in procedures and methods

* provides supervision of each discipline by a person who understands discipline.

There are also some disadvantages:

* no clear focus on customer.

* the view of the big picture is distorted by functional orientation.

* no logical focal point for a project.

* functional objectives could override company goals.

* slow communications and decision making.

2. Matrix Organization. This is a change to the functional organization to improve harmony while still keeping technical strength. There are two lines of authority - vertical and horizontal. The vertical chain of command resembles the functional organization. The horizontal part is broken down by project. See Figure 8-2 for an example of a matrix organization.

The functional part of the organization is permanent, while the project part is temporary. Each project has people from the functional areas assigned. Depending on the project, they may be assigned part time to several projects or full time to only one project. When a project is finished or their specific job done, the people in the project will be assigned elsewhere. They may go directly to another project or back to their function to await assignment.

In a sense, a person has two bosses - a functional and a project boss. Many companies distinguish this by saying the functional boss is responsible for technical details. In contrast, the project boss may be only assigned responsibility for administrative details. This involves accountability for meeting budgets and schedules. Yet, it is sometimes difficult to distinguish the two and conflicts occur. A matrix organization often has the following advantages:

* project provides customer focus.

* common objectives for all those in the project despite the functional area they came from.

* more effective utilization of technical resources in that demands are more in tune with availability.

* improved flow of information both horizontally and vertically through the project organization.

* technical interchange of information among projects.

* project members have a home base - their functional organization.

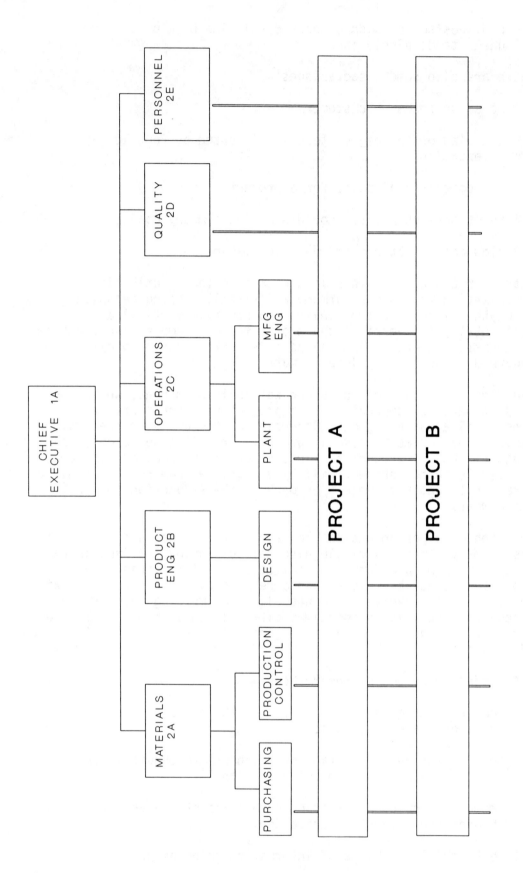

Figure 8-2. Matrix organization used in some companies.

* breakdown of department barriers that impede progress.

There are, however, some disadvantages to this type of organization:

* potential conflict from workers reporting to two bosses.

* complexity of the structure of the organization creates some confusion on borderline issues that may be either functional or product in nature.

* overhead cost is higher since two different management structures, functional and project, are necessary.

* Priorities among projects for resources are a problem often that can only be settled at the top.

3. Project organization. This type of organization is shown in Figure 8-3. It is often used in large companies, like defense contractors, who ordinarily work on a project basis. Each project stands on its own, staffed with the resources necessary to accomplish its mission. Often, the project is concerned with design and does not ultimately concern manufacturing. The functional organization is assigned work not concerned with projects. Specialized areas, like a tool room, may contract with a project organization and perform the services of a supplier. A project organization also may be involved in bidding. If the bid is accepted, a specific project organization is created and staffed to handle the work. In this way, progress of the project is not hampered by competitive pressures among functional areas. A major advantage is that workers in a project are dedicated to a specific goal. Motivation and dedication are high to achieve that goal. A disadvantage is that when a project is finished, there may not be another project that can use the workers immediately.

The major advantages of a project organization are:

* clear focus on customer.

* accountability is clearly defined.

* excellent control over resources.

* good reaction time.

* strong commitment to schedule and budget goals.

The major disadvantages of a project organization are:

* focus on project not company goals.

* limited technology transfer among projects.

* sharing of resources among projects difficult.

* possible duplication of effort with other projects.

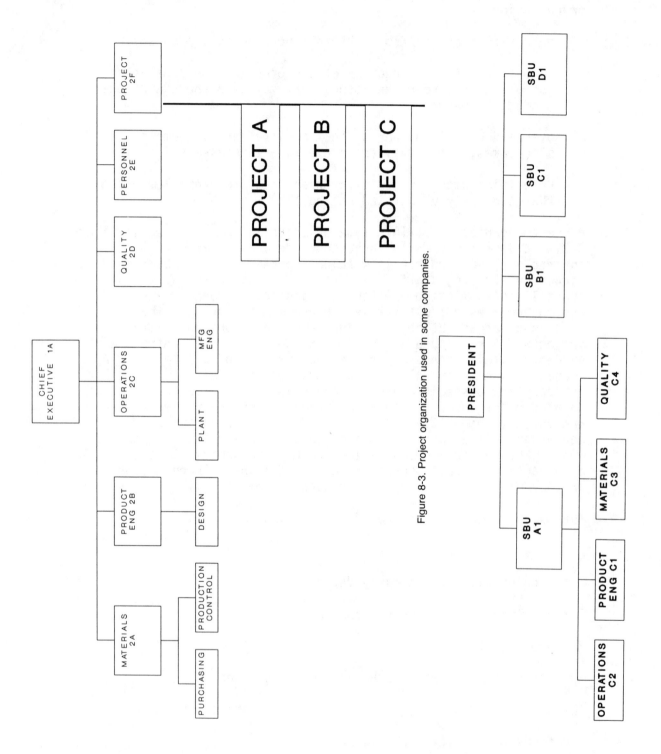

Figure 8-3. Project organization used in some companies.

Figure 8-4. Small business units used to break up a large company.

162

4. Small business units (SBU). Many large companies have found the reactions within their functional organizations sluggish. In many respects, the entrepreneurial spirit was gone. To regain it, a company is broken into the equivalent of smaller companies called small business units. This is shown in Figure 8-4. Each SBU is a company in itself. The SBU's are staffed with the various disciplines required to operate as a separate company. The functions in the company disappear and are found in each SBU.

    SBU's differ from project organizations in how long they are expected to last. A SBU is expected to last as long as the products are viable. A project organization has a limited lifetime. It ceases when the project is done. Also the project organization differs from SBU's in that they may use the functional areas of the company as suppliers. The advantages and disadvantages of SBU's are similar to that discussed for the project organization.

5. Improvement organization. This is a somewhat recent organization structure. Many companies adopted it to get a fast start on improving quality. A quality council and ad hoc improvement teams are superimposed on the existing functional organization. It is shown in Figure 8-5.

    The quality council is composed of the heads of the major functions and top officer of the company. This council jointly evaluates how well the company is dealing with customers. As a result of these analyses, ad hoc improvement teams are initiated for short-term projects. The members of these teams are part-time. They are from the various functional areas that have an interest in the project.

    This type of organization has a strong customer focus. Many companies feel that the main reason for a quality council is to ensure this customer focus. The secondary reasons are to remove barriers among departments and obtain a strong consensus on direction. This is transmitted to the rest of the company by actions. Teams are formed to address problem areas. These actions often are like a catalyst in changing the culture of a company. More will be included later in this chapter on quality councils and ad hoc improvement teams.

INDICATORS OF SUCCESSFUL CHANGE IN ORGANIZATIONS

There are characteristics that a successful organization should be like. By successful, it is meant that the company will likely succeed in having a strong continuous improvement effort. On one hand, the characteristics may not be possible considering the practicality. But, they form a good starting point for understanding where the organization of a company stands.

The characteristics are:

1. Customer focus. The priority of everyone in the company must be the customer. This includes a relentless dedication to improve the products that the customer receives.

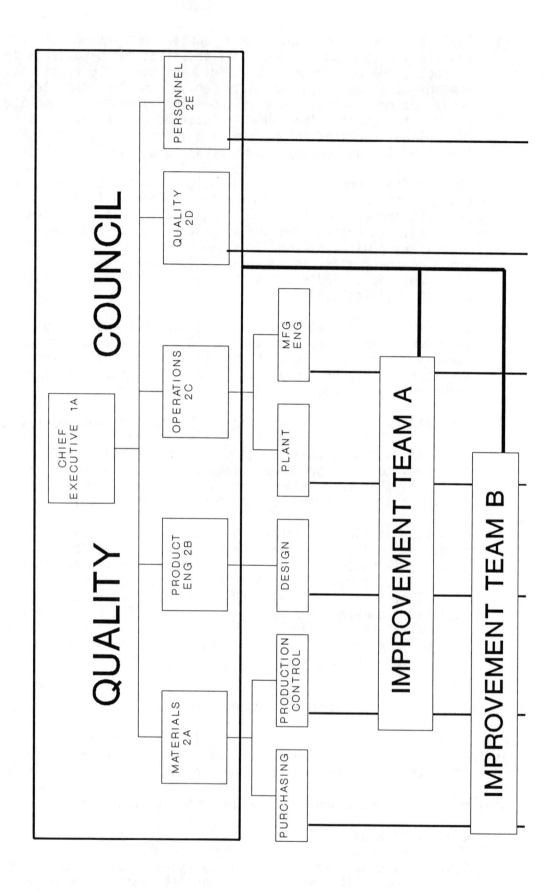

Figure 8-5. Improvement organization breaks down department barriers.

2. Management commitment. The bottom line is that management must walk like they talk. Actions must be directed toward improving the products. There cannot be a relapse. The workers will see this and quickly assume that management is not serious.

3. Change. Change should be taking place on a wide-scale. Not all change works. But people are willing to try things and some changes really help.

4. Management philosophy. Old management styles should be disappearing and replaced by more involvement of the workers. People feel that they are a vital part of the company.

5. Risk taking. Risk should be recognized as a part of being in business. People should be able to take risks and know that they will not damage their careers. Because of this, problems are being solved quickly.

6. Information. There should be a good flow of information in the company. People should feel informed and trusted. They should have the information needed to do their job and to help in planning the future.

7. Roles. The role of each person in the company should be clearly defined in the organization chart. Everyone ought to be aware of where they must go for help or information.

8. Team work. The organization should encourage team work. Controls should be relaxed to permit self-direction of projects by people working cooperatively.

9. Strategy. The strategy of the company should be clearly represented in the way resources are intermeshed. In this way, a strong message is given to everyone on the framework of future actions to support strategy.

10. Tasks. The form of the organization should be designed to do various routine tasks in an effective manner.

11. Decision making. The organization should be designed to drive decision making to the lowest level possible. The best decisions are usually made by those that will be personally affected. Attention should be placed on an organization that will get decisions quickly.

12. Stability. To encourage a feeling of belonging and strong dedication, the organization should not be changed frequently without strong reasons. Where a change is required, extensive efforts must be made to pave the way.

13. Innovation. The organization should provide for the constant development of innovative approaches for products and processes. This insures the future competitiveness of a company.

14. Trust. The organization should promote a high degree of trust among its employees. One part of the organization must not be

pitted against another in an adversal relationship. Teamwork and cooperation must prevail throughout the organization.

15. Problem solving. The company should have a problem solving process that is widely understood and used.

QUALITY COUNCIL

If the "improvement organization" is chosen, the first step is to appoint members to the quality council shown in Figure 8-5. The members of this council should be the heads of the major functions in the company. It should also include their leader--the top manager in the company. This way, the key decision makers in the company are brought together with a common purpose--continuous improvement. Also, the people on the council have the power to add or reallocate resources necessary for any changes. A consensus on plans, should eliminate conflict.

If the company is unionized, it is logical to also include the top officer in the union. This will help in getting the "buy-in" of the workers. It also will get contrasting viewpoints in the discussions that will help to make better plans. Membership on the council should probably be around seven to nine persons. If the council is much less than this, discussions may be shallow and all options may not be considered. If it larger, discussions are likely to linger on too long and actions will not be as timely.

The quality council is the driver of continuous improvement in the company. This is shown in Figure 8-6. In this role, the quality council also acts as

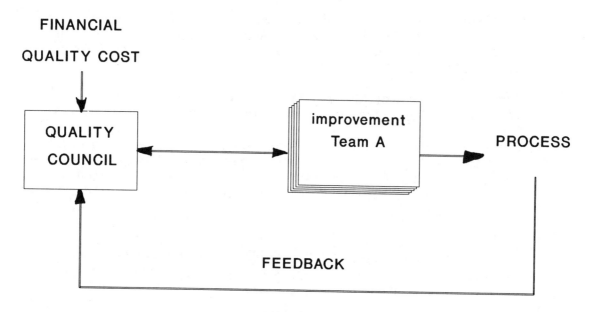

Figure 8-6. Improvement organization.

a facilitator to the improvement teams. It must provide the vision, direction and assistance to the teams in order to make necessary changes happen. This takes a long-term effort which is quite intensive for everyone on the council. To be effective, members can expect to devote a significant portion of their time in discussions and leading the teams. The dedication and attitude of the council members will have a great influence on the rest of the company. Relentless dedication and a positive attitude will act as a catalyst in the continuous improvement effort.

Also important is the ability of each member on the council to see problems from the customer viewpoint. This ability to act, in a sense, as an agent of the customer will greatly enhance improvement efforts and the overall effectiveness of the company. For most people, this is a new role and perhaps creates a certain amount of discomfort. Many of today's managers likely reached their leadership position by achieving production goals. Quality was sometimes compromised in the reward system of the past. But the new mindset can be learned and absolutely must be adopted for the company to survive.

A major roadblock to the effectiveness of the quality council is that the role of each member is usually a new experience. There is no past practices to rely upon. Often an outside facilitator is used in council meetings to help make this transition. The outside facilitator lacks interest in the outcome of any discussion. The focus of this person is devoted only to "how" the discussions take place. This person can be a positive influence in keeping activities on track. A major training effort also has to take place. To be successful, each member must realize that they need this training. The types of training that should be considered are:

1. Problem solving. The company should adopt a process for solving problems and the council should encourage its use. To do this, each member must understand how it works. This knowledge will aid the council in carrying out its goals. A strong problem solving approach is the foundation for continuous improvement.

2. Organization change. Techniques for management to use in changing the organization are valuable for the members of the quality council to know. Through these techniques, power bases in the company can be handled and conflicts minimized. In addition, these techniques can help promote team work and dedication to needed changes.

3. Team development. Teams are the implementors of changes needed by the quality council. It is important that the teams be started with the maximum likelihood of success. After starting, the teams will probably need to be facilitated by the members on the council. This facilitation includes, among other things, assuring the flow of ideas and the positive handling of constructive criticism. Also, guidance must be offered to have the commitment and involvement of each member on the team. Help in doing this can be obtained from a knowledge of team development techniques.

4. Continuous improvement. Concepts of continuous improvement need to be known and used by the quality council. How to focus on improvements through techniques such as quality cost is mandatory in efforts of the quality council. The importance of a long-term focus, instead of looking for quick gains, must be ingrained in the operating philosophy.

5. Tools for improvement. Members on the quality council must know

the strengths and weaknesses of the various tools used in improvement. This is necessary to provide advice to the teams as they seek change. These tools range from those that are used as needed to those that are constantly used. Analytical tools, such as "fish-bone" diagrams, are used as needed. Other tools, such as control charts, may be in constant use by those on the factory floor.

6. Cost monitoring. The use of cost reports showing the financial health and opportunities of improvement in the entire company are important. A comprehensive quality cost study, as well as other financial reports, may also be useful to demonstrate this. These reports may not have been widely shared before among all the members of the quality council. Sharing not only these reports but the meaning behind them is critical to the improvement efforts. Different views on approaches are gained from analysis by people from the different functions in a company.

The quality council provides focus on the proper priorities for improvement initiatives. Teams are formed to implement needed changes. The typical role of the quality council regarding the teams is:

1. Focus. The quality council identifies the preliminary direction of the team effort. Often this is an iterative process. As the team solidifies and gains additional information, fine-tuning occurs. Through consultation with the quality council the scope and objectives are fixed.

   The scope concerns the boundaries of the effort. This must be carefully considered. Normally, changes are needed in several functional areas and the scope must recognize this. Too small a scope which does not recognize all contributors to the problem, may not result in a solution. If the scope is too large, the project may be slowed with unnecessary details and be very chaotic.

   Objectives are important, too. These also may be firmed up by an iterative process between the team and the quality council. Objectives must be measurable. They must also be stated so that it is known by everyone concerned when they have been reached. Teams are formed with the notion that they have a limited life. A team must be disbanded when the objectives have been reached. This releases the members on the team so they can pursue other improvement opportunities.

2. Resources. Members of the quality council, collectively, control the resources of the company. First, they must staff the teams with the right people to do the job that is envisioned. As the team develops and more information is gained, it may be necessary to change the people that are on the team. Usually, team members perform their regular duties, too. Priorities must be established for the time needed for the team. Sometimes, parts of the regular jobs must be reassigned to others in the company.

   As the team realizes that funds are required to accomplish objectives, this must be dealt with by the quality council. Cost and benefits must be examined. If the changes are justified, then funds must be allocated. Alterations of plans may be necessary to reach agreement on justification. Such alterations may be identified through joint discussion among members of the quality council and team.

3. Facilitates progress. The quality council monitors the progress of each team as they proceed toward their objectives. In a sense, they must be like a trusted advisor. Without showing any indication of control, they should provide advice about different ways to approach things. The quality council must be sensitive to the needs of the team and attempt to provide them. Normally, review meetings are scheduled to facilitate this interaction. During these sessions, it is important that conflict and criticism is carefully handled.

The quality council must provide a positive climate for continuous improvement. This is not easy. The most critical aspect is that the actions of the members of the quality council must support the improvement philosophy that has been adopted by the company. This must not only exist in meetings of the quality council but also in the performance of their regular jobs. These actions carry the real message to the employees. A consistent approach to improvement will be adopted by others in the company based upon these actions. Other ways of spreading the message are through such things as training, newsletters, and employee involvement groups.

TEAMS

Ad hoc improvement teams are the implementors of what is desired by the quality council. Members of the teams are usually chosen from each function concerned with the outcome of the project. This way, department barriers are broken down. Each member on the team has a common objective of achieving that desired by the quality council. Department objectives are put aside in team meetings to reach a consensus for what is best for the company.

In pursuing the objectives, the team may do the following tasks:

1. Identify the problem if this has not already been done by the quality council. If it has, the team may be asked to verify the problem.

2. Estimate the size of the problem. This may be determined by dollars wasted, unhappy customers, or some other measure.

3. Develop alternate solutions to solve the problem. Evaluate the costs and difficulties inherent in each solution.

4. Evaluate the solutions to find the best one for the company. Financial and other criteria may be used.

5. Suggest action to the quality council.

6. Implement the solution acceptable to the quality council.

7. Check results to verify if the objective was achieved. Alterations may be needed to fine-tune the change.

In setting up teams, making objectives that will not take too long may be desirable. This helps ensure the effort will be fast moving and there will be less danger of the project lagging. Often, the tasks listed above are not all done by a single team. Some people in the organization may be better at planning. They may be assigned the initial tasks. Others may be better at putting things in place. They may be assigned the latter tasks. Members or the entire team can change as different phases are completed. In other situations where continuity is important, the team and its members will stay in place for all the tasks.

For some companies, a "sponsor" is assigned to each team. The "sponsor" is a member of the quality council who usually has a strong interest in the outcome. This assures a good working relationship. Seeking advice from one individual is usually easier than waiting for the quality council to meet. However, the "sponsor" does not supervise the team. This person is only a facilitator to help the team around road blocks. By virtue of the high position of the "sponsor" in the functional organization, needs of the team can be quickly addressed. Priorities can be given for resources needed by the team. The typical responsibilities of a sponsor are:

1. Provide counsel in adjusting the scope and objectives of the team. This will be approved by the quality council later on.

2. Examine the progress and activities of the team and make suggestions for improving efforts.

3. Remove artificial barriers in a company that hurt team progress.

4. Help in justify and obtain needed resources.

The "sponsor" may attend the early meetings of the team. This may be extremely helpful in providing background and clarification. Often, the focus of the team is improved through this early contact. The "sponsor" must be careful, however, to not act as a team member or leader. The function of the team must be carried out by the members of the team to assure maximum effectiveness.

Members of the team must be selected carefully, they should all have a direct interest in the project. Teams range in size from three to ten members. Any less than this would not be a team. Any more would probably slow down progress with too much debate. The leader of the team is sometimes appointed by the quality council. Often this individual has skill in managing and sometimes is a supervisor in the functional organization. The companies that do this feel that a strong team results from having a strong leader.

Other companies do not appoint a leader. They feel that a person will naturally emerge as a leader. Acceptance of the leader by the other members is almost a certainty in this situation. However, the natural selection process could promote serious conflict at the beginning, slowing overall progress.

Factors that are important to consider when selecting team members are:

1. Knowledge and skill of the person in relation to needs of the project.

2. Ability of the person to adapt to being a team player.

3. Degree of effect that the outcome of the project has on the person.

4. Philosophy of person about continuous improvement.

5. Regard of the person for needs of customer.

6. Desire of person to be on that specific project and team.

7. Availability in view of other commitments.

The team leader has some important responsibilities. This includes keeping the project on track and conducting meetings. A critical element is accepting ideas without anyone feeling threatened. Often, an outside facilitator is assigned to help the team get off the ground. This person is only interested in how the meeting is conducted, not the outcome. Reports to the quality council may be prepared by the team leader. A better approach is to involve the entire team in reporting. Efforts are then reinforced and progress is improved. Sometimes, a secretary is appointed to keep notes of important decisions and schedule meetings.

Involving all members in team meetings is critical. A consensus cannot be achieved without full attendance. With time being scarce in any company, this is a constant challenge. Management must support a policy where team meetings are among the highest priority activities. Many companies have found changing members on teams as the project moves ahead to be disruptive. This must be weighed carefully against the benefits of making the change.

Training of the members on the team is an absolute necessity. Members must understand their role and the philosophy of the company relative to continuous improvement. Other types of training that should be considered resembles in general the type that recommended for the quality council:

1. Problem solving.

2. Organizational change.

3. Team development.

4. Continuous improvement.

5. Tools for improvement.

6. Cost monitoring.

SUMMARY

In many respects, the suggestions in this chapter are techniques to get people together. Each person in a company can make a vital contribution to its success. The key is organization. As a company grows in size and age, togetherness is sometimes hard to accomplish. A challenge for management is to design the right organization to make it happen.

BIBLIOGRAPHY

Badiru, Adedeji B., Project Management in Manufacturing and High Technology Operations, 1st ed. Wiley Interscience, 1988.

Hendricks, Dale, "The Element of Successful Organizational Change." Industrial Management, January-February 1990.

Kezsbom, Deborah S.; Shilling, Donald L., and Edward, Katherine A., Dynamic Project Management, 1st ed. New York: John Wiley and Sons, Inc., 1989.

Lawler, Edward E. III, "High Involvement Management," Jossey-Bass, 1986.

Rubenstein, Albert H., Managing Technology in a Decentralized Firm, 1st ed. New York: John Wiley and Sons, Inc., 1989.

CHAPTER 9

TRAINING FOR IMPROVEMENT

In this chapter. . .

OBJECTIVES OF TRAINING

HELPING TO CHANGE INDIVIDUALS

CONTINUING EDUCATION

MAXIMIZING APPEAL FOR TRAINING AND EDUCATION
   Employees at Large Urban Companies
   Employees at Small Nonurban Companies
   Employees Who Are Older
   Other Factors

SOURCES OF TRAINING AND EDUCATION OFFERINGS
   Professional Societies
   Consultants
   In-House Classes
   Educational Institutions

APPROACH FOR TRAINING AND EDUCATION

DETERMINATION OF TRAINING NEEDS AND OBJECTIVES
   Before Delivery
   Delivery
   Evaluation

SUMMARY

Appendix information

Training effectiveness questionnaire
(Courtesy of Ann Arbor Consulting Associates) A-39

9
Training For Improvement

This chapter is about training. It also considers continuing education undertaken by the employees in a company. Conceptually, training is different from education. Training is concerned with teaching skills, while education conveys knowledge. This distinction shows that individuals can have knowledge about a certain subject but may not have the ability to apply it. Before it can be applied, the individuals must be trained in the skills to apply that knowledge. Many offerings are combinations of education and training: knowledge is conveyed to show why certain skills are needed. This is followed by training in skills.

In recent years, many companies have changed their perspective of the work force. Instead of viewing employees simply as a cost of doing business, they now recognize workers to be a resource or asset. This broader perspective is a major factor in the current large investment in people by many companies. Spending to improve the performance of employees has never been greater. This investment is seen as affecting performance over a long period--perhaps even over the entire career of the employee. Like a capital investment, this expenditure may have a rewarding payoff. This viewpoint is also influenced by the switch in focus of companies from the short-term to the long-term. Investment in employees is not only justified when looking at the long-term, but may be mandatory. The long-range success of companies is seen as strongly dependent on the quality of the work force.

Much of the investment is in employee training. This involves improving the ability of a person to do a job; training ranges from basic math and reading skills to approaches for continuous improvement. Many companies are doing this while the employee is on company time. To encourage professional employees to stay abreast of technology and improve their knowledge, continuing education programs are supported. These range from sending employees to seminars given by professional organizations to paying the tuition for those in degree programs at universities.

Driving this change in perspective by management is overwhelming evidence that people, not investment in capital equipment, directly caused most of the rapid economic growth from 1948 to 1982. During this period, the Gross National Product in the United States increased at an annual rate of 3.2%. A recent study shows that one third of this growth was due to better education of the work force. Half the annual growth came from innovation by the work force. Innovation was made possible by the increase in education level. Only 15% of the annual increase resulted from buying capital equipment.

Employees also agree with the new perspective. The 1990 ASQC Gallup survey reports that employees feel that the most important thing a company can do to achieve higher quality work is to provide training in job skills. Another vote of confidence for training is a major labor contract negotiated in 1990. This agreement diverts up to five dollars for each hour worked to a fund for training employees.

The cost of training by U.S. firms in 1989 exceeded $50 billion. This is about 10% more than in 1988. Just in the U.S., over 17 million training offerings are available. Most of these are delivered. Well over 15 million people attend a training offering each year.

The amount a firm spends for training ranges from 2-5% of budget. Typically, about half of that amount focuses on quality related issues. A major vehicle builder invested over 600 hours for each employee in training prior to opening a new truck assembly plant. This was about 2 million hours of training for the 3000 people involved. Most of this was before selling the first truck. The training ranged from group dynamics in teams to problem solving and enhancing productivity.

Many companies now provide training in basic mathematics and reading skills. This is necessary to build the proper foundation for performing the job. It is estimated that up to 30% of the work force lacks basic skill in reading, writing and arithmetic. This is a major impediment to achieving gains in quality. A large corporation in the electronics industry is investing several hundred million dollars in the next five years just for training in basic skills. Interestingly, this effort concerns both employees on the factory floor and those in offices.

Extensive training is not a short-term phenomenon. The need for training will intensify in the future. Based on U.S. Labor Department study, more than three-quarters of the people attempting to join the work force in this decade will have limited basic skills. Even more troublesome is that they will be competing for only 40% of the available jobs. These are jobs on the lower-tier of the skill level. But most of these lower-tier jobs will require solid reading and writing skills. Obviously, massive training will be necessary. The remaining one-fourth of the new job seekers that are more qualified will be sought to fill 60% of the available jobs. It is alarming that there will be a shortage of people who are qualified to perform higher skilled jobs. But even people in upper-tier skill levels will need training. This will help them adapt to new technologies that are expected. One study shows that as many as 50 million workers will need to be trained and retrained in the next 12 years. This includes 20 million who are new to the job market and 30 million current workers. Indeed, training will be a significant investment for companies in the future.

OBJECTIVES OF TRAINING

In general, the objective of training is to support the needs of the organization. These needs are found in the strategic plan and various other plans cascading from it. The payoff for training should be improved performance of an organization. Some of this may be immediately seen in lower costs and better quality. Other training will have a long-term effect. For some companies, training may be needed just to stay in business.

A considerable amount of training often takes place before employees join a company. Much of this training is supported by state funds and is furnished as an incentive for a company to locate in a particular area. Often this training includes various hurdles through which job seekers must pass to gain employment. This is intended to ensure a qualified employee.

In the past, the effects of training were disappointing, because the objectives were unclear. It may have appeared as something that looked good, or it may have been used as an award to someone for doing a good job. Another major reason for training being ineffective was that the ideas taught were not accepted by the rest of the organization. As an example, improved management techniques may be taught to an individual. But if the associates of this individual do not accept the changes that are necessary, the new techniques will be quickly discarded.

To avoid past mistakes, it must be recognized that all training requires an identifiable objective. The objective that is identified should support what the organization is trying to achieve. For many companies, the objective may not have an immediate payoff. It will, however, support what the company is trying to achieve in the long-term. Long-term needs are typically found in the strategic plan and the various department plans that cascade from the strategic plan.

A perplexing part of training is that it is a two-way street. The commitment of the company is not enough. There also must be a desire by those being trained to learn the skills offered. Training effort will be wasted if it is not wanted. Several approaches to training are currently being used to address this problem. At one extreme, a company only offers training to volunteers. Through this method, it is felt that only those who want the training will be involved. Using this approach, only a portion of those persons needing training will receive it.

At the other extreme, a company dictates what training each employee must take. Not completing the specified training could affect salary increases, promotions and even continued employment. This is intended to provide an incentive for workers to want to be trained. With this approach, the company can schedule needed training for everyone in the work force. But the training effort may still be wasted for those who feel forced to take it.

In the past, it was observed that the most effective training occurred when the employees in a company perceived that the company may go out of business. Their future was in jeopardy, and motivation for seeking better skills was high. This situation was present in industries where offshore competition caused severe erosion of domestic markets.

To achieve effective training, there must be a desire by the participant. A major challenge to a company is to present positive incentives that will be attractive to those who need to attend. Many companies are paying employees to take training, by having it on work time. Others are paying overtime for classes after work. But this is typically not enough. Positive incentives also must be identified that are clearly important to the unique situation of each employee.

A company may view training as being of two types--helping to change individuals, and changing the organization. The differing objectives of each are described below.

HELPING TO CHANGE INDIVIDUALS

From the start of training efforts by companies, most of the training focused on individuals and skills. Much of this was because of company organization and the reward system. Jobs were designed for individual contributions; performance was judged on individual performance. Whether persons were successful or not depended on how they performed individually. Now, the importance of how people work together is widely recognized. An increasing part of training funds are now devoted to group activities and how the individual can contribute in the new role.

Training in the past was on skills concerning:

1. New employees who had little or no experience.
2. Existing employees for new jobs.
3. Machines that are new to the company.
4. Newly appointed supervisors.
5. Employees undergoing training for skilled trades.

The retraining of existing employees was made necessary by improved technology. This was needed by companies to improve productivity. Numerical control equipment and manufacturing cells are now widely used. Sensors are used to trigger controls for manufacturing parts. Machines are more sophisticated and complicated to run. New skills are required to run and maintain the machines. Much labor-management activity in the past decade focused on ways to retrain workers displaced by technology. For some, the training was in a new career, different from the past job. Another major training effort concerned quality issues to improve quality of products.

In the past decade, there was also extensive training needed for office personnel. A large part of this was in computer skills. For secretaries, word processing is now solidly entrenched. Most engineers use a computer to solve problems. Many office workers in a company are part of an integrated computer system and must use the system daily. This training was necessitated by the need of companies to improve office productivity. Training in quality issues also extended to those in the office.

Other training concerns accelerated the ability of existing employees to handle higher-level responsibilities. Often this is an output from career planning for an individual. It may range from being assigned to a variety of jobs, to being enrolled in a fellowship program at a prestigious university. Often used is a mixture of on-the-job training, outside seminars, and coaching by a mentor.

Training for improving individual skills needs to be focused. The objective for the desired skills must be clearly identified. Also, the aptitude and desire of the employee for the new skills must be gaged. If these factors are compatible, the training likely will be successful. This can be measured by the performance of the employee in the job that requires the new skills. In the past, there have been troubling differences among employees undergoing the same training. Much of the differences in performance can be attributed to the degree of compatibility of the factors just mentioned.

Helping to change organizations is also significant. There is an increasing part of training being devoted to the changing of organizations. This emphasis coincides with the recognition of the importance of team work and the culture of organizations. Companies are undergoing dramatic changes. Many of these changes started in the early 1980s in response to erosion of markets by offshore competition.

Teams, composed of members from several functions, were successful in making solutions that were best for the company. This contrasts to past practices that promoted solutions that were most favorable for a particular functional area. Also, it is widely recognized that an organization must change its culture to foster continuous improvement. This is needed to get necessary gains in productivity and quality. The change in culture involves the way things are done in a company. Often, the new ways of doing business are dramatically different from the past. Massive training is needed in the skills necessary for the new ways of doing business.

For some companies, early training consisted of lectures on why changes were needed and how things were to be done. For the most part, this was a failure. Change was not promoted because the people hearing the lectures really did not feel involved. People, unlike machines, cannot be easily reprogrammed unless they feel that they are an important part of the decision making process. Sometimes the changes talked about were contradicted by almost every action taken by management. In a large sense, management needed to "walk like they talked."

The failure of this type of training promoted a new direction. Change was recognized as only being possible through strategic planning and the involvement of the entire organization in these plans. Details of this are covered in Chapter 6. The objectives for training needed to focus on knowing the concepts and having the needed skills for continuous improvement. Decisions regarding changes in how the business is to be run are outside the domain of training. This must be handled within the organization by involving affected employees. But training has a vital role in providing concepts and skills in using the tools for continuous improvement.

The job of training in changing organizations is immense. Understanding the concepts of group processes and the behavior of organizations is vital for top management, as well as members of teams. The skills necessary to build effective teams are also vital to top management and team members. Technical skills must be developed in many employees. Top management may go to outside seminars and workshops seeking skills necessary to proceed toward their objectives. Inside training may be targeted for developing skills in employees regarding problem solving and data analysis.

The scope and objectives of the necessary training are closely linked to the strategic plan and the other plans cascading from it. Since strategic plans are different for each company, training details for each company are very different as well. For this reason, it would be a mistake to emulate too closely the training plans of another company without a sound reason for doing so. In making training plans, it must be remembered that training should support, but not supplant the job of management.

For many companies, the skills needed for continuous improvement are not widely possessed. Since the concept is new to the company, massive training is likely. This extends from top management to those on the factory floor. The scope is much larger than that for individual training. The length of the training is also much longer than it is for individual training. It may continue, in one form or another, into the future. Transferring skills may not be successful the first time and retraining may be necessary. As the skill level of the organization increases, more sophisticated skills may be necessary. For example, after mastering SPC, training in Taguchi Methods or design of experiments may be in order. Upon mastering this, training in Quality Function Deployment (QFD) may be appropriate. Another factor complicating this type of training is that often an offering involves several functions in a company. Agreement on outcomes and performance measures may take much more intensive discussion. Providing this broad-based training is a challenging assignment.

CONTINUING EDUCATION

For all persons in the work force, continuing education is vital. The knowledge gained helps a person adapt to new technology, the changing nature of an existing job, higher level responsibilities and new careers. For manufacturing professionals, continuing education is particularly important.

Most professionals try to keep their knowledge current. If they did not, they would not be able to work successfully in the fast-changing environment. Many professionals are involved in activities that add to their knowledge base. The activities are designed to share knowledge among a broad-base of professionals. This is done, for example, by conferences and meetings of professional organizations like the Society of Manufacturing Engineers. Seminars are a means for professionals to share their specialized knowledge with a larger group. Often, this knowledge is "state-of-art" and critical to getting needed productivity and quality improvements. Formal courses at local universities, that may lead to degrees, are also a part of continuing education. These courses may be job-related, or just contribute to a broader knowledge base.

Continuing education is probably the most visible of the efforts to upgrade employees. Enormous amounts of money are spent by companies to get educational offerings by professional societies, schools, and outside consultants. The format of this effort may include such things as courses, technical books, papers, videotapes, workshops, or seminars. In reality, these offerings are bought and sold in a competitive environment. Currently, there is no coordination among the multitude of entities furnishing the services. Strategic planning for continuing education is left up to the individual company and each person involved.

Some believe that 50 years ago, completion of a four-year curriculum could prepare a person for the changes during an entire career. Technology was not changing at a rate that was difficult to keep up with. Today, the changes in technology can be overwhelming. To keep up with the changes, continuing education is mandatory. For example, the half-life of what is learned in a mechanical engineering undergraduate program is estimated to be about four years; half of what was learned is obsolete and must be updated by continuing education only four years after graduation.

In general, an undergraduate education is not intended to prepare a graduate for a specific career. It's purpose is to offer an option to pursue several career paths. For example, a manufacturing engineering graduate may plan to pursue a career as a production engineer or an equipment engineer. Both require the same knowledge base, but are different in the skills required. Also, undergraduate education is generally not geared to a specific industry. This increases the job options for the graduate. More specifically, the goals of an undergraduate engineering education are:

1. Prepare graduates to contribute to the practice of engineering.
2. Prepare graduates to pursue advanced degrees in engineering.
3. Provide a base for career-long learning and professional development in support of career objectives.
4. Prepare graduates to be informed, effective and responsible participants both within the engineering profession and in society.

On-the-job experience after graduation gives skills and knowledge necessary for the specific job for which the engineer is employed. In a sense, this is an apprenticeship giving the new engineer the skills necessary to apply the knowledge gained in school. As an individual proceeds on the career path, additional knowledge and skills are required. Continuing education provides this.

Many engineers take on management duties early in their careers. This requires additional knowledge that some obtain through an advanced degree in business. Others attend management and other specific workshops. The new concepts and skills may be, for example, the following:

1. Managing and working effectively with others in a company.
2. Performing analysis of product markets.
3. Speaking and writing in a more concise and convincing style.
4. Finding the priorities of potential financial investments.
5. Assessing business opportunities.
6. Conforming to or attempting to change regulatory constraints.
7. Acting as an interface to the public sector in representing the viewpoint of the company.

Obtaining the knowledge and the skills to apply these concepts often takes some form of continuing education. Some of this can be dealt with in undergraduate education, such as communication skills. But often, additional effort is required through continuing education.

Today, nearly all companies are influenced by rapid technological change. The composition of the work force reflects this change. There are fewer low-skill jobs. Most jobs require an understanding of concepts and use of sophisticated skills. Many jobs are entwined with a computer system. Machines are run by computer programs; they are linked to each other with networks. Information is provided by computer to run plants. Employees are called on to input data into the computers and use the information provided to do their jobs. Other people must write the programs and fix the computers and equipment. Still other employees must design and fine-tune the sophisticated computer systems that are being used. Modern technology has changed the way employees are used. With this change, educational requirements are increased for almost all occupations.

From a global viewpoint, companies need:

1. New employees who have a broad base of knowledge and the capability to adapt to future technology.
2. Educational resources that can adapt quickly to the needs of industry for new and existing employees.
3. A way for successful professionals to share their methods and skills with other professionals.
4. A means for improving the knowledge and skills of existing employees, that can be adapted to individual needs.

In the past, there has been a tremendous variety of continuing education offerings promoted through companies. For larger companies, these ranged from specific short-course training to formal graduate degree programs. The diverse and flexible programs often resulted in doubts about the effectiveness of the offerings. The programs may have lacked effectiveness if they were not tailored specifically to the needs brought out in a company's strategic plans. There were few offerings that had direct application to the job. Too many were in the "nice-to-know" category and lacked immediate application. To assure the effectiveness of continuing education, offerings must support the strategic plan of the company and the departmental plans cascading from it.

MAXIMIZING APPEAL TO EMPLOYEES FOR TRAINING AND EDUCATION

Factors that motivate employees to participate in training and educational offerings were identified through a study conducted by the National Research Council and are listed as follows:

Employees at Large Urban Companies

The top reason given was to prepare for increased job responsibilities. Perhaps this reflected the perception that a large organization had many opportunities for career growth.

Employees at Small Nonurban Companies

The most important reason these employees gave was to obtain the background to do their job better. Perhaps promotions were felt to be more limited than in larger companies. The next most important reason was to prevent obsolescence in their job.

Employees Who Are Older

The primary motivation for older engineers is to become better at their current job. Perhaps this is influenced by their perception of future promotional opportunities. Interestingly, few older engineers took part in offerings. Less than half of them attended, but offerings are attended by two-thirds of the younger engineers.

Other Factors

1. Employer sponsored courses are favored by employees over courses from outside sponsors.
2. The perceived usefulness of the offering to meet the real needs of the employee is critical. This helps form an opinion about the course by the employee.
3. Highly targeted short courses that focus on new and developing technologies are favored.
4. Perception by employees that attending noncredit short courses, workshops, seminars and conferences is very useful.

The study also found that the primary reason for not attending offerings is travel distance. A one-way distance of over fifty miles is felt to be too far. Other important reasons for not attending were lack of time and the inconvenient location of the offering. The financial support given by a company was also important. Lack of support sent a message to the employee that discouraged attendance.

SOURCES OF TRAINING AND EDUCATION OFFERINGS

People gain new knowledge and skills during their careers in three ways. The first method is by "on-the-job" experiences. The second is by professional development; this includes reading magazines and books and attending seminars, workshops, technical meetings and conferences. The third way is by formal educational programs given by schools and universities. Funds are often provided by companies through direct payment or tuition reimbursement for courses satisfactorily completed. In the past few years, state governments provided funds, often matching in nature, for training. By matching, it is meant that the company must provide some funding. Much of this type of financing is for training new employees in skills for a recently relocated plant.

ON-THE-JOB EXPERIENCES. The most important gain of knowledge and skills is while doing the job. Studies found that employees rate a challenging work assignment as the top learning experience. This implies that the company is very important in the development of an employee. A company must look to itself first before delegating the training and education task to others.

As repeatedly shown in studies, the supervisor is key to the how the employee feels about the company. The great responsibility placed upon a supervisor extends to the effective training and education of an employee. It is up to the supervisor to provide the right environment for motivating the employee to learn new concepts and skills. This is done by providing progressively more challenging assignments for the employee. Coaching by more experience associates will help. But, in a sense, the employee under going training must be allowed to fail at times without penalty. With this atmosphere, the experience will be more rewarding and contribute more effectively to personal growth. Experiences on the job have a close correlation to the needs of the company regarding employee knowledge and skills.

Another study identified how engineers keep up to date using new methods on the job. The most useful way was through contact with coworkers. Some contact was coaching and other contact concerned discussion of ideas about an assignment. Printed information, such as technical papers and supplier catalogs, rated high as providing needed information and analysis skills. Handbooks and computer bases of information also rated high as enhancing "on-the-job" training. Contact with others not in the company was not considered as a major contributor for many companies. Outside contacts were rated lowest as a contributor in defense companies; contractual constraints concerning secrecy prevented discussions with outsiders.

PROFESSIONAL SOCIETIES. Organizations like the Society of Manufacturing Engineers and the American Society of Quality Control are major contributors to the career development of employees. Experts share their knowledge with others through such things as seminars, papers at conferences, workshops, home study materials, books and magazines. Some feel that networking among the members is the most valuable benefit. Often, the offerings concerning education and training directly address areas of weakness needing the most attention.

The strength of a professional society in providing education and training lies in its purpose for existence. That purpose is to serve the needs of its members. Because of this, offerings are targeted to real needs. Advisory committees composed of members, provide guidance for course development after the needs of the market are analyzed.

The composition of membership is also a strength. Many different industries and government agencies may be represented by the members. Because of this, the professional society can choose instructors from a large and diverse pool of specialists. These experts can also address many different topics of interest including new and emerging issues.

Although there is no regulation of courses offered by an outside agency, quality control is often assured by a peer advisory group. This group has a stake in the success of the offering from both a personal and professional point of view. Feedback is obtained from attendees, usually by formal surveys. These are analyzed and shared with the advisory group and the instructor to help improve performance. This review places the stature of society courses somewhere between company in-house classes and formal degree programs at universities.

Often a professional society can identify the various career interests of its members. Analysis of these interests can lead to a targeted array of offerings of great help to the members. Both technical and nontechnical issues may be important. A professional society can present both types.

Training and education offerings by a professional society are viable alternatives for a company to consider. Often, needed specialized training is only offered by professional societies. If there is enough interest, courses can be scheduled on-site. In this way, more people may receive needed training than if employees had to travel to the offering. There also may be financial advantages to this arrangement.

CONSULTANTS. The growing demand for education and training has encouraged many offerings by consultants. They may have a company name or be identified by the name of the individual involved. Because there is no overseer to accredit the offerings, the quality varies widely. Qualifications and references should be checked carefully to help assure the expected quality of the offerings.

There are advantages to using qualified consultants for providing needed offerings. Often because of a modular approach to units of instruction, courses can be quickly customized to meet the unique needs of a company. In addition, consultants are usually flexible about where they will conduct the training and how many employees need to be involved. Often, coaching can be arranged after the offering to help the participants implement the new concepts. Consultants often stress relevance during the training that is accomplished by workshops in which the participants practice the new skills.

IN-HOUSE CLASSES. The roots of in-house classes go back a long way. Early use of this technique was with apprentice training. Today, a very popular use involves training new employees. Some efforts today are by wholly owned subsidiaries of companies; other efforts are by organizations that are independent of the company. Over the years, in-house classes have attempted to cover gaps in traditional education, and meet needs that others could not deliver.

Several large companies use a mixture of courses originating inside and others offered by local educational institutions. For example, General Electric has dozens of specialized courses by corporate entities and hundreds of other courses from local schools. Most are engineering courses, but, there are classes offered in finance, marketing and employee relations. The curriculum changes constantly to meet new needs of the company.

Courses may be given by instructors in the locality or broadcast widely through such means as satellite linkages. The instructors may be experts within the company or from outside. Other in-house classes may use videotapes. This way students can view tapes when they wish and material can be reviewed by reruning of the tape.

The courses used by one company for in-house classes differ from another company because of diverse needs. Some courses are taken on a noncredit basis. For others, employees receive full college credit that may be transferred to degree programs. Employees taking the in-house classes usually get a notation of completion in their personnel records. Some companies grant certificates for a series of courses. A few companies grant degrees after completing a specialized program.

In the past few years, several companies have established institutes. Many institutes are devoted to training in quality. The training is given to everyone in the company including top management. Usually classes are organized so that the participants have a common interest. Often, they are workshops ranging from a day to several weeks in duration. Company employees act as instructors and facilitators of discussion groups. Some institutes offer training to suppliers of the company.

Another approach used by some companies is assigning the responsibility for classroom training to the supervisor of each group of individuals being trained. One company trained 9,300 employees by this method. The most important benefit of this approach is consistency after training is completed. The supervisor and subordinates have a common understanding about the approaches learned. Differences in perspective can be worked out during the classroom sessions. This is particularly important in courses intended to help change the culture of a company. Another benefit is that the concepts and skills learned are considered important because of who taught the offering. Also, the supervisor, by teaching the concepts and skills, becomes more bonded to the approaches and will likely insist on their use.

EDUCATIONAL INSTITUTIONS. Schools provide many courses for the training and education of employees. The availability of formal degree programs, often at the graduate level, is well-known. Short courses, both at college campuses and other locations, are offered in interest areas of the faculty. Employees also can enroll as special students taking a few courses that may be of use. Special programs are offered so that employees can gain skills in the basics of mathematics, reading and writing.

Community colleges are particularly successful in customizing courses and seminars that are offered on-site at a company. These customized courses are specifically related to jobs that must be handled in a company. They are not general or speculative in their use of course material. The courses concentrate on making participants skilled in doing specific tasks.

Teachers from primary and secondary schools are often sought to provide basic education in mathematics, reading and writing skills. Companies may provide these opportunities after work or during work hours. Often, special arrangements are made to make the offerings readily available to second-and third-shift employees.

To target offerings to the needs of industry, advisory committees are often used by educational institutions. The committee consist of industrial leaders in particular disciplines. Current and future needs for specific knowledge and skills often result in improvements in the educational system. Graduates who meet these needs are widely sought by companies. By hiring these candidates, the need for further training by companies is minimized. To have the most effectiveness, industry advisory committees and educational institutions should consider the following:

1. Industry must identify and prioritize its needs for training and education. The priorities should be in terms of short-and long-term needs. Collaborative efforts should be considered where needs cannot be handled solely by educational institutions.
2. The strengths and weaknesses of various academic organizations should be recognized. In general, universities having a strong research base are better at teaching fundamentals than applications. In contrast, technology programs and community colleges are better at applications. Basic skills in mathematics, reading, and writing may best be taught by primary and secondary teachers. Once the strengths of various academic organizations are clarified, industry can better target its requests for help.
3. Programs should be designed to minimize the time it takes for an employee to master the learning objectives. This is the job of the educational institution. It is a major challenge for educational institutions since there is little experience in doing it. It also has an important reward for industry, where the time available is scarce.
4. There must be recognition by the educational institution that it is competing with other sources offerings needed by industry. A consultant may be more competitive in the time required for training and the cost of the offering. Both are important to industry and must be addressed when programs are developed. A company must maximize its use of resources. The greatest cost in training is the

wages of the employees while they are in the classroom.

5. The educational institution also must recognize that it is competing with others in the timely development and delivery of courses to companies. Managers within a company are typically pushing to start training quickly. Consultants can often add temporary staff to speed the development. Unfortunately, educational institutions with full-time students have limited time available for development of outside programs.

Students who are employed full-time present a different classroom make up than those in formal full-time degree programs. In classes having employed students, there is often a large contrast in background; also there may be a large spread in ages. The students in a full-time program are usually similar in background and age. Very often, the employed student faces noticeable family and community responsibilities. Also, the priority with the employed student is the job, with the classroom sometimes taking a back-seat.

For these reasons, employed students require a more flexible structure than full-time students. They need the ability to alter their learning effort as job and family pressures change. There is also a conflict between theory and practice. Employed students are usually more interested in applications with just enough theory to help understand the problem. The student focuses on specific outcomes, as does the employer. Maintaining a balance between practice and theory is challenging to the instructor.

APPROACH FOR TRAINING AND EDUCATION

In a sense, the suggested approaches for identifying training and education activities are different from those used by most companies in the past. For the most part, preferences about training in the past were provided by the individuals who desired the training. Management decided the specific training to be done based largely on these preferences.

Training in the past was decided through a highly decentralized decision making process at the lower levels of an organization. There was little consideration of widespread training in topics that would be best for the company. Training in the past was directed mostly toward what was good for the individual and the function in which the person worked.

The focus of training has changed during the past decade. Many companies faced huge competitive pressures, often from offshore producers. The survival of many companies required a change in the way they did things. Cultural change was needed to close the gap on quality and costs. Massive training efforts were required involving all employees.

A third dimension was added in the past decade to the reasons for training which encompasses those elements needed by the company to meet its strategic plans. Meeting these plans is absolutely necessary to assure survival in a highly competitive environment. In reality, the third dimension does not conflict with the other two. To survive, a company also needs to provide training in what is best for an individual and what is best for a functional area. Often, a training offering can meet all three goals. The three dimensions of training are illustrated in Figure 9-1.

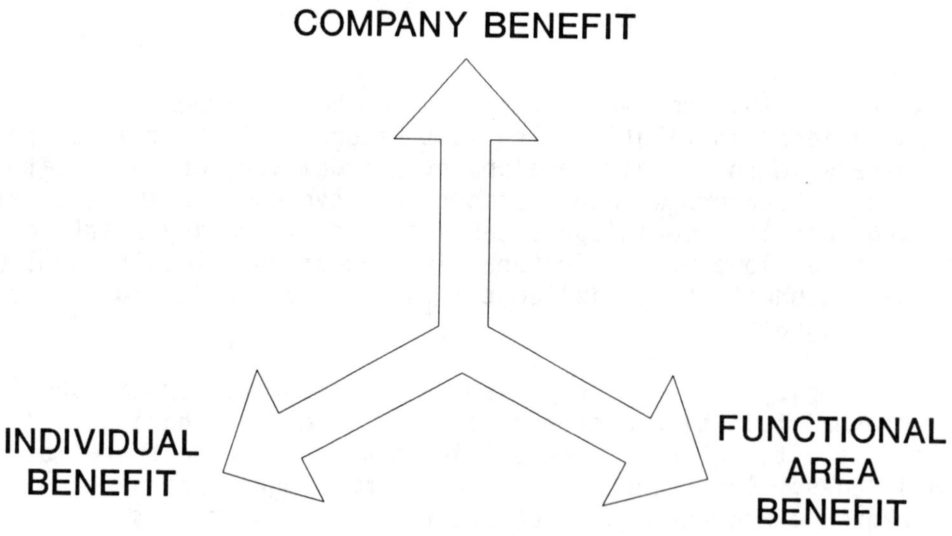

COMPANY BENEFIT

INDIVIDUAL
BENEFIT

FUNCTIONAL
AREA
BENEFIT

Figure 9-1 The three dimensions of training.

The new focus for training also shifted the responsibility for developing the training program. No longer can this responsibility be placed with each supervisor. It must rest with members of the top management team to assure that it supports the strategic plan. A human resource training plan is developed from the strategic plan. The human resources committee that makes this plan typically involves the head of each major functional area. This committee seeks input from others in the company. The outcome is a broad based plan for training of the entire work force. The focus is long-range and adjustments are regularly made to meet new circumstances. Specifics may differ for some personnel to meet special needs.

DETERMINATION OF TRAINING NEEDS AND OBJECTIVES

The foundation for determining training needs and objectives is the company strategic plan and the other plans that cascade from it. The process for doing it is called a needs analysis. The manner of preparing the needs analysis will differ for each company. A conceptual approach is as follows:

1. The desired outcomes of the strategic plan and plans that cascade from it must be understood.
2. The current capabilities of the organization must be assessed in view of the desired outcomes.
3. Organization capabilities needed to obtain desired outcomes must be understood.
4. The difference between current and needed capabilities must be assessed.
5. Desired outcomes that can be influenced by training or education should be identified. Typically, these appear where employee capabilities need to be upgraded. There are outcomes that cannot be helped by training or education and require other actions by management.
6. For each outcome that can be helped by training or education, the following should be understood:

   a. The general nature of the training.

    b. The indicators that show that current knowledge and skills are
       not satisfactory.
    c. The performance measures related to desired training outcomes.
    d. Other measures that can help in determining if the prospective
       training is effective.
    e. The breadth and depth of the prospective effort.
    f. The estimated timing and cost for developing and delivering the
       training. An important part of the cost is the wages of those
       being trained.
    g. An understanding of how the training will be used on the job and
       supported by it. If there is little use of the training on the
       job, skills will soon be lost.

7. Survey existing course offerings that meet learning objectives for
   prospective training.
8. Identify those course offerings that may need to be developed for
   the prospective training and the learning objectives of each
   course.
9. Identify specific training needs for groups of people or
   individuals. Only those employees who will gain needed skills
   should be trained. In doing this, it is important that the current
   capabilities of each individual are known. It is also important
   that any special training needs desired by an employee are
   considered.
10. Prepare training plan for an intensive review by those involved and
    approval.
11. After approval, start the execution of the plan.

BEFORE DELIVERY. Prior to delivery of the course offering, it is important
that those being trained understand why they are being trained. It is also
important that participants understand what is expected of them during the
training. They should know the learning objectives and performance measures
for the training.

They should understand how the training relates to the desired outcomes of
the strategic plan and the plans resulting from it. Discussions should
cover how the skills and concepts learned will be useful on the job.
Specific ways that they will be useful should be outlined. Any concerns
that an employee has should be dealt with in a constructive way.

DELIVERY. To be effective, training must consist of clearly defined
learning objectives arranged in a well thought out sequence. Often, a
lesson plan for each learning objective is used as a guide to the
instructor. A typical lesson plan may consist of the following parts:

1. A clear description of the learning objective.
2. A comprehensive list of the material and equipment needed by the
   instructor to convey the objective.
3. A comprehensive list of what is expected from the student both
   before and during the exercise. This may include reading a section
   of a book or working a problem. Often it includes the mastery of
   previous learning objectives that are in essence prerequisites.
4. A step-by-step plan for how the objective will be conveyed from the
   instructor to the student.
5. A method for evaluating whether the students have mastered the
   objective. This is a measure of the effectiveness of the education

or training that is taking place. To provide a proper environment for learning, the evaluation probably should not be used to judge the student.
6. A plan for retraining students who did not master the objective the first time.

Conceptually, learning is seen as a two-step process. It is the reception and processing of information. Information is received from both external sources and inside the human mind. External information is observed through human senses--the eyes, ears, nose and nerves. More effective learning occurs as more senses are involved.

Simultaneously, the human memory provides other relevant information that is merged with the observed information. The human mind now sorts the information at hand. Some information will be processed and the remainder will be ignored. The processing step ranges from memorizing the surviving information to taking action based on the information. Usually, reasoning also takes place. Learning occurs at this point. The effectiveness of the learning experience is based upon the outcome. It is a comparison of what is learned from external sources versus expectations.

Complicating the learning process are the many different ways a student learns. These are illustrated in Figure 9-2. The best way is different for each student. Training and education are difficult because there is no best way for all students in the classroom. The best way for a particular student to learn may be understood by considering these questions:

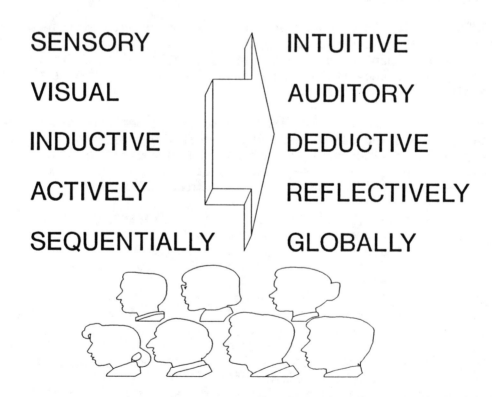

SENSORY	INTUITIVE
VISUAL	AUDITORY
INDUCTIVE	DEDUCTIVE
ACTIVELY	REFLECTIVELY
SEQUENTIALLY	GLOBALLY

Figure 9-2. The many different ways in which students can learn.

1. What type of information is favored?

   a. SENSORY--external sources through sight, sound, smell, feel and
      taste OR
   b. INTUITIVE--insights and hunches.

2. For sensory information, which is preferred?

   a. VISUAL--pictures, diagrams, and graphs OR
   b. AUDITORY--words and sounds.

3. What flow of information is favored?

   a. INDUCTIVE--facts and observations are discussed first followed by
      concepts that are implied OR
   b. DEDUCTIVE--concepts talked about first followed by observations
      supporting the concepts.

4. What is the preferred way to process information?

   a. ACTIVELY--by discussions in groups, asking questions OR
   b. REFLECTIVELY--by thinking alone.

5. How does understanding normally occur?

   a. SEQUENTIALLY--in a series of steps OR
   b. GLOBALLY--in large jumps such as holistically.

Further complicating the learning process is the style of teaching. This is
illustrated in Figure 9-3. The styles used differ for each instructor.
Also, any particular offering may contain several different styles. It is
rare when a single teaching style is used. An understanding of the
different teaching styles may be obtained through these questions:

1. What type of information is favored by the instructor?

   a. CONCRETE--factual OR
   b. ABSTRACT--conceptual or theoretical.

2. How is the information presented?

   a. VISUAL--pictures, diagrams, films, demonstrations OR
   b. VERBAL--lectures, readings, and discussions.

3. How is the presentation organized?

   a. INDUCTIVE--facts and observations are discussed first followed by
      concepts that are implied OR
   b. DEDUCTIVE--concepts talked about first followed by observations
      supporting the concepts.

4. How do the students take part in the presentation?

   a. ACTIVELY--asking questions, making comments,
      discussions in groups OR
   b. REFLECTIVELY--by thinking alone just watching and listening.

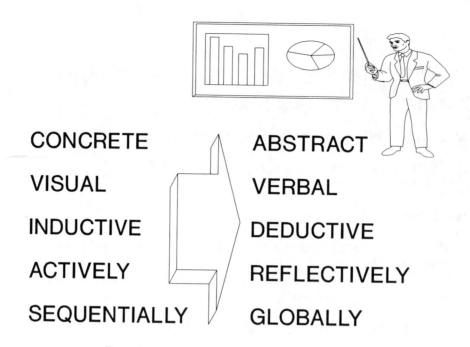

CONCRETE	ABSTRACT
VISUAL	VERBAL
INDUCTIVE	DEDUCTIVE
ACTIVELY	REFLECTIVELY
SEQUENTIALLY	GLOBALLY

Figure 9-3. There are many different types of teaching styles.

5. How is the information presented?

   a. SEQUENTIALLY--in a series of steps OR
   b. GLOBALLY--in large jumps such as holistically.

Ideally, the teaching style should match the best way a student learns. This can be done in "one-on-one" situations such as on-the-job training, but in a classroom or workshop situation, each student may need a different teaching method to optimize learning. This, of course is not possible. The strategy used is to present the material using a variety of methods. Guidelines that may be helpful in this situation are:

1. Relate the material presented to other parts of the course, other courses, and the personal experiences of the student.
2. Present a mixture of information that is concrete, abstract, sensing and intuitive.
3. Balance the amount of material having practical problem solving with other material concerning concepts.
4. Mix illustrations of an intuitive nature with those that are sensing.
5. For describing concepts, use both inductive and deductive approaches for explaining the same concept.
6. Use visual material before, during and after the presentation of verbal material.
7. Provide video tapes for viewing and "hands-on" demonstrations to show concepts and practice skills.
8. Use computer-assisted instruction.
9. Minimize lecturing and provide periods that students can just reflect on the material.
10. Provide frequent opportunity for students to be active. Short team exercises in class are good for this.
11. Provide some open-ended problems that need analysis and synthesis.
12. Maximize the opportunity for the cooperation of students on assignments.
13. Praise creative solutions even if they are not correct.

There are many styles through which a student learns. Including the above techniques in a presentation should help address the many needs of those in a class. The proper mix to use depends on each situation. In a sense, it is a judgment call by the instructor using feedback sensed from the students.

EVALUATION. The effectiveness of the training can be evaluated by the performance measures developed during planning. These will show if learning objectives were achieved. For example, a simple exercise could be given to see if participants know how to construct and interpret a variable control chart. If not, retraining may be necessary. At a minimum, future offerings must be revised.

Using performance measures provides direct answers to whether training was successful. Where new skills are the objective, tests should be given after the employee returns to the job. These may be simply watching the employee applying the new skills. On the other hand, behavioral changes are difficult to measure and often cannot be directly tied to training.

Tests can be given to find out if employees remember the concepts and procedures taught. These can tell if the employees can express on paper what they learned in class. However, written tests cannot predict if the things learned will be used on the job.

Traditionally, training offerings are evaluated by a survey or interview. A typical survey is shown in the Appendix (Training Effectiveness Questionnaire). If it is filled out immediately after a training offering, results may be skewed. This is because of the "halo" effect. The "platform" skills of an instructor may have a great influence on results. Because of this, the effectiveness of the technology transfer may be masked. To avoid this, the survey should be administered several months after the training. Often, this method of evaluation tells the popularity of the course and not its ability to transfer technology.

SUMMARY

Training and education are tools that management can use to nourish continuous improvement. They can provide concepts and skills that would otherwise not be available to the work force. They are, in reality, tools that can help bring about needed change for a company to survive.

The next chapter discusses the building of teams.

BIBLIOGRAPHY

Akoodie, Mohammed, and Rourke, T. Frank, "Achieving Excellence in Training." Quality Conference Transactions (Minneapolis). Milwaukee: American Society for Quality Control, 1987.

Alexander, Philip C. and Munro, Roderick A., "Continuous Improvement in Training." Quality Conference Transactions (San Francisco). Milwaukee: American Society for Quality Control, 1990.

Anderson, Robert M. Jr., "From Co-existence to Collaboration and Competition," Engineering Education, American Society for Engineering Education, May 1987.

Burleson, Alan L. and Pridgen, A. Wade, "Using Line Management to Lead Quality Fundamentals," Quality Conference Transactions (Dallas). Wilwaukee: American Society for Quality Control, 1988.

Cranch, Edmund T., "Continuing Engineering Education in the United States: An Overview and Assessment." Engineering Education, American Society for Engineering Education, May 1987.

Felder, Robert M. and Silverman, Linda K., "Learning and Teaching Styles in Engineering Education," Engineering Education, American Society for Engineering Education, April 1988.

Gilbert, Jay, "Continuing Education: Seeking the Cutting Edge," Engineering Education, American Society for Engineering Education, May 1987.

Hayner, Anne M., "Getting Technical Training into Gear," Manufacturing Engineering, Dearborn, MI: Society of Manufacturing Engineers, September 1989.

Jones, Russel C., "Continuing Development to Enhance the Utilization of Engineers," Engineering Education, American Society for Engineering Education, May 1987.

Maynard, H.B., Editor, Chapter Eight - Training, Handbook of Business Administration, McGraw Hill Book Company, 1967.

Schneider, George, Jr., Mishne, Patricia P., "Keeping Up in an Uphill Struggle," Manufacturing Engineering, Dearborn, MI: Society of Manufacturing Engineers, October 1988.

"Special Report - Needed Human Capital," Business Week, September 19, 1988.

Stauffer, Robert N., "Getting Manufacturing Education Up to Speed," Manufacturing Engineering, Dearborn, MI: Society of Manufacturing Engineers, September 1989.

Willenbrock, F. Karl, "The Need for Career-long Education," Engineering Education, American Society for Engineering Education, November 1988.

CHAPTER 10

TEAM BUILDING

In this chapter. . .

PART-TIME TEAMS

FULL-TIME TEAMS

TRUST
1. Reprisal
2. Failure
3. Providing Information
4. Not Knowing
5. Giving Up Control
6. Change

COMMITMENT

COMMUNICATION

CONFLICT
1. Emphasizing a "Win-Win" Solution
2. Creating a Positive Atmosphere
3. Focusing on the Issue
4. Reaching Consensus
5 Use of External Help

TEAM BUILDING
1. Develop a Mission Statement
2. Agree on Operating Principles
3. Prepare Team Action Plan

TEAM LIFE CYCLE
1. Team Building
2. Team Development
3. Team Maturity
4. Team Completion

Appendix information

Sample meeting agenda
(Courtesy of Charney & Associates, Inc.) A-41--A-44

10

Team Building

This chapter deals with establishing teams. Teams are composed of several individuals pursuing a common objective. When that objective is met, the team is disbanded, and members reassigned.

Teams are important to many organizations today. They are being used increasingly by manufacturers faced with the changing nature of business. In the last decade, there has been an erosion of consumer confidence to the products manufactured by offshore competition. This prompted a change in management approach. The use of teams is widely believed to be the best way to tap the people power of an organization.

Properly designed, teams have the following advantages for the company and team members:

1. Members of teams that help achieve organizational goals will be more concerned with the success of the company.
2. By participating in decisions regarding organizational goals, team members are more committed to reaching them. There will be much less resistance to needed change.
3. Performance is improved because members of teams feel more in control of their destiny, and less subject to arbitrary actions. There is less need for heavy staff involvement, and intense supervision.
4. Working with other disciplines, team members increase their understanding of the needs of others, and make wiser decisions.
5. Being on a team provides members a chance to satisfy higher-level needs concerning self-esteem and self-actualization.
6. A team allows each member to stand on an equal footing, breaking down status differences. This creates open and honest communication about issues.
7. Techniques for effectively dealing with people can be learned in teams, and team members become role models for the rest of the organization.
8. Problem solving, and other skills are developed better by members of teams.
9. Better decisions result from bringing into focus the diverse resources of the members on a team.

For most companies, the positive effects of team technique will far outweigh the following negative factors:

1. Wages may need to be increased to correspond to the new skills that are acquired.
2. Training costs are usually much higher, to develop the new skills associated with meeting the objectives of teams.
3. Support expenses, such as travel, may increase. Often, less staff and supervision is needed, offsetting this cost.
4. Middle management typically feels threatened because of its perceived loss in power, and usefulness to the organization.
5. Staff personnel also may feel threatened, and resist the change.
6. Nonproductive time increases as team business takes more time.
7. Decisions may be slower because more people need to understand, and agree with plans.
8. Unhappiness may result if outcomes do not meet expectations. Change takes a considerable time to implement, and is not a short-range phenomenon. Results from some changes may take years to notice.
9. Some workers will have trouble working as team players. Many workers, for most of their careers, have been part of a system where individualism was rewarded.

PART-TIME TEAMS

Many teams are a part-time effort for their members. Time spent with the team must be taken from the regular job. The majority of teams dealing with improvement are part-time. Each member is linked to a different area of the company; this is an important strength of improvement teams. Through this linkage, outcomes needed by the team can be more easily obtained. Part-time teams were discussed in previous chapters.

FULL-TIME TEAMS

There are other teams that are full-time. They range from such applications as "skunk works" to employee involvement teams on the factory floor, and in offices.

The term "skunk works" is sometimes used to describe a small group of highly skilled people sequestered from the rest of the organization. Usually, they are asked to design a new product, or process quickly. No organizational constraints are imposed. Without these constraints, innovation is high, and the project is completed promptly. At this point, the "skunk works" is disbanded. Participants return to their original function.

Employee involvement teams recognize that people are the key to competing in the world marketplace. Studies show that meaningful participation by employees in a business has a positive effect on productivity. One study of auto plants showed that adding technology without involving workers was not successful. When computer-based technology was accompanied by involvement of workers, results were much better.

The long-standing practices of dividing labor are out of date. No longer can work be divided ahead of time into simple, repetitive tasks, done by unskilled workers under close supervision. The survival of companies depends on involving workers in making decisions regarding how work is divided. Workers involved in planning make things even better. A multinational electrical manufacturer achieved improvements in productivity of 50% or greater by using worker teams for planning changes in technology.

In many companies, there is a transition to work teams that manage themselves. Management will be involved in training the team members and providing information. This way, employees and management are no longer adversaries. There will be less resistance to change and, in fact, many changes will be suggested by the worker teams.

Work teams have been used successfully for years in many countries; most notably in Japan and Sweden. Copying their practices, however, generally was not successful in the U.S. An example of this is the quality circle concept. The culture in the U.S. is different. It is now recognized that U.S. workers need a larger voice in things left up to management in other countries. A sharing of power with management must occur.

Typically, work teams decide how work will be divided. They often estimate production rates that are higher than those found by industrial engineering techniques. Engineers take on a consulting role, and provide advice to the team. The members of the teams learn a variety of jobs, and are more flexible. Some work teams even maintain their equipment and work area to reduce downtime. There are plants that run with less than half a dozen job classifications with improved efficiency. Workers on the teams may be involved in hiring decisions, and rate the performance of the members on the team.

Work teams provide jobs that are more challenging because they are designed by those on the team. Workers, in a sense, have control of their destiny. Under these circumstances, workers are committed, and perform better. Unfortunately, labor unions may see this as an erosion of their influence, and a threat to their existence. This perception is also often shared by multilayered middle management. A major challenge to any company is to deal with these perceptions in a positive manner.

TRUST

Critical to any company is a feeling of trust by their employees. Distrust causes people not to share ideas. Cooperation is also lost when it is unclear in what spirit it will be used. Success in continuous improvement depends on using the creativity of each employee to solve problems. Unlocking this creativity is contingent on providing a climate of trust where individuals do not fear consequences that may result from the sharing of ideas.

In the past, trust in many companies did not widely exist. For example, workers were penalized for errors that may not have been their fault. The result of this practice ranged from doing as little as possible to not taking any chances. For these employees, it was often more important to avoid risk than to make a contribution. The survival of companies today depends on the contribution of each employee. Today, a company cannot afford to simply turn off this contribution by a culture of distrust. Trust cannot be mandated. Trust must be built over a period of time. The actions of every employee toward others form the base of the trust inherent in a company. In a sense, it is part of the culture of a company. Trust results from the way the company wants each employee to treat others. This starts with top management, and extends throughout the company. Specific rules cannot be written down. It must be part of a value system that is inside each employee.

Feelings of trust are most likely in a company where employees receive support from each other. To have trust, there must be mutual understanding, and acceptance of individual differences. Also, risk-taking must be encouraged, and failures accepted as a potential byproduct.

Trust promotes honesty. This is necessary to expose problem areas and deal with them. Many chronic problems today continue because the people involved are afraid of the consequences of dealing with them. In many ways, lack of trust is a cancer destroying the long-range viability of a company. More importantly, lack of trust limits the true potential of individuals within the company. For a company to survive, this cannot be allowed.

To deal with lack of trust, its causes must be understood and minimized. One way of dealing with this is to describe the causes as "fears" existing in varying degrees in any company:

1. REPRISAL. This fear is characteristic of an organization that manages by intimidation. Threats are made to control outcomes. These threats range from job loss to embarrassment in front of peers. Where no open threats exist, they are imagined, further stifling the progress of an organization. There is a lot of pleasing the boss by agreeing with anything that is said. Debating issues leading to better solutions is overtly discouraged.

2. FAILURE. Often, fear of failure is based upon perceptions of reprisal. Failure is not accepted by the organization as a potential outcome of risk-taking. Rather, it is seen as weakness by the people involved. Employees are convinced that any failure may destroy their career and future raises. Typically, an organization becomes paralyzed, in that new ideas are not tried. Being part of an effort is not desirable unless the effort is sure to be a success. The company work force is always on the defensive and will not take action to make things better. Often "CYA" activities consume a disproportionate amount of time.

3. PROVIDING INFORMATION. This fear is often described as "shoot-the-messenger." Unfavorable information is often not desired by those receiving it. Going back to at least ancient Greece, the typical reaction is to blame the messenger. Employees pointing out issues that should be dealt with are instead labeled as malcontents. This limits the generation of new ideas, and discourages dealing with pertinent issues that affect the survival of a company.

4. NOT KNOWING. Many managers feel that possessing more information than others gives them power. The additional knowledge is perceived to provide wisdom that others do not have. Also, lack of information is perceived as a weakness. Yet, by not sharing information freely, much effort is often wasted by second-guessing.

This takes the place of admitting to a lack of knowledge, and asking for what is needed. In a company that does not freely share information, employees begin to distrust those controlling the information, and question their motives.

5. GIVING UP CONTROL. In the past, companies with functional organizations evolved into power bases. Decisions were made favoring those having the most power. Often, power was defined by how much a manager controls; this could be both people and resources. Improvement efforts today require reallocation of resources. If managers believe they will lose power, this issue may be paramount. The message sent to others in the organization if this occurs will be adverse. Employees will doubt that the company really wants to improve.

6. CHANGE. In the journey of continuous improvement, there are many unknowns. Certain business risks must be taken, and outcomes may be dependent on factors that are not under the control of a company. But constant change is needed for a company to survive. It is natural for employees in a company to fear the unknown, but trust can be achieved through sharing plans and logic with all employees.

Addressing the issues just outlined takes a basic change in the culture of most companies. Achieving this change has been discussed in previous chapters of this book.

COMMITMENT

To get commitment, employees must have a shared vision of the company, its mission, and its goals. There also must be a widespread consensus about the need for improvement, and the way it will be done.

This must start with top management. The message they send to the organization by their actions is critical. Employees generally mirror the attitudes and behaviors of the managers of the organization. Management absolutely must act the way they talk. Quality and continuous improvement must be the driving force, from the top of an organization to the factory floor.

Achieving continuous improvement requires a common value system in employees. This value system is centered on a high commitment to achieve improvement, both personally and for the company. That value system requires a change in attitudes and behaviors on the part of employees not working up to their potential.

Companies are changing their approach to the way they achieve commitment. They realize that employee commitment is needed to achieve goals. In these companies, traditional approaches to management are being discarded. Instead of control, management is assuming a support role. They realize that commitment is a two-way street. To receive it, management must demonstrate it by providing challenging work, a good work environment, and training for needed skills.

In these types of companies, managers are really facilitators. Their objective is to provide the tools and atmosphere to help workers reach full potential. Removing roadblocks slowing the progress of teams is a high priority. Commitment of employees can be best obtained where they feel confident of their abilities. Also, employees must have management support in reaching both personal and company goals.

COMMUNICATION

Improvement efforts require open communication among employees. All employees, from top management to those on the factory floor, need to value the power of open, direct, and frank communication. In reality, this is the way that all issues are exposed so they can be dealt with. If ideas for improvement are never expressed, it is unlikely that the full potential of the company will be reached.

This type of communication calls for more than willingness to express ideas. It also requires active listening, and efforts to understand the ideas expressed. A key part of listening is assuring that no criticism or punishment will occur as a result of the sharing of knowledge. If adverse consequences are perceived, communication will be throttled. Without communication, improvement will be difficult to achieve.

CONFLICT

Conflict is a vital part of improvement activities. The most innovative and lasting improvements are often generated by involving a variety of differing viewpoints. This is a major strength of cross-discipline improvement teams. Ideas generated on the first round of any discussion may not survive. They often inspire new and better ideas as the discussion continues, however. The importance of conflict was pointed out sometime ago in a saying attributed to Robert Frost, who said, "if two people always agree, one of them is unnecessary."

Unfortunately, conflicts also can get out of hand, and cause much damage. Causes of conflict include:

1. Schedules.
2. Project priorities.
3. Resources.
4. Technical opinions.
5. Performance trade-offs.
6. Administrative procedures.
7. Personality conflicts.

Many ways exist to deal with conflict. The least desirable method is to retreat from it, because the source of the conflict remains and will likely surface again at an inopportune time. The best approach is to confront conflict, and seek the best possible solution.

Unlike technical problems, focusing on the source of the problem likely will not resolve the conflict. Rather, experience has shown that the focus must be on solutions. Managing conflict for constructive results requires:

1. Emphasizing a "win-win" solution. Most people were brought up in a competitive environment. Sports are a good example: somebody has to win, and somebody has to lose. In a company where there must be a united effort, this posture is often disastrous. Conflict may exist only because of the need to win, not because of the idea offered.

   To achieve improvement, many companies now recognize that all parties involved should benefit. In essence, there must be "win-win" solutions wherever possible to achieve company goals. By working to eliminate a win-lose atmosphere, cooperation improves. Potential solutions are rated on their merit -- how they meet the goals of the company, not the narrower goals of each functional area. Solutions are sought that benefit everyone in different ways.

2. Creating a positive atmosphere. The key to having an effective improvement effort is maintaining a positive atmosphere during conflict. Often, this is done by emphasizing the goals of the company that are common among the parties involved. For best results, common goals should be in quantitative terms, not subject to interpretation that may cause further conflict.

   The discussion should not place blame on individuals who are involved. To do so, creates a defensive atmosphere that will not support improvement efforts. The focus should be on improving conditions so errors cannot occur in the future. Emphasis should be placed on what is said, not who said it, and on what is right, not who is right.

   Also beneficial is having the team identify the positive outcomes that will occur when company goals are achieved. Often, these are found to benefit all functions involved in "win-win" situation. Another helpful technique is setting a target date for completion of the task. This will limit procrastination, and increase collaboration among the parties to meet the target date.

   Arguments and emotional outbreaks should be avoided. These can lead to resisting solutions, and may cause deep resentment. Maintaining an atmosphere where all viewpoints are considered is necessary. This is difficult, since strong personalities may not easily tolerate other ideas. Experience has shown that calm and rational discussions focused on the issue causing the conflict result in wise, workable solutions.

3. Focusing on the issue. When a conflict starts, other peripheral issues are added by the parties. These do not really relate to the conflict, and cause the discussion to be chaotic. Efforts should be made to keep the parties focused on the issue concerning the original conflict. Other issues not directly related can be discussed later after solving the original conflict.

4. Reaching consensus. The priority for a team should be to reach consensus. This is where all parties accept the outcome of a discussion. It is based more on support of the outcome than on full agreement. Often, it is a compromise among the parties to get a "win-win" solution. It usually requires flexibility among the parties, and adjustment of original expectations.

Support is often lacking when reaching decisions based on a vote. Those who vote against something may not adopt the majority viewpoint. If everyone can accept an outcome through consensus, the likelihood of success is increased.

5. Use of external help as a last resort. The best results occur if the members of a team can resolve conflict among themselves. Sometimes, this takes an intensive effort. If all efforts fail, external help may be needed.

First, a facilitator should be considered. A neutral third party, called a facilitator, can lead meetings of the team. Usually, facilitators can promote rational thinking and understanding among the members. New avenues can be explored, leading to more viewpoints. Often, these discussions lead to a consensus among the team members.

If the outcome is critical, an arbitrator may be chosen by the team members. This is only suggested after unsuccessfully trying a facilitator. In this scenario, the arbitrator makes the final decision after hearing all viewpoints. It is important that the decision of the person chosen be accepted by all team members. Usually, the arbitrator is a member of management.

TEAM BUILDING

The process of team building is, in reality, laying the cornerstone of a team. It is a process in which several diverse individuals are bonded together in a team. The effectiveness of a team depends on how well the bonding takes place. The strength of any team depends upon building on the differences of each member, and focusing on common goals. Gaining agreement on the common goals is an important element in the bonding process. The differences of each member help assure well-tested solutions.

Members of the team are selected from several functional areas in a company. Sometimes, the team also may include suppliers, as well as customers. The members form a natural work group whose skills are collectively needed to reach a goal.

Many questions are in the mind of a new team member at the first meeting. Some of them are:

1. What will I do?
2. Who is the leader?
3. How will I fit in with the others?
4. What is going to happen in the meetings?
5. What is in this for me?

In the effort to get the team established, these questions may not be asked. Nevertheless, they must be answered promptly to properly set the foundation for what is to come.

Most companies pursuing continuous improvement use a facilitator for team building. Approaches differ, depending upon the facilitator. Though different, they produce the same result--bonding of the team members. Each approach is generic in nature, and works in a variety of applications. A typical approach is:

Step 1. Develop a mission statement.

Usually, several hours are spent by the members of a team to develop a mission statement. It is an intense discussion about such questions as, "Why is the team in existence?" Typically, conversation also takes place about whether each team member is needed.

Input may come from a steering committee about what needs to be done. Through discussion, a common understanding of goals is reached by all team members. Also, the role of each member is clarified. Teams draw on the diverse backgrounds of each member to make sure that all aspects of a situation are considered. Also, the issues can be tested from many points of view. Often, the project assigned by a steering committee is redefined during the discussion. For example, the project may be to reduce scrap by a certain percentage. The team may find during the discussion that specifications were based on similar parts produced over a period of years. It may not be clear that the specifications reflect the needs of the current customers, or if warranty is also a concern. The project scope may be widened to first identify customer needs, and then reflect the needs in the specifications. After doing this, the process capability can be evaluated, and steps can be taken to assure that the process conforms to the needs.

Whenever a group of people gathers, there are many preconceived notions regarding solutions. Because of this there are many arguments, and decisions become difficult to reach. By discussing the mission, it is likely that the focus of the group will change to what needs to be done. Preconceived notions will take a back seat. The attention of the group will be focused on a common objective, and agreement is more likely to be readily obtained. A common focus can rally the strengths within the team, and focus them toward achieving goals. In essence, the mission focuses on where the team needs to go by sorting out many of today's hot issues.

Step 2. Agree on operating principles.

After understanding what the team is to do, team members can concentrate on how they will operate. This will establish the culture of the team. The way the team does things will be discussed and agreed upon. Some of these operating principles may be:

1. Each member will tolerate the ideas of others, and try to understand them.
2. Consensus will be used to decide approaches.
3. Each team member has an equal status.
4. A leader to conduct meetings will be selected by consensus of the team members.
5. Meetings will be conducted in a professional manner with a high degree of mutual respect.
6. There will be an agenda for the next meeting prepared at the end of each meeting.

7. Agenda items will be assigned to appropriate team members, who will prepare material in a timely manner.
8. The generation of ideas will be separate from the evaluation and selection process.
9. During the generation of ideas, there will be no criticism.
10. Important parts of meetings will be put in the minutes.
11. Responsibility for minutes will be rotated among team members who will send them out prior to the next meeting.
12. Meetings of a short duration (not more than two hours) will be scheduled frequently in a room that assures privacy.
13. All team members will be invited when reporting to the steering committee.
14. Official communication from the team will be coordinated by the leader.
15. Provide timely training for the members in group interactions and problem solving.
16. Use a trained facilitator where appropriate.
17. Celebrate successes.

Step 3.   Prepare team action plan.

The next step in the team building process is to reach agreement on the approach to be taken. The approach must satisfy the common objectives of the team. It is a listing of steps needed to achieve the team's goals. The team members having prime responsibility for each step must be defined. The listing should include the critical information, and decisions required. Also, when each step will start and be completed should be clarified. Details on this were covered in Chapter 7.

A critical part of the action plan is specifying the deliverables. This is a tangible output of the team that can be easily seen. It is usually in the form of a report. Ideally, each step should have a deliverable. At a minimum, the final step must include a deliverable. The final step may be, for example, issuing a report with a recommendation to the steering committee. This deliverable signals that the team has completed its mission, and can be disbanded, or assigned another project. A sample agenda for meetings is included in Appendix A.

TEAM LIFE CYCLE

A team, like anything else, has a life cycle. Expectations for a team should consider the phases in this life cycle. Results cannot be expected until members are transformed into a team. The life cycle can be looked at as being comprised of four phases:

1. Team Building. In this phase, members typically feel unsure of what to do. Efforts to identify a common objective help to unify the members in an approach that is acceptable. Output from the team is often not noticeable. Much assistance is needed from the steering committee, and trained facilitators.

2. Team Development. Teams gain momentum during this phase. Relations among the members evolve into mutual respect and cooperation. Conflicts are often noticeable, and are a natural outcome of the

maturing of the relationships among the members. There is a small but growing output from the team. Reliance on the steering committee and facilitators is decreasing.

3. Team Maturity. The members work well with each other and output often exceeds expectations. Typically, advice from the steering committee is not needed, and the team proceeds on its own.

4. Team Completion. At this point the mission is accomplished. Often, disbanding the team offsets the feeling of accomplishment, and members hope to work together again in the future.

The next chapter discusses how priorities are set to achieve effectiveness in continuous improvement efforts.

BIBLIOGRAPHY

Babcock, Daniel L., Managing Engineering and Technology, Englewood Cliffs, NJ: Prentice Hall, 1991.

Berg, Deanna H., "Building Team Commitment to Quality," Quality Congress Transactions (Dallas). Milwaukee: American Society for Quality Control, 1988.

Bowman, Joseph C., "Leading by Example." Quality Progress, November 1989, p. 38.

Caplan, Frank, "The Use of Teams in Achieving Quality," Quality Congress Transactions (Baltimore). Milwaukee: American Society for Quality Control, 1985.

Denton, D. Keith, "Four Steps to Resolving Conflicts." Quality Progress, April 1989, p. 29.

Dingus, Victor R. and Hrivnak, Dave, "Tennessee Eastman Department Raises Quality, Customer Service Through Employee Teamwork." Industrial Engineering, July 1988.

Jones, Louis and McBride, Ronald, "Team Approach to Problem Solving, Taps," Quality Congress Transactions. Milwaukee: American Society for Quality Control, 1987.

Jones, Louis and McBride, Ronald, An Introduction to Team Approach Problem Solving. Milwaukee: Quality Press, 1990.

Lawler III, Edward E., "High-Involvement Management," Jossey-Bass, 1988.

Linell, Eric R., "Are We Part of the Team, or Part of the Problem," Quality Congress Transactions (Baltimore). Milwaukee: American Society for Quality Control, 1985.

Lowe, Theodore A. and McBean, Gerald M., "Honesty Without Fear." Quality Progress, November 1989. p. 30.

Scharf, Alan, "How to Change Seven Rowdy People." <u>Industrial Management</u>, September/October 1989.

Spartz, Donald, Management Vitality: The Team Approach. Dearborn, MI: Society of Manufacturing Engineers, 1984.

The Ernst & Young Quality Improvement Consulting Group, Total Quality An Executive's Guide for the 1990s, Quality Press and Dow Jones-Irwin, 1990.

"The Payoff From Teamwork," <u>Business Week</u>, July 10, 1989.

Wolkensperg, Kazmer A., "Participative Leadership: Teamwork American Style," Quality Congress Transactions (Baltimore). Milwaukee: American Society for Quality Control, 1985.

CHAPTER 11

SETTING PRIORITIES

In this chapter. . .

FINANCIAL TECHNIQUES

COST ACCOUNTING PRACTICES

OTHER SOURCES OF COSTS

NONFINANCIAL FACTORS

APPROACH
1. Identify Factors Important to Deciding Priorities
2. Rank Factors According to Importance
3. Select a Rating System
4. Develop Weights for Factors Used in Deciding Priorities

11
Setting Priorities

Industry is undergoing a major change. This change is necessary to offset competitive pressures that occurred in the last decade. Technology is being modernized; systems are being used that can tap the vast information processing capabilities of today's computers. For many companies, basics are being revisited, leading to innovative ideas from much of the work force.

Historically, the right combination of resources necessary to instigate change never seems to be present at the same time. This is true in even the largest companies. Part of these resources involves the use of money for modernizing existing facilities. Another part includes the right type of people to facilitate change. Time also must be available for the work that must be done. Today, the pressure for more resources has never been greater.

Rational choices must be made about the type of change to be implemented. Needs must be assessed and ranked, and solutions chosen wisely. These subjects are addressed in this chapter. The necessary changes enabling the company to survive must take priority. This requires a global viewpoint and long-range focus. Department needs must be measured on the basis of how they support company strategy. Also, short-term profits may need to be sacrificed for long-term benefits.

Decisions about priorities should be made by top management. They can focus in on the needs of the entire company. This responsibility should not be delegated, otherwise decisions are made favoring one department over another. Such decisions usually do not fully support company needs. In general, priorities are reflected in the:

1. Funding of operating budgets to support tasks having a strategic significance.
2. Assigning the proper resources to do these tasks. Resources include such things as people and equipment.
3. Providing direction and support to the organizations and people that are directly and indirectly concerned.

To decide priorities, consensus must be sought from all major disciplines in the company. This consensus must be reached in a team setting by focusing on all factors in the business. The collective wisdom of all those involved will reduce the risk of making decisions that could prove unfavorable. There also are great risks in not gaining support for decisions. Those not agreeing may not work aggressively to make the decision successful.

Getting dependable information on which to base decisions is vital. Direct labor, for example, is no longer considered a viable driver of productivity improvements. For many companies, direct labor has eroded to between 5-10% of total cost. Other costs have become more important. Direct material may be from 40-70% of total cost. Overhead cost may be two-to-three times greater than direct labor cost. In many companies, white collar workers outnumber those on the factory floor. Yet, direct labor savings are still being used by some companies to assign priorities. Improvement opportunities are often not pursued as a result, leading to further deterioration in competitiveness.

Tools for assigning priorities to projects are changing a great deal. New techniques adopt an approach that evaluates many factors which are not necessarily financially based. These factors are difficult to quantify in financial terms. They do, however, suggest the degree of support for the strategic plans of a company. The use of these broad-based tools for assigning priorities is being emphasized in many forward looking companies. A recent survey found about half are using subjective evaluations to supplement financial techniques. About 10% are currently using these broader-based methods as a primary way of assigning priorities.

FINANCIAL TECHNIQUES

Despite this trend, financial tools are still being widely used by companies as the sole determiner of investment priorities. Further survey results reveal that about half the companies use only financial techniques for assigning priorities. These include the payback method and traditional engineering economic techniques, such as internal rate of return (IRR) and net present worth (NPW).

The payback method estimates the time it will take for the savings or profits to offset the cost of the investment. Many companies insist that an investment be offset within 24 to 36 months. The period often varies with economic conditions. When conditions are bleak and money is tight, it may be less than 24 months. For several projects, the one having the shortest payback time usually has priority. Critics of this approach point out that it does not properly allow for varying cash flows at different times. Its simplicity, no doubt, accounts for it being used by one-third of the companies recently surveyed.

IRR is the interest rate that would need to be realized for the value of the expected future cash flow to equal the initial investment. As a minimum, the IRR must be greater than the interest rate needed to get the capital for investment. For several investments, the one with the higher IRR is usually given priority. This approach was being used by over half the companies responding to a survey.

NPW is the net value of the savings and expenses in terms of today's money. Future cash flow is discounted to today's value using a threshold rate of interest. The threshold rate reflects the minimum expected from an investment. Positive future cash flow offsets the initial investment. The net value is called NPW. The NPW must be positive to provide a good investment. Normally, the project with the higher NPW is given priority when comparing several investments. Of the companies surveyed, 14% used this technique.

In general, financial evaluation techniques have the following steps:

1. Finding the initial investment and other costs during the lifetime of the project.
2. Finding the savings and incremental revenue over the lifetime of the project attributable to the investment.
3. Analyzing the financial benefit to the company using techniques such as payback, ROI or NPW.

Details of these techniques, and others, can be found in any engineering economics book.

The traditional engineering economy tools were developed some years ago as a means of deciding how obsolete factory equipment would be replaced. They are mainly concerned with cost avoidance and replacement of somewhat inexpensive capital assets. Past use emphasized the expense part of the profit equation rather than revenue creation. Whether they are appropriate for assigning priorities, for broader-based and extensive investments affecting both cost and revenue, is debatable. The usefulness of engineering economic tools also is questionable when dealing with multiple objectives and environmental uncertainties. Dealing with inaccurate estimates of cost is also a concern.

The use of financial techniques alone for determining priorities is currently being questioned by both financial and manufacturing professionals. There is a feeling that decisions based only on financial tools are partly responsible for a downturn in productivity gains during the past decade. In other words, wrong decisions may have resulted from not considering more factors in assigning priorities. This concern centers on placing needed investments in new technology on the back burner during the past decade. This happened when short-term financial targets could not be met.

COST ACCOUNTING PRACTICES

Accurate cost information is needed to make reliable decisions from a financial viewpoint. Traditional cost-accounting approaches may not be adequate. Many people feel that accounting is more "art" than "science." Cost estimates are developed by judgment and consist largely of allocated costs; the true costs are rarely known. For most companies, costs are a rough approximation. This situation makes decisions, based only on financial techniques, risky. It may be that an awareness of this situation influenced half the companies recently surveyed to use nonfinancial factors in decision making.

Approaches may be consistent within a company for developing and allocating costs. This consistency is believed by some to allow valid comparisons. Comparisons still may be misleading, however, if the items being compared are not alike in shape, processing, volume, and resources required. Alternative approaches are not always alike.

A recent report by the National Association of Accountants (NAA) suggests that a major problem in accounting for costs is due to the erosion of direct labor in companies.

A substantial part of production costs has shifted to overhead for many companies. Overhead costs are assigned from cost pools. Many cost pools contain the salaries and wages of employees not directly concerned with producing the product. Increasing use of white-collar workers has enlarged these cost pools. Also contributing to the larger pools are such things as increased maintenance expense and depreciation for new technology.

Traditionally, the cost pools are allocated on a percentage basis. Many companies use direct labor as the base, applying a percentage for the overhead pool. The make up of the cost pool regarding resources that are included is not clear to most people in the company.

Even more serious is the size of the cost center to which the overhead rate is applied. For many companies, this consists of the entire plant. For others it may be several departments. Within these cost centers can be a variety of diverse operations. For example, the cost center may include a machining department, a pressroom, and an assembly area. Each of these may involve different efforts by those resources accounted for in the cost pool. For most companies, the even application of overhead masks the uneven application of resources in a company.

Use of overhead in the manner just described is called full costing. The use of full costing may exist because it is an easier way for accountants to provide cost information for external reports. In essence, it hides the real cost of specific operations. Not only are the type of costs in overhead unclear, the amount of each type for specific operations is unknown. Dissimilar operations that use the same amount of direct labor will have the same allocated overhead cost. In reality, the costs of operations requiring few resources are overstated. The costs of operations requiring many resources are understated. This has serious implications for decision makers using costs developed in this manner.

Academicians in accounting have long advocated variable or direct costing for internal use in a company. This would avoid the full-costing problems just described. To do this would involve reducing the types of costs in the traditional overhead base. The costs that would be removed could be treated as variable and not fixed. Examples may be scrap and rework that vary considerably for different products. This concept is justified on the basis that the only relevant costs for decisions are those that can be changed. Fixed costs, for the most part, have already been incurred and cannot be changed.

Recently, the concept of variable or fixed costing has been seriously challenged. In the short term, fixed costs do not change, but in the long-term, they will. Today, decisions concerning priorities often have long-term implications. This viewpoint emphasizes the importance of considering fixed costs in decisions having a long-term influence.

Just emerging as a viable concept is activity-based costing. This technique discards the idea that such bases as direct labor are the drivers of overhead costs. Rather, it is assumed that overhead costs are incurred because products need resources. These resources include design, engineering, production setups, distribution, marketing and service. Activities cause overhead costs by triggering the consumption of these resources. Costs are different for products because unlike amounts of resources are needed. They do not differ in cost as reflected in traditional allocations of overhead costs. Development of this concept should prove beneficial to decision makers.

OTHER SOURCES OF COSTS

There are other sources of costs besides those in formal financial records. For example, many companies have detailed scrap and warranty reports that may provide needed information. Other costs can be obtained through special studies.

Some companies have found quality cost techniques useful in deciding what continuous improvement efforts to launch. These techniques are described in previous chapters of this book. A big benefit is that they can help identify the full impact of failure costs. Many times, only a portion of these costs may be apparent to decision makers.

Direct labor may contain scrap allowances and rework operations. Employees in staffs may spend much time on failure analysis of both internal and external failures. Quality cost techniques can do a good job of identifying the full impact of waste. Otherwise, much of this may be considered a normal part of doing business. Many companies have found, through quality cost techniques, that waste is several times what was previously thought.

NONFINANCIAL FACTORS

There are many factors, not easily quantified, that are critical to the survival of a company. Examples are:

1. Revenue enhancement through improved quality.
2. Impact of customer satisfaction on future sales.
3. The effects of proliferation of products on costs and sales.
4. Infusion of technology in products and processes to provide a foundation for future progress.
5. Investment in people, such as intensive training, to lay a foundation for future progress.
6. Development of the supplier base and its impact.
7. Effect of concepts, such as quick change tools and JIT, on future revenue.
8. Impact on customers of decisions, and their effect on the generation of future revenue.
9. Effect of decisions on employee turnover and potential retraining costs.
10. The gain or loss of a competitive advantage and its impact on revenue.
11. Support of strategic plans in a timely manner.

This is, of course, a partial list and is general in nature. Each company is distinct and has different external forces acting on it. Efforts should be made by a company to identify the specific factors applicable to its situation. These can be used to make better decisions in ranking improvement projects.

APPROACH

An approach that may be used by the top management of a company to establish priorities is based on the "nominal group technique." This technique has often been used in the past to arrive at a group consensus regarding things that are difficult to quantify. Each person in the group is given an equal voice in making the decisions. When this occurs, the participants will likely agree with the outcome. More important, they will feel committed to the direction that is determined through using the technique. The steps are:

STEP 1 - FIND THE FACTORS IMPORTANT TO THE COMPANY IN MAKING A DECISION CONCERNING PRIORITIES.

A free flow of ideas concerning those factors important to the company is sought in this step. Brainstorming is often used during a meeting of persons involved in deciding priorities. Each person in the group is expected to contribute as factors come to mind. It is important that the factors are not critiqued at this stage. To do so would inhibit obtaining a complete list. The factors are usually written on a flip chart or blackboard as they are offered. In this way, an idea may prompt others. When no further factors are forthcoming, the next step takes place.

STEP 2 - RANK THE FACTORS ACCORDING TO IMPORTANCE.

The factors important to the company, found in Step 1, are edited so members of the group can vote on the ranking. Initially, each member works independently of the team.

Members are asked to select, for example, the five most important factors. Scores are assigned by each member to the five factors selected. The top ranked factor could be assigned a score of "5" and the lowest a score of "1." Then, those factors between would receive scores of "4," "3" and "2." The factors selected and the scores assigned will likely differ for each individual.

After scores are assigned, they are consolidated and provide the basis for the ranking by the team. Factors having a higher consolidated score are likely more important in decisions concerning priorities. The list of factors is again edited, placing them in order of the consolidated scores. Typically, many factors have low scores and can be removed from consideration by the team. The remaining factors are discussed and the ranking adjusted accordingly.

STEP 3 - SELECT A RATING SYSTEM FOR HOW IMPROVEMENTS WILL AFFECT EACH FACTOR.

An improvement effort could have either a positive or negative affect on factors that are important to a company. For example, the impact of a specific automation project may be a two-edged sword. On one hand, it could improve profits. If not properly handled, however, reduced

216

flexibility in reacting to orders could decrease customer satisfaction.

There is no rating system that is best for all companies. Rather, a system must be developed to meet the particular needs of each company. Primarily, it must be meaningful to those making the assessments. One rating system is shown in Figure 11-1. It attempts to place in perspective the relative impact of both positive and negative outcomes. Larger scores are given when the impact on a factor is greater. Those improvements having a negative impact are given minus scores. Where there is no impact on a factor, a score of zero is assigned. Positive scores are given where impacts are good. The point scale is subjective and should be meaningful to those making decisions on priorities.

Figure 11-1. A rating system shows how improvement affects a company.

STEP 4 - DEVELOP WEIGHTS FOR EACH FACTOR THAT WILL BE USED IN DECIDING PRIORITIES.

Various factors have different levels of importance for decisions made by a company. The weight for each factor should reflect that level of importance. This difference in importance is reflected in the ranking of factors discussed in Step 2. The consolidated score for each of the factors should be a help in assigning a relative weight. For example, a factor receiving a higher score should have a higher weight. The following illustrates this:

FACTOR	WEIGHT
CUSTOMER SATISFACTION	10
COMPETITIVENESS	5

In this example, the factor of customer satisfaction is considered by the company to be twice as important as competitiveness for assigning priorities. This is a judgment call based upon the conditions within each company. For another company, facing different conditions, it may be the reverse.

STEP 5 - DEVELOP A CONSISTENT APPROACH TO DECIDE PRIORITY OF IMPROVEMENTS.

Agreement should be reached on a consistent approach for summarizing improvement proposals. The approach must be meaningful to those persons making the decision. For most companies, the approach will be looking at both financial and nonfinancial factors. Figure 11-2 illustrates a form to help do this. Financial impact is described in payback and engineering economic techniques. For this company, an improvement proposal must support the strategy of the company. This support is shown on the form. The exceptions are if the proposal is required to meet governmental regulations or involves safety reasons. This is also noted on the form. Other nonfinancial factors are listed to help evaluate the proposal. The other factors have weights reflecting the relative importance of each to the company in deciding priorities. The proposal is rated on how it will affect each factor. The rating is multiplied by the weight for each factor to provide the full impact. Total points for the nonfinancial factors are calculated for comparison to other proposals.

PRIORITY ASSESSMENT
Improvement Project

Objective: *Upgrade product line XYZ*

Financial Impact

PAYBACK:	*3.2 years*
IIR:	*12.1%*
NPW:	*$240,000*

Supports strategy: *Item 2a. Provide products exceeding competition*
Required for regulation: *No*
Required for safety: *No*

Other factors:

	WEIGHT	RATING	TOTAL WT X RATING
CUSTOMER SATISFACTION	*10*	*5*	*50*
PRODUCT PERFORMANCE	*8*	*3*	*24*
TECHNOLOGY	*7*	*3*	*21*
COMPETITIVENESS	*5*	*3*	*15*
REVENUE	*3*	*1*	*3*
TOTAL POINTS			*113*

Figure 11-2. A form used for summarizing improvement proposals.

The next chapter will discuss setting goals.

BIBLIOGRAPHY

Badiru, Adedeji B., "A Management Guide to Automation Justification."
Industrial Engineering, February 1990.

Diaz, Andres E., "The Software Portfolio: Priority Assignment Tool Provides
Basis for Resource Allocation." Industrial Engineering, March 1986.

Downing, Thomas, "Eight New Ways to Evaluate Automation." Mechanical
Engineering, July 1989, p. 82.

Ford Corporate Quality Office, "Planning for Quality," Dearborn, MI: Ford
Motor Company. April 15, 1990.

GOAL/QPC, "Memory Jogger," 2nd ed. Goal, 1988.

Hendricks, James A., "Accounting for Automation." Mechanical Engineering,
February 1989, p. 64.

Johnson, H. Thomas, "Managing Costs: An Outmoded Philosophy." Manufacturing
Engineering, May 1989, p. 42.

Jones, Louis and McBride, Ronald, An Introduction to Team Approach Problem
Solving. Milwaukee: Quality Press, 1990.

Long-Becker, Linda C. and Landauer, Edwin G., "Service Assessment Matrix: A
Measurement Technique for Service Group Evaluation."

Sullivan, William G., "Models IE's Can Use to Include Strategic, Non-
Monetary Factors in Automation Decisions." Industrial Engineering, March
1986.

CHAPTER 12

GOAL SETTING

In this chapter. . .

DEVELOPING GOALS
   1. Measuring Progress
   2. When To Take the Measurement

SOURCES OF DATA
   1. "Hard" Data
   2. Perceptions of Employees
   3. Perceptions of Customers
   4. Performance Measurements

COMPANY GOALS SUPPORTING STRATEGIC PLANS

CRITERIA FOR SETTING CONTINUOUS IMPROVEMENT GOALS
   1. History
   2. Technical Studies
   3. Market Studies
   4. Benchmarking

12
Goal Setting

This chapter is about setting goals. Often, the terms "goals" and "objectives" are used interchangeably by those in a company. In this case, both terms mean the same thing. This is the context in which the term goal will be used in this chapter.

A goal is what an activity is aimed toward, and the goal is the result. In a way, it is the "bottom line" of why a project is undertaken. Goals can also be set to foster activity and gage progress along the way. Goals for gaging progress are used in projects of long duration.

It is critical that goals be quantitative and measurable. Otherwise, it may not be obvious whether the goal has been achieved. It is important that all those involved in the project agree with the goals and measurement methods to maintain credibility. Without this, more time may be spent arguing about a goal than achieving it.

Goals must be achievable and challenging. Those too easily reached invite complacency and quick loss of interest. On the other hand, goals that are impossible to achieve may cause contempt before a project gets off the ground. Historically, the latter approach to goal setting was widely used to inspire outstanding achievement. Sometimes it worked, as in the space program in the 1960s. Goals for the space program set by NASA proved ultimately challenging, but possible. Many feel that goals should be set with a "road map" for completion in mind. This way, the likelihood of success is increased.

Goals are used to evaluate continuous improvement efforts to keep them on track, or to indicate if changes in direction may be required. Developing goals usually involves two issues:

1. How the progress and results can be measured along the way.

Usually, a baseline reflecting what is currently happening needs to be developed. For example, rework may now be 5% of factory cost. The baseline is 5%. The goal may be to "reduce rework by 40%." When this is done, rework can be expected to be at 3% of factory cost. The percentage of factory cost is used for the measurement of the goal.

Sometimes, development of a baseline suggests that the original goal should be changed. In the example just given, the goal could be changed to "reduce rework from 5 to 3% of factory cost." This may be more tangible to those involved.

2. When to take the measurement.

Often, the time for measuring progress is when the improvement is done. Assume that the results for the rework improvement are expected by January 1992. The goal would be modified to: "reduce rework from 5 to 3% of factory cost by January 1992." Historically, a goal with an open-ended time frame is of little use in motivating progress.

Finding sources of data for establishing goals could be challenging. The sources can be generally classified as:

1. "Hard" data. This data is found in reports published by different disciplines within the company. Sources include financial records, or quality control reports. Information in these reports is sometimes suspect and caution should be exercised when using it.

2. Perceptions of employees. Data from employee surveys may be useful. This can be supplemented with structured interviews, or group discussions. In using this type of information, it must be recognized that perceptions sometimes are not based on facts.

3. Perceptions of customers. What a customer feels about a product is found in market surveys. This information is very important because perceptions greatly influence buying patterns.

4. Performance measurements. Many companies are using key indicators of performance. These are measurements made at critical points that show how well things are going. Sometimes, they are part of a manufacturing process. Often, they are part of a business system. They are usually very reliable because of their wide use, and acceptance in the company.

COMPANY GOALS SUPPORTING STRATEGIC PLANS

In a company, broad goals are established first. The goals, taken together, should make sense for the company. With rare exception, there is probably no goal having priority. Rather, the goals are likely balanced in relation to each other. Each goal supports the others. Any inconsistencies are sorted out when developing the goals.

These goals are targets that must be achieved to satisfy strategic plans. In a sense, goals are markers along a path that direct actions and chart progress. These goals are usually very broad in nature and require the active contribution of most functional areas.

The functional areas in the company must develop specific goals to support the achievement of the broader goals. Goals cascade down the organization, and are ultimately reflected in goals for each individual. Progress often depends on the achievement of the specific goals by each individual. For a company, the broad goals usually address the following areas contained in the strategic plan:

1. Share of the market.

A company will target a certain share of their market sector for their product line. Competitors have the remaining share. The size and success of the company is directly related to the market share that can be obtained. An example of a goal would be:

"Gain a 5% increase in market share for product line A by January 1992."

2. New products.

Introduction of new products is required to replace those no longer viable. Without this, a company will not survive. Many companies find that one-quarter of their product line was developed within the last five years. This requires setting goals for developing new products continuously. A typical goal could be:

"Introduce an electronic-based product line B by the 1993 model year to replace the mechanical version."

3. Quality and productivity.

Gains in productivity have long been a goal of most companies. These gains allowed wage increases to be given without accompanying price increases. Quality improvement is now recognized as a key contributor to these gains. Reduction in failure cost directly increases productivity. A goal could be:

"Reduce failure cost by 25% by July 1993."

4. Resources.

Goals are set for needed resources. These may include people, buildings, and equipment. Financial commitment also is required to allow these resources to be obtained. An example goal is:

"Build new 100,000 square foot plant in location to serve Pacific Rim market by 1991."

5. Organizational performance.

Goals are developed by management to carry out the needs of the organization. The key to success of any company is the effectiveness of management. Philosophies of management have changed dramatically in the past decade, bringing about widespread change. A typical goal could be:

"Train all managers in group dynamics by July 1991."

6. Worker performance.

A lot of effort has been expended lately to increase worker performance. This includes more involvement in decision making and a raise in status within the company. Goals are set to secure progress in this area. A goal that is typical is:

"Expand worker teams to 80% of the work force by January 1992."

7. Profits.

Goals are set on profits to be expected for a company and its individual product lines. This serves as a target to guide strategy within a company on a wide range of subjects. An example goal is:

"Increase gross profits as a percentage of investment by 5% before the 1992 calendar year."

8. Social responsibility.

More than ever before, goals are being set concerning the social responsibility of a company. This includes responsibility, for such things, as the community and environment. A typical goal is:

"Provide a specific number of hours of release time for employees to contribute to community activities during the next calendar year."

9. Customer satisfaction.

Most companies realize that continued success depends upon identifying the needs of the customers and satisfying them. This covers both product offerings and servicing the product during its expected life. An example goal is:

"Increase proportion of customers rating products and service good or better by 10% during the 1992 calendar year."

CRITERIA FOR SETTING CONTINUOUS IMPROVEMENT GOALS

History

Past performance is used by many companies in establishing goals. In some companies, similar activities are compared by performance. The resulting performance of the best activity sets the goal for the remaining activities. Where comparisons are not available, an improvement in performance by an arbitrary amount is often set by management. The goals are often set in economic terms, such as percentage reduction in scrap costs.

There are advantages to using history as the criteria for setting goals; often the goals are more palatable to those involved because:

1. The relationship between the goal and past performance is usually understood, so the goal is perceived to be obtainable.

2. There is knowledge of why past performance was not better. This can

be used to improve performance and meet the goal.
There is a major disadvantage, however, to using past performance to
set goals. This approach may perpetuate poor performance. Needed
gains may be hindered by current practices that go unquestioned.
Goals may be set too low. If they are, the pace of improvement may
seriously lag behind competition.

In a sense, this approach is a projection of past practices into the future.
Adjustments are made for modest improvements that will likely occur. There
is usually little effort to adjust goals to reflect the needs of the market.
For continuous improvement efforts, this approach to goal setting may prove
inadequate.

Technical Studies

Technical studies rely on the scientific collection and analysis of data.
An example of this is design of experiments (DOE). Experience shows that
goals based on this method are more successful than those using more
traditional methods of analyzing data.

Goals developed through these criteria are expressed in technical terms and
are not economic based. For example, the goal may be tighter tolerances on
certain key dimensions of a product. This requires improving process
capability.

Despite their good track record, goals are often attacked by those that must
implement them. A frequent complaint is that these goals were developed
under laboratory conditions and do not represent the "real world." Often,
this perception is due to a lack of understanding of the methods used in
developing the goals. By joining all parties concerned in the earliest
stages of development of the goal, this may be avoided.

Market Studies

An important criterion for goal setting is marketplace activity. Of major
importance is finding out what is the top quality product in the market
sector supplied by a company. This should include other factors such as
performance and field service. If the top product is not produced by the
company, goals must be set to reach higher levels. Obviously, these goals
are attainable. They are being met now by a company.

A company cannot succeed by merely being a follower. When they can react to
higher quality in the marketplace, competition has further improved. A
company must set goals to exceed the status of competition.

Much of the data on how a product is seen in the marketplace is based on
customer perceptions. Sometimes, perceptions are felt to be not based on
facts. This may occasionally be the case. Yet, despite how ill-founded
they may be, what a customer buys is based on perceptions. Dealing with
these perceptions is vital to the survival of a company.

Benchmarking

Developed in the past decade, benchmarking holds promise for being the most effective way of setting goals. This criterion measures products, internal business functions, and services against the leaders in performance and quality. The practices of the leaders are then examined and this knowledge improves the company.

Many companies in the past have limited innovation to their products, or services. Benchmarking also focuses on the processes within the business functions. With this added dimension, innovation is encouraged throughout a company.

Benchmarking is a continuous process. Measures of performance against the leaders are usually maintained in a database and periodically updated. It fits well with continuous improvement for this reason. Company progress is continuously tracked against the leaders. Benchmarking also provides goals that are attainable.

Sometimes, the leading companies are competitors. Competitors include any business that provides the same type of product to a market. In other cases, the leading companies may provide for completely different markets. Regardless, a company, despite the market served, may have demonstrated superiority in a particular business function. For example, a manufacturing company may look to a mail order firm for the best practices concerning distribution.

Historically, focusing only on competitors was inadequate. Part of this was the difficulty of getting information. This narrow focus diverted attention from the improvement of business functions in a company. Early on, business functions were compared only to competitors. Not all business functions in a competitor are strong, however.

Superiority over competition can be achieved if most business functions are better. This realization expanded the focus of benchmarking to seek out the best business functions no matter where they existed. Industries serving different markets and service firms were excellent sources for setting goals for each business function.

In a sense, gaining information for benchmarking should be a "win-win" situation. Both companies should gain from sharing information. Open discussion of practices can result in both parties gaining from the critique. Competitors must be careful not to address sensitive issues. The best way to do this may be by focusing only on practices.

Goals are developed based on the actions of the leaders. These goals can be achieved. They are being accomplished by other companies. A typical approach to benchmarking may be:

1. Identify the measures for benchmarking. They may include product, service, and business function performance and quality measures.

2. Select leading companies to be studied. They may be competitors or other companies having a reputation of being leaders in a certain area.

3. Estimate the value of the measures for each relevant company.

4. Set internal goals based on measures found in the leading companies. Typically, goals are set to meet, or exceed the performance of the leading companies.

5. Attempt to find practices that lead to superior performances at the leading companies. Often, this can be determined easily in companies that are not competitors. Some feel that this step should be taken before setting goals. This way, they feel the goals will be clearer and more meaningful.

6. Adopt practices that appear to offer improved performance.

Obtaining the best measures for setting goals may be tricky and require intense discussions. An example of this concerns inventory management. Two measures are commonly used.

One is "months supply." This is the inventory needed to offset an error in forecasting the demand. If the demand is higher than the forecast, there still will be inventory to supply it. This approach reflects the stockpiling of inventory.

The second measure is "inventory turns." This is the number of times during a period of time that an inventory must be replaced. This measure reflects the velocity of the use of inventory. It is much different from stockpiling of inventory.

Which measure is chosen depends a great deal on the practices of the industry. However, a company that wants a competitive edge may want to challenge these practices. Then the opposite measure may be chosen.

There are many benefits to a company that uses benchmarking to set goals. Some of these include:

1. Direct support continuous improvement in identifying realizable goals that have "workable" solutions.

2. Focus attention on "workable" solutions that are now being practiced in other companies.

3. Increase awareness of changes occurring outside the company. Sometimes technology breakthroughs found in other industries are adopted much sooner for applications within the company.

4. Helps shift from a mind set of complacency to a sense of urgency to meet that being realized by the leading companies.

5. Helps motivate a more global view of improvement and de-emphasize the "not invented here" (NIH) syndrome. In many companies, employees are more willing to adopt new ideas originated outside of their industry.

6. Focuses resources through setting goals motivating improvements with high potential.

7. Provides a ranking so management can prioritize efforts.

8. Promotes a stronger manufacturing base by sharing the best practices among companies.

Setting realistic goals is critical for the continuous improvement effort of a company. Focusing on the world outside the company for these goals seems the answer. Benchmarking appears to provide it.

The next chapter will discuss problem solving.

BIBLIOGRAPHY

Babcock, Daniel L., Managing Engineering and Technology. Englewood Cliffs, NJ: Prentice Hall 1991.

Camp, Robert C., "Benchmarking: The Search for Industries Best Practices That Lead to Superior Performance - Introduction." Quality Progress, January 1989.

Camp, Robert C., "Benchmarking: The Search for Industries Best Practices That Lead to Superior Performance - Part III." Quality Progress, March 1989, p. 76.

Fray, Earl, "The Evolution of Performance Measurement." Industrial Management, September-October 1988.

Juran, J.M., Quality Control Handbook, 4th ed. New York: McGraw Hill, 1988.

Maynard, H.B., Handbook of Business Administration. New York: McGraw Hill, 1967.

Schneiderman, Arthur M., "Setting Quality Goals." Quality Progress, April 1988.

Sedam, Scott M., "Quality Measurement - How to Corner a Greased Pig," Quality Congress Transactions (Dallas). Milwaukee: American Society for Quality Control, 1988.

The Ernst & Young Quality Improvement Consulting Group, "Total Quality," Dow Jones-Irwin, 1990.

Williams, Harry E., "Productivity, Costs and Quality." Manufacturing Systems, April 1986.

CHAPTER 13

PROBLEM SOLVING

In this chapter. . .

TYPES OF PROBLEMS
1. Analytical Problems
2. Judgmental Problems
3. Creative Problems

ROADBLOCKS TO PROBLEM SOLVING
1. Perception
2. Emotion
3. Culture

CREATIVE PROBLEM SOLVING

BRAINSTORMING
1. No Criticism or Evaluation
2. Group Results
3. No Constraints
4. Many Ideas - Short Time

STEPS IN PROBLEM SOLVING
1. Define Problem
2. Find Possible Causes
3. Determine Root Cause
4. Find Possible Solutions
5. Pick the Best Solution
6. Implement Solution
7. Checks Results

13

Problem Solving

Problems are, in a sense, opportunities for continuous improvement efforts. Through problem solving, quality and productivity are improved. A major step during this process is deciding on the best solution among several alternatives.

The most critical step in any continuous improvement effort is defining the problem. This takes a great deal of time, and the real problem usually differs from what is initially viewed as a problem. Discussion in a team setting helps focus thoughts properly. This is often a long iterative process, but is worthwhile. Solutions that work require identifying real problems that must be resolved.

TYPES OF PROBLEMS

Problems can be thought of as either analytical, judgmental, or creative. In the manufacturing environment, problems are usually a combination of these, with perhaps one type being prevalent. The dominant type often influences the way in which the problem is perceived and dealt with.

Analytical Problems

Solutions to analytical problems can be found through formulas, computer programs, or logic. Much of the education of an engineer is directed toward solving this type of problem. There is usually an answer, and often there may be only one.

A major challenge may be finding the best way of reaching a solution. Some methods of doing this are simple and easy to use. An example is finding the cost of doing a rework operation if the required time and frequency are known. Other methods of reaching solutions are complex and lengthy in nature. Production scheduling is an example of this. For most companies, this requires the use of a powerful computer.

Another major challenge is realizing the difference between analytical problems in a school setting, and those in a company. Usually, problems in a company are not clear, and are intertwined with many qualitative factors. Data may not be readily available, and may be too costly to collect. A purely analytical problem in a factory setting is rare.

Judgmental Problems

Judgmental problems are solved by choosing the best solution in view of the circumstances. This type of problem calls for a decision often based only on "gut reaction." Facts are non-existent or inadequate for solving the problem. There may be no time to gather supporting data, yet the decision must be made immediately.

On a factory floor, problems of this type occur constantly. The success of a company often depends on the collective wisdom of those confronted with problems of this type. An example is whether to shut down a machine for repairs immediately, or wait until the end of the shift. On a more global basis, strategic planning can primarily be considered resolving judgmental problems. The judgment of the management team is critical in deciding the best strategy for a company.

Creative Problems

To resolve creative problems, innovative solutions are required. Solutions are not obvious from normal thought patterns. For most people, conventional thinking must be supplemented with creative problem-solving techniques. Such a technique is brainstorming, which is described in this chapter.

Many improvements in manufacturing have been conceived through a creative problem-solving process. Typically, many possible solutions are generated that must be sorted out. Many will seem far-fetched, and appear unworkable in the present environment. There will, however, usually be one or more solutions that are truly innovative, and will have a positive impact. Solutions to these types of problems are essential to preserve the future competitiveness of a company.

ROADBLOCKS TO PROBLEM SOLVING

Many roadblocks exist that stop or slow progress in solving problems. Some are caused by external forces, like information that is difficult to get. For example, assume that information is critical to solving a problem. One approach may be not to pursue it because of the difficulty. In this case, progress in solving the problem is stopped.

A way around the difficulty must be identified. Often, this requires a change in the way things are done. Continuous improvement requires dealing with these roadblocks.

Perhaps the most difficult roadblocks lie within people. They are often called mental blocks. A person may not be aware of them, but they can be dealt with in a positive manner, once recognized. Success depends on the willingness of a person to change the way they think. Mental blocks can be generally classified as due to:

234

Perception

A mental block concerning perception involves a preconceived notion, formed largely because of experiences. A person typically assumes that a new situation is almost identical to something in the past. This shapes the viewpoint adopted by the person.

Complications set in when people find it difficult to change viewpoints once they are formed. In a team setting, other viewpoints are presented that are often more plausible. Dealing with this mental block requires considering viewpoints of others before forming an opinion. Where an opinion has been already formed, a person must be willing to alter it when warranted.

Emotion

Mental blocks due to emotions are often tied to anxiety, insecurity, and confusion about issues. This may translate into an attitude that is not very positive about the situation at hand. There is usually little logic reflected in the actions of a person having this mental block. In this case, issues are fought with strong emotions, and it becomes difficult to hold discussions in a productive manner.

Another byproduct of this is withholding information. A person may feel that information could be used in harmful ways. On the other hand, it may be critical to the discussion taking place.

Minimizing this mental block is often a two-way street. The individuals involved must gain the trust of the person with the emotional block, and any rationale that relieves anxiety, insecurity, and confusion must be sought. Taking time to do this will enhance the team's progress toward continuous improvement.

Culture

An individual with this mental block typically wishes to preserve the status-quo. There is strong resistance to change. Often the individual sees security for the future as being possible only by keeping the same culture in a company.

During the past decade, many companies experienced crises by not changing fast enough to stay competitive. Employees in these companies now realize that change is the only way to ensure security for the future. Although effective, this was a hard lesson. A company maintaining status-quo will not survive.

As the culture in a company changes to support continuous improvement, maintaining status-quo will no longer be an option. Training and knowledge of the issues facing a company also will help minimize this type of block.

CREATIVE PROBLEM SOLVING

Creativity is not limited to a few people. Most innovative ideas are generated by a creative problem-solving process that can be used by almost anyone. Through this process, ideas are synthesized into useful applications. Typically, creative problem solving begins with vague ideas in a somewhat chaotic form. During the process, ideas are structured and organized into a more useful design.

There are more than a dozen techniques for the creative problem-solving process. One that has been widely used during the past several years for quality efforts is the "fishbone" diagram, described in Chapter 5. The most popular technique, however, is brainstorming. This can be used to both help define a problem more precisely and arrive at possible solutions. Its popularity stems from its simplicity and ease of accomplishment. Brainstorming will be discussed later in this chapter.

All of these techniques have the same weakness. They do not conclusively evaluate "cause and effect." This must be determined separately. Tracking the possible sources of a failure is one example. Through creative problem solving, several possible reasons may be found. Determining which is the actual reason for the failure takes a separate analysis.

Adapting to the unstructured nature of this approach is often the most difficult part of creative problem solving. The following suggestions may help:

1. Begin with the confidence that the outcome will be useful. Initially, it is not clear what the outcome will be, but a person should have a positive attitude, and believe that a useful result will come about. Often, this confidence comes only after being in a creative problem-solving effort more than once.

2. Mimic the imagination of a young child. A vivid imagination will add much to the creative problem-solving process.

3. Display tenacity in the pursuit of solutions. Creativity is hard work and often a lengthy process. Thomas Edison once remarked that creativity is 95% perspiration and 5% inspiration.

4. An open mind is essential. Ideas must be accepted from all sources. Often, the best ideas come from those who know little about the circumstances because their thoughts are not hampered by preconceived notions. Ideas from blue collar workers on the factory floor have a high degree of success. Floor workers are most familiar with the manufacturing processes and their inherent problems.

5. Ideas should not be judged when first offered. The flow will stop if ideas are criticized. In a creative problem-solving process, many notions are off the mark, but they may cascade into other ideas that come closer to the solution.

6. The scope of the creative problem-solving process must be identified by establishing boundaries for the effort. By focusing on a limited area, creativity is enhanced, and the results are focused and more appropriate.

BRAINSTORMING

Since its development many years ago, brainstorming has been a group
activity. Normally, four to eight people are involved. Because of this,
brainstorming fits well with team activities for continuous improvement.

The objective of brainstorming is to develop an exhaustive list of ideas
about a subject. Responses are sought in an atmosphere that induces a free
flow of ideas from a group of people. One idea may start a chain of other
thoughts. As ideas are offered, a facilitator writes them on a flip-chart
or blackboard for everyone to see. This allows the others in the meeting to
concentrate on creating new ideas.

The number of theories generated varies somewhat with the size of the group.
Often, over 100 ideas are identified, some very innovative, and which would
otherwise not have developed. Teams may use brainstorming, for example, to:

1. Redefine a problem statement to reflect the possible real problem.
2. Find possible causes of problems.
3. Find possible problems causing a symptom.
4. Find possible solutions to problems.
5. Find alternative approaches for analyzing issues.
6. Find alternative manufacturing processes and test methods.

Brainstorming is most useful on subjects that are specific in nature: where
the scope, or boundaries, of the subject is limited. Other desirable
aspects of brainstorming are:

1. Open-ended outcomes.
2. Problems are handled verbally.
3. Analytical calculations or graphical solutions are not required.
4. More than one plausible solution.
5. Members on teams are generally familiar with the situation.

The simplicity of brainstorming is reflected in its four fundamental
principles, which are:

1. No Criticism or Evaluation. There must be a free flow of ideas, not
   subject to criticism during the brainstorming session. This
   principle also mandates that there be no evaluation or analysis of
   ideas during the session.

2. Group Result. The conclusion should be that of the whole group.
   One idea starts a chain of other ideas, and each chain is a result
   of mutual associations among all the thoughts presented. This way,
   the final ideas are not generated by any one person, but are built
   on the ideas of all participants in the session.

3. No Constraints. All ideas must be divulged, no matter how odd they
   seem. Any idea, no matter how peculiar, may influence the
   generation of another. That new notion may be a key ingredient in
   the ultimate outcome.

4. Many Ideas - Lack of Time. Many ideas should be generated in a
   somewhat short time. They need only consist of several key words
   that can be written down quickly. Rapid generation of ideas will

bring uninhibited new thoughts to the session. When the development
of ideas slows, it is time to stop. Typically, over 100 ideas may
be put forth in half an hour.

Sometimes, the facilitator needs to ask key questions to start the process;
the pace may need to be quickened when the stream of ideas slows. These
questions can often be prepared before the session. Some typical questions
could be:

1. What can we add?
2. What can be deleted?
3. What can be modified?
4. What can we combine?
5. What can we substitute?

STEPS IN PROBLEM SOLVING

There are many approaches to this process. They are generally similar,
differing only in minor details. A typical step-by-step approach for
continuous improvement is explained as follows:

STEP 1 - Define the Problem

Defining the real problem often takes as much effort as solving it, but this
time is well spent. The initial investment avoids wasted effort solving the
wrong problem.

The problem statement is the foundation upon which the solution is built.
The statement must be easily understood by anyone involved in the effort.
It is first used for finding the possible causes of the problem. The
following questions may help in developing a valid problem statement:

1. Who is having the problem?
2. What does the problem concern?
3. Where is the problem happening?
4. When does the problem occur?
5. Are there any obvious reasons for the problem?
6. What are the specific circumstances when the problem happens?
7. What is the magnitude and severity of the problem?
8. Can the type of problem be classified?

These questions are deceptively simple. To properly answer them usually
takes considerable effort, ranging from analyzing data to talking with those
who have experienced the problem. Tools for analyzing the data are
discussed in Chapter 5. Brainstorming may also be useful in defining the
problem. It could, for example, help develop potential answers to some of
the questions just mentioned.

STEP 2 - Find Possible Causes

After the problem is stated, all possible causes of the problem are
identified. Tools such as the "fishbone" diagram, discussed in Chapter 5,
and brainstorming are useful. Often this is an iterative process. Causes
from the initial findings are reviewed with those experiencing the problem,
and this usually identifies additional causes.

STEP 3 - Determine the Root Cause

The next step begins by sorting the list of possible causes to find the most likely candidates, which is often accomplished by a simple process of discussion. The most likely causes will then be analyzed by, for example, experimental methods. The root cause of the problem is then sought. While there may be several possibilities, a root cause is the real cause of the problem. If the root cause is eliminated, the problem will not reoccur. Identification of the root cause is required to take permanent corrective action.

STEP 4 - Find Possible Solutions

After the root cause or causes are found, different ways of fixing the problem are identified. Again, the "fishbone" diagram or brainstorming may be used. Talking with individuals involved in the problem is another source of possible solutions.

STEP 5 - Pick the Best Solution

Initially, the possible solutions should be reviewed to select those likely to be most effective, and these solutions should be evaluated. Make both economic and qualitative assessments, and seek team consensus on the best solutions.

STEP 6 - Implement the Solution

The best solution is then put into place. An evaluation should be made to assure that the root cause of the problem is eliminated. If not, the study should be reopened starting at STEP 2.

STEP 7 - Check Results

Periodically, the problem should be reassessed. The purpose is to assure that permanent corrective action is in place. If the problem still exists, the study should be reopened.

Continuous improvement efforts require permanent resolution of problems. This means directly addressing the root causes of all problems. Chronic problems exist only because root causes were never found. To achieve continuous improvement, they must be eliminated.

The next chapter will discuss rewarding successes.

BIBLIOGRAPHY

Barr, Vilma, "Brainstorming and Storyboarding." Mechanical Engineering, November 1988, p. 42.

Deland, Terry and Meyer, Michelle, "A Revolutionary System for Solving Quality Problems," Quality Congress Transactions (San Francisco). Milwaukee: American Society for Quality Control, 1990.

Dieter, George E., Engineering Design. New York: McGraw Hill, 1983.

Ford Power Train Operations, Team Orientated Problem Solving, 2nd ed. Dearborn, MI: Ford Motor Company, 1987.

Goetz, Victor J., "Steps in Problem Solving - Back to Basics," Quality Congress Transactions (Anaheim). Milwaukee: American Society for Quality Control, 1986.   •

Hyde, W.D., "How Small Groups Can Solve Problems and Reduce Costs." Industrial Engineering, December 1986, p. 42.

Iizuka, Yoshinori, "Key Points For Success in Problem Solving," Quality Congress Transactions (San Francisco). Milwaukee: American Society for Quality Control, 1990.

Jones, Louis and McBride, Ronald, An Introduction To Team Approach Problem Solving. Milwaukee: Quality Press, 1990.

Schoonmaker, Amanda L., "Creative Block-Busting," Quality Congress Transactions (Toronto). Milwaukee: American Society for Quality Control, 1989.

Ward, Richard A., "Engineering Problem Solving Teams Equal Excellence," Quality Congress Transactions (Anaheim). Milwaukee: American Society for Quality Control, 1986.

Wortham, A. William, "Problem Solving in Quality Control Areas Creates Synergistic Ripple Effect." Industrial Engineering, July 1986, p. 78.

CHAPTER 14

REWARDING PERFORMANCE

In this chapter. . .

PERFORMANCE APPRAISAL SYSTEMS

MOTIVATION

TYPES OF REWARDS
1. Financial Rewards
2. Performance Based Plans
3. Skill Based Scales
4. Merit Raises

PROBLEMS WITH FINANCIAL REWARDS

REWARDS THAT ARE TANGIBLE BENEFITS

REWARDS THAT ARE INTANGIBLE BENEFITS

REWARDS THAT ARE NEGATIVE IN NATURE

INNOVATION

14
Rewarding Performance

Most people would agree that rewards are vital to assure continuous improvement. Tailoring and administering these rewards, however, is a subject of much controversy.

Reward systems of the past were tied to individual performance. In a sense, competition among people formed the strength of traditional organizations. Today, this is clearly different in a company seeking continuous improvement. Working together as a team is the strength of this type of organization. Teamwork is the key to continuous improvement.

The efforts of an individual often cannot be distinguished in a team environment. Yet, the contribution of individuals has a great impact on the collective success of the team. Competition among individuals may destroy the close working relationships needed. It cannot be condoned or rewarded.

The superior performance of a company depends on the contribution of each person toward collective goals. It is important to remember that new technology is selected, designed, and put in place on the initiative of many individuals. Systems that stamp out waste are designed and implemented by individuals working together.

A big lesson learned in the past decade was that a company cannot improve by simply throwing money at problems. Buying unprecedented amounts of technology without involving the people who have to make it work was ill advised.

Problems are best answered by the people who must make the solutions work. Often, these problems are solved through basic, inexpensive changes. To be successful in this effort, an active and relevant reward system is mandated.

PERFORMANCE APPRAISAL SYSTEMS

Traditionally, the basis of many reward systems is the performance appraisal of individuals. Usually, this is an annual event. It is a process by which a company sets performance measures and evaluates individual progress against the measures. For some businesses, they are based on company goals. For others, they represent desired traits and are often meaningless in achieving company improvements. Many combine the two.

A recent survey shows that performance appraisals are used for the following purposes:

1. Merit raises.
2. Bonuses.
3. Promotion considerations.
4. Documentation for legal protection.
5. Counseling.
6. Training and development.
7. Staff planning.
8. Retention and discharge decisions.
9. Validation of selection techniques.

The most widespread use of performance appraisals is for compensation issues. Some experts feel this hinders the counseling of employees during the appraisal process. Clearly, help in improving performance by counseling should be a strength of the process. With a salary adjustment in the balance, however, an employee may become defensive, and blame others for any difficulties. The ensuing stress often dilutes any counseling effort to the point of futility.

In many companies, the ratings of the appraisal process drive each employee to conform to the norm of the organization. In other words, the ratings motivate employees to maintain the "status quo." This stifles innovation and chokes off motivation, self-esteem, and cooperation with others in the company.

In the past decade, performance appraisals have come under attack. Leading the charge is Dr. W. Edwards Deming. Using statistical process control principles, he challenges the value of continuing to rate individuals. He blames most problems on the systems in which people work. To get continuous improvement, the systems need to be appraised and improved. Ratings of individuals result in undue pressure and mask the real issues.

A recent example, previously discussed in Chapter 4, concerns the work of designers at a major car company. The designers were under pressure to reduce engineering changes occurring after release of the design. A process control chart was set up to analyze the system in which the designers worked. The result was that most of the engineering changes were due to the system. Charting indicated that only one of 17 designers needed help. Clearly, the system was the culprit and had to be changed.

There is further evidence for the claim that most performance variation is due to the system in which the individual is operating. At best, performance rating identifies those who do well in the system. These are the people who do not "rock the boat." Rating does not really identify those who challenge the system to do better, nor does it adequately suggest those who need help. This includes both those in need of greater skills and those who should be encouraged to "rock the boat."

Also, Dr. Deming feels that individual performance appraisal methods reward competition, not teamwork. In competition, there is a "win-lose" syndrome. If somebody wins, someone else has to lose. This must be replaced with a "win-win" culture that fosters teamwork, and encourages everyone to feel they have achieved something when a decision is made. With a "win-win" culture, the company will make more dramatic progress toward achieving strategic goals.

In the future, performance appraisal must concentrate on evaluating systems, not individuals. Improvements in methods and technology will then enhance continuous improvement. Rewards should be based on group performance and, to a lesser extent, individual contributions to a team.

Some companies are developing new performance appraisal processes in view of the constructive criticism of Dr. Deming. Early results show that there is improved teamwork. Characteristics of the new appraisal processes are:

1. Ongoing appraisals instead of periodic.
2. Open communication with no surprises.
3. Mutual responsibility shared by the supervisor and employee.
4. Ownership of the process is by employee's management, not personnel.
5. Documentation is downplayed.
6. Shift to system problems that employee can help with.

There is still much work to be done in this area. The legal implications of providing documentation for personnel decisions seem to be a major roadblock to doing away with individual appraisals entirely. Yet, this is a major objective of the philosophies of Dr. Deming.

MOTIVATION

A great deal of research has been done to identify the factors that motivate employees. The top factors are:

1. Achieving both personal and company objectives.
2. Being recognized in the minds of others for this achievement.
3. Having potential for advancing in the organization.
4. Doing work that is challenging.
5. Having potential for personal growth.

Interestingly, direct financial rewards are noticeably missing from this list, but recognition for achievement is near the top. One could easily conclude that a simple pat on the back by management is more powerful as a motivator than money.

Rewards are often misunderstood by management. They must be customized to each situation and individual. A complication is that a person may need something different each time recognition is due. Still, rewards can be successful in motivating people if:

1. People believe that meeting the objectives of the company will lead to receiving rewards.
2. There are criteria for deciding who is to receive rewards that are clearly understood by each employee.
3. The distribution of rewards is fair and equitable to all employees.
4. Management clearly understands the impact of rewards on those not receiving them.
5. Employees are involved in deciding issues that influence their lives

at work. This could be a way of providing broad-based rewards for many people. Examples are such things as benefit changes and flexible work times.

Rewards help reinforce desired actions, and such reinforcement aids in sustaining and accelerating continuous improvement activities.

When giving rewards, the following questions should be answered and emphasized during any presentations:

1. What is the specific achievement being rewarded?
2. What is so important to the company and its employees about this achievement?
3. How was the specific achievement accomplished?

Often, the answers to these questions are summarized on a symbolic object such as a plaque. Such a token extends the life and meaning of the occasion. The plaque is usually treasured, and given a special place where it can be seen by others, and the impact of the reward will likely last well into the future.

TYPES OF REWARDS

Rewards could be classified in many different ways. They may be viewed as one of the following types:

1. Financial rewards.
2. Tangible benefits.
3. Intangible benefits.
4. Negative rewards.

FINANCIAL REWARDS

Most in management feel that direct financial rewards are necessary to provide a stimulus for improvement. In recognition of this, many companies have performance-based plans including profit-sharing. Also used are skill-based pay scales and merit raises.

Performance-Based Plans

Financial reward plans have included commissions, incentive pay, piece work, and executive bonuses. Typically, these plans emphasized quantity, not quality. Clearly, they are inappropriate in continuous improvement efforts. Because of the quantity component, attempts to match these plans with quality objectives have not worked well.

Recently designed plans base rewards on company performance. Company performance depends on many factors, including quality. Unfortunately, some factors are external, and may not be controllable, such as economic conditions. Because of this, rewards may not be sufficient in spite of outstanding efforts by employees.

The major problem with the new plans is not how to maximize the pot of money available for rewards, but rather how to distribute rewards in an equitable manner. This is often a controversial issue within a company, and controversy can detract from the primary purpose of the reward.

Executives usually partake of a large share of the pot as bonuses and deferred compensation, which recognizes the magnitude of their impact on the destiny of a company. Arguably, however, all employees have a large effect on a company's future. In recognition of this, many companies are now rewarding all employees with a share of the profits. This is usually much smaller than the share given to the executives.

The issue of individual versus group rewards is still to be solved. Group rewards are an attempt to equally recognize all the people contributing to a system. An example is profit-sharing. Usually, part of the profits are equally divided among all employees. For executives, however, bonuses are still often determined individually.

Skill-Based Pay Scales

Employee skills are critical to the success of a company. Skill-based pay scales are intended to encourage each employee to gain new abilities. As new skills are demonstrated, the pay is adjusted. This may involve such things as cross-training in a new job or acquiring knowledge in problem solving. The payoff is the ability of each employee to make superior contributions to continuous improvement.

Important side benefits are more flexible employees and the possibility of fewer job classifications. Many companies are making sizable productivity and quality improvements by reducing the number of job classifications. Some plants are run with as few as three different classifications, instead of the traditional 15 to 30 classifications. Scheduling and downtime for maintenance is no longer a big problem for these companies.

Merit Raises

Raises based on performance have been part of the compensation package of most companies for many years. They reward individual performance. With continuous improvement, the intention must change to rewarding for team contributions. Separating out the relative contribution of each individual on a team might not only be tough but also unwise. It is likely that new merit raise plans will equally reward all team members based on the general performance of the team.

Problems With Financial Rewards

A study shows that financial rewards do not rank high on the list of motivators. This is because they are perceived differently by the company, and the persons receiving them. As an example, merit raises are often expected by individuals regularly. Bonuses and profit-sharing, once received, also are expected regularly, and the amounts of future financial rewards are expected to be greater than in the past.

Financial rewards usually are not perceived as a unique event by an individual, but they must be by a company. Different people will be sharing in each round of financial rewards, and the same people that shared before may get less, not more.

Future financial rewards depend directly on the success of the company in the marketplace. Often, this is because of external factors not under the control of the company, such as an economic downturn. As a result, financial rewards usually are far less dependent on the specific contributions of people. This is often not willingly accepted. Financial obligations of individuals frequently increase with the expectation of continued rewards. When the rewards do not come, or if the amount is less than expected, financial hardship may occur. Perplexingly, the result is unhappiness, the opposite of the goal of any reward system.

Profit-sharing as a reward by one automobile maker was first received with great joy. But it was treated as added compensation by employees. Some used it for a down payment. The added monthly payments created another burden on their regular paychecks. To catch up, these employees began anticipating their profit-sharing for the next year. When the following year's profit-sharing amount was less, there was unhappiness and financial discomfort.

TANGIBLE BENEFITS

Tangible benefits include life insurance, health care, cost of living adjustments, time off for vacation, and retirement programs. These have been part of employee benefits for many years, and are often modified to provide more extensive coverage. Yet, they are a huge expense for a company, perhaps adding 80% to the base wage. The original intention was to reward employees and relieve the anxieties that would arise without this type of coverage. Unfortunately, tangible benefits are now taken for granted and provide little incentive for improved performance.

Recently, tax laws have allowed for the addition of cafeteria plans as a fringe benefit, and some employees can now select from custom packages of fringe benefits. For example, a married couple where both work may not need duplicate health care coverage. Elimination of one plan may allow more life insurance to be purchased with the savings. This recognizes that rewards often must be tailored for each individual. There is no indication, however, that the cafeteria plan has a positive effect on motivation.

INTANGIBLE BENEFITS

Intangible benefits include flex time, reserved parking spaces, and separate executive dining facilities.

Flex time is a somewhat recent innovation. It allows employees to work when they want within certain limitations. Some feel that this reward does provide positive motivation. Employees often pick the time of day when they work best, and they may feel more self-directed, and less inhibited in their actions.

Other intangible benefits tend to send a message that higher management is not really in partnership with everyone else in a company. For continuous improvement, this is a chilling message. As a result, many companies have eliminated reserved parking spaces and separate dining facilities for management. Where this has happened, teamwork has noticeably improved.

NEGATIVE REWARDS

Negative rewards send negative messages, and stop motivation. An example is silence, when recognition is obviously in order. As previously discussed, being recognized for an achievement is a powerful motivator. Keeping silent is, in essence, a slap in the face, and may slow or stop future contributions.

Other questionable practices include reprimand systems that give employees time off for errors. Earlier in this chapter it was stated that poor performance is often the fault of the system, not the individual. For continuous improvement, processes and systems must be refined. People need not be punished. They need to be involved in defining problems, and helping improve situations.

INNOVATION

The key to effective rewards in the future is innovation. Clearly, many past rewards are no longer appropriate in companies seeking survival. Rewards in a continuous improvement culture must motivate the teamwork and creativity of the entire work force. They must also encourage trying new things despite the possibility of failure. Taking risks is a crucial part of improvement.

As an example, a company gives a small cash reward to the manager who makes the biggest mistake of the month. The object of the reward is to get people to take risks. If a person makes a mistake, others must be told about it quickly to break the natural reluctance of people to admit their mistakes. Another company gives a plaque to an employee who challenges the wisdom of management. The objective of this award is to encourage speaking out against bureaucracy, which can choke innovation and continuous improvement.

The next chapter concerns avoiding failure.

BIBLIOGRAPHY

Dingus, Victor R. and Justice, Russell E., "Celebrating Quality." Quality Progress, November 1989, p. 74.

Hayes, Robert H.; Wheelwright, Steven C., and Clark, Kim B., Dynamic Manufacturing, The Free Press, 1988.

Hillkirk, John, "Employees Blunder into Rewards," USA TODAY, May 22, 1990.

Lawler, Edward E. III, "High Involvement Management," Jossey-Bass Publishers, 1988.

Moen, Ronald D., "The Performance Appraisal System: Deming's Deadly Disease." Quality Progress, November 1989, p. 62.

Shell, Richard L.; Souder, H. Ray, and Damachi, Nicholas, "Are IEs and Managers Prepared to Motivate Today's Technical Workers?." Industrial Engineering, August 1983, p. 58.

Tickel, Craig M., "Reward Systems: Inhibitors to Implementation." Quality Congress Transactions (Dallas). Milwaukee: American Society for Quality Control, 1988.

CHAPTER 15

AVOIDING FAILURE

In this chapter. . .

ROADBLOCKS TO CONTINUOUS IMPROVEMENT

TOP MANAGEMENT INSIGHTS

MANUFACTURING INSIGHTS

MEETING INSIGHTS

15
Avoiding Failure

Avoiding failure when pursuing continuous improvement involves more than considering the ideas contained in this book. It requires planning, judgment, insight, and innovation. Internal and external factors acting on companies differ widely, and create unique needs. Modeling the continuous improvement efforts of another company would be a mistake. It would also be an error in judgment to believe a specific approach is available that would work for your company.

Ideas and concepts can be obtained from other companies and seminars, and can be found in technical publications. Specific approaches, however, must be tailored to each company, beginning with strategic planning by the top managers. This provides a focus for the company, extending into the future. The strategic plan provides consistency, since it is directed toward common objectives. Specific projects are launched throughout the company based upon the strategic plan. People from various disciplines are joined into teams to achieve specific improvements. The management of these groups forms a steering committee to unify the various factions, and strengthen the company.

This general process moves the culture of a company toward a customer focus, while each employee becomes attuned to the battle for survival. Many fundamental changes are required, and may include the organizational structure, the way people think and act, and even the value system. Change is not easy, but it is absolutely necessary for survival.

ROAD BLOCKS TO CONTINUOUS IMPROVEMENT

A recent study identified those factors that may slow, or even stop progress on continuous improvement activities. The most important elements are:

1. Lack of awareness of the program by all employees.
2. Lack of understanding of why, and how it is being done.
3. Insufficient, or ineffective training.
4. Inadequate planning before launching the program.
5. Lack of cooperation among functional areas.
6. Lack of coordination among functional areas by teams.
7. Resistance to change by middle management.
8. Lack of appropriate rewards, or incentives.

9. Ineffective leadership skills for the changing culture.

Each of these areas is discussed in detail in various chapters of this book. When embarking on continuous improvement efforts, progress in each area should be carefully tracked. If results are not adequate, corrections should be made promptly.

TOP MANAGEMENT INSIGHTS

Continuous improvement requires commitment from top managers, and that they believe in the new approach. It is absolutely necessary that they give the right message to the rest of the organization. They must believe what they say.

Decisions by top management must be made using the same criteria as that used by others in the organization. Concern for delivering quality products must be a priority, as well as a way of life for the entire company. Quality cannot be sacrificed for short-term profits.

Top management is accepting great risk by setting up a continuous improvement culture, because profits may erode during the transition. For most companies, however, there is no choice. If they are to survive, change cannot be delayed or ignored. Often, a financial return from the change will be several years away. Until then, there are many additional expenses. Massive training is usually required, and planning and team meetings take a great deal of time. Productivity may suffer until efforts take hold, and quality increases.

To achieve effective transition, top management must support:

1. A long-term commitment to continuous improvement. During the initial transition, profits may be affected, but top management cannot allow this to slow progress. They must assure that the transition proceeds without delay, in spite of economic downturns, and reduced sales.

   Most believe that the journey on continuous improvement will never end. Improvements must be relentlessly pursued for the future. The resources deployed must be consistent and focused. The effort cannot be started, stopped, and restarted. Once halted, it will be difficult to regain the dedication of employees, and the fight for survival may be lost.

2. A commitment to the necessary money and resources. Much of the funding will be invested in employees to increase knowledge and skills. In a sense, this must be viewed as a capital investment. Although it will be spent in the short term, the positive effects will last for a considerable amount of time. It will furnish the foundation for sustained effort.

   Provisions for resources also need to be made. While increasing the work force may not be necessary, priority for continuous improvement must be established. This means that all functions in the company must support the availability of people for the teams. The heads of the various functions must dedicate a sizable portion of time to providing guidance.

3. The duty to learn new techniques at all levels in the company. Time must be devoted not only to learn, but to develop confidence in new approaches. Various techniques must be sorted out to find those that best suit the company. Consistent effort must be made to practice the principles that are important to continuous improvement. This new demand placed on the time of top management will be both challenging and rewarding.

MANUFACTURING INSIGHTS

Over the years, the manufacturing function has developed a strong sense of teamwork, which eases the transition to continuous improvement. Most would agree that manufacturing floor employees and support staffs are a close-knit bunch. Although there is controversy, people in manufacturing act as a team. Everyone must do their job for the product to be successfully manufactured, and this takes coordination. Issues are constantly being laid out on the table, and action is swiftly taken.

Conflict has developed strong processes and business systems. The innovation that has occurred over the years has forged powerful alliances and mutual understanding. Openness is a hallmark of those in manufacturing, and these traits are needed in a continuous improvement culture. This may better equip manufacturing professionals to deal with the new culture than people of other disciplines.

There are other traits of manufacturing that must be modified for continuous improvement. Most companies have a few of these traits. They are:

1. Fixing problems quickly without identifying the root cause. The ingrained reaction of manufacturing personnel is to make repairs immediately. Often, no time is taken to determine the cause. Keeping machines running under all circumstances was of paramount importance in the past. Quantity produced was the main issue then.

   Today, quality is recognized as more important than quantity. Often, a quick fix is not permanent, and the trouble recurs. A permanent solution is possible only when the root cause of a problem is found.

2. Fixing something only if it is broken. From this point of view, everything that is not broken is ignored. In essence, this philosophy says to deal only with surprises, and to wait until they happen.

   This ignores the fact that although a machine is running, it could run better. Continuous improvement strives to enhance processes, and one should be alert to all possible avenues to success.

3. Handling risk by using hidden safety factors. Manufacturing may take tremendous risks because of a lack of concrete information. Therefore, safety factors are used.

   Plants are built with excess capacity to handle unknown sales surges, and safety stock is added to inventory in case of quality problems. In fact, schedulers sometimes only put 80% of jobs into production plans just to be able to handle any last minute emergency that may arise. If these contingencies do not occur, resources are wasted.

In the new culture, concrete information may be more readily available, and the need for safety factors reduced. Cross-discipline teams should share information freely, and reduce risks by examining the company as a whole.

4. Not taking action without the prior agreement of the plant manager. Traditionally, plant managers have been in charge. Since they are responsible for all plant activity, many managers require employees to seek permission before anything is attempted.

   Through the use of cross-discipline teams, decisions are made on a company-wide basis. It is important that the decisions be made by those in the team meeting.

   The plant manager must trust the teams to make the best decisions for the company. However, in some cases, this may not be the best plan for manufacturing alone. The use of "veto power" by plant managers in this case would be counterproductive.

MEETING INSIGHTS

Meetings are the keystone of continuous improvement. Most important changes occur because of a consensus developed in meetings. Only then can top management formulate strategic plans, and steering committees gain agreement on team goals. It is critical that meetings be effective.

Unproductive meetings are often listed near the top of employees' lists of annoyances. Nothing is more frustrating than wasting time, and unproductive meetings have had a long, chronic history.

This waste is very costly. Consider that a two-hour meeting of 10 persons averaging $50,000 annually, including benefits, costs the company $500. Five such meetings weekly would cost $125,000 each year in salaries and benefits. The potential losses posed by ineffective meetings can be substantial.

A recent study indicated that the major causes of unproductive meetings are:

1. The agenda has not been prepared ahead of time. A meeting with no agenda generally drifts, and lacks an obvious purpose. Each new topic brings only knee-jerk responses designed to please those in attendance.

   The people who should have contributed lacked the notice necessary to prepare for discussion. This results in people leaving perplexed, wondering why they were invited.

   An agenda should be distributed in advance, with the most important topics appearing first. It should clearly identify who is responsible for each topic. The number of items should not exceed an amount that can be covered in the time allotted for the meeting, and the list should be followed closely.

2. Key people are missing. The attendees must be able to discuss the issues, and decide upon solutions. If inappropriate people are in

attendance, another meeting will need to be scheduled, wasting a great deal of time. There are several possible causes:

a. Meeting was not given a high priority by the managers of missing people.
b. Meeting was not given a high priority by missing person.
c. Check was not made to ensure everyone could attend.
d. Agenda was not sent out giving notice of meeting.
e. Those not in attendance did not notify the meeting planner that the scheduled time was inconvenient.

Every effort should be made to confirm attendance before a meeting. Where there are conflicting priorities, the steering committee should be consulted. If attendance problems cannot be resolved, the meeting should be rescheduled.

3. Supporting material is not available. Sometimes agenda topics are discussed with no supporting documents, resulting in confusion and poor decisions. Remember, meetings are for sharing information.

   Data must be summarized so findings and conclusions can be made. Visual aids and handouts enhance information.

4. Team members are not fully prepared to discuss issues. To make good decisions, it is important that each team member be prepared to challenge or support every proposal, and share the reasons.

   Snap reactions must be avoided. Wherever possible, input must be based on logical reasoning and factual evidence. Only then can a consensus be properly reached.

5. Dominating personalities choke off discussion. A controlling member may discourage quieter participants from joining the deliberation. Dominant individuals may have the first and last word, and team members may discount their opinions because of their demeanor.

   Usually, a facilitator is needed to bring the situation back under control. The problem is corrected through counseling to ensure that each team member gets equal time to share ideas. Opinions of each team member must be considered equally important. A few members cannot monopolize meetings so that decisions are made on the basis of who talks the loudest and the longest.

6. The meeting becomes an arena for personal attacks. Such behavior is clearly out of place. Continuous improvement concepts concentrate on processes, not people. Faulting individuals only breeds defensiveness, and halts progress. A facilitator can prevent this situation by establishing ground rules that address such behavior.

7. Facilities are not adequate. Meetings may be unsuccessful simply due to the environment. The room may be too small, too hot, too cold, dirty, uncomfortable, or the furniture may be placed awkwardly. Theater-type seating is not conducive to discussions.

   Facilities should be investigated in advance, and corrections made before the meeting.

8. The times established for a meeting is inconvenient for members. Members may be distracted, and lack full concentration if they should be elsewhere. Timing may be poor if meetings are held on weekends, before the shift starts, or if they continue into the night.

   Where possible, meetings should be held during the workday, and the time should always be determined by the team members. Exceptions to these general rules must be based on options freely chosen by the team.

9. The meeting may have outside interruptions. When they occur, maintaining the flow of thought may not be possible. If key personnel are called away, the meeting may be thwarted.

   Conference rooms should not have telephones, and meetings should be held in private rooms. No one should be summoned from a meeting except in an extreme emergency.

10. No decisions result from holding the meeting. Often, the only decision is to have another meeting. Issues are not accurately identified, and consensus is not reached.

    Meetings should involve the entire team before a decision is made. Agendas must clearly identify the issues, and should time run out, the topic under discussion must be first on the next meeting agenda.

    Consensus may require discussions that are long and tense, but these discussions must progressively narrow the gap between opinions. After each meeting, members should be able to summarize what was actually accomplished.

11. The meeting is chaotic. This may occur because the leader is unprepared, or unable to maintain the group's focus.

    Conducting meetings is often not a natural talent. Initially, facilitators may be necessary to help the leader gain skill.

12. Meetings do not start or end on time. Often, they continue past the allotted time, potentially making team members late for subsequent commitments.

    Time is a precious resource. Team members must be punctual, and the team leader must begin and end sessions as originally planned.

    Meetings need to be constantly evaluated. Surveys to a cross-section of employees may identify opportunities for keeping them on track, and improving results.

The next chapter concerns maintaining perspective in continuous improvement.

BIBLIOGRAPHY

Axley, Stephen R., "Toward Productive Meeting: Advice from the Firing Line."
Industrial Management, September/October 1988.

Chu, Chao-Hsein, "The Pervasive Elements of Total Quality Control."
Industrial Management, September/October 1988.

Feitner, Charles E. and Weiner, Steven E., "Models Myths and Mysteries in
Manufacturing." Industrial Engineering, July 1985, p. 66.

King, Joseph P., "Executive Survival Guide to Meeting Requirements."
Quality Congress Transaction (Minneapolis). Milwaukee: American Society
for Quality Control, 1987.

Stimson, Richard A., "DoD's Drive to Adopt TQM: Barriers to Success,"
Quality Congress Transactions (Toronto). Milwaukee: American Society for
Quality Control, 1989.

CHAPTER 16

KEEPING IT IN PERSPECTIVE

In this chapter. . .

AUDITS
1. The Top Officer
2. Cross-Functional Audit Team
3. Auditors External to the Company
4. Company Audit Professionals

GENERAL FORMS OF AUDITS
1. Product Audits
2. Process Audit
3. System Audit

GROUND RULES FOR AUDITS

Appendix information

A quality system survey report
(Courtesy of Ford Motor Company) A-45--A-47

Appendix B: Quality--Both Home and Abroad
              By Edith Holmes
              Presented at the SME Fabricating
              Composites '90 Conference B-1--B-7

16

Keeping It In Perspective

In large part, perspective is maintained by developing a vision of the company's transformation through continuous improvement. Visualize a road map of the company's path, and use markers along the way to indicate progress.

Experts feel a company that has matured in continuous improvement will have certain characteristics that were defined by the vision:

1. Striving to improve all procedures, even routine tasks.
2. An obsession with excellence, demonstrated by constant improvements in costs, productivity, and quality.
3. Paramount effort toward satisfying the customer.
4. A growing number of long-term customers.
5. Suppliers that are full partners in the process of continuous improvement.
6. Full involvement in self-directed, cross-discipline teams that make decisions about company direction.
7. Complete understanding and full use of the tools of continuous improvement.
8. Problems are often anticipated and prevented during planning stages.

Keeping continuous improvement in perspective requires recognition that the journey to a company's maturity is a long one. For most companies, if not all, ultimate goals will be barely visible on the horizon. The basic tenet of continuous improvement is the ongoing nature of the effort. It is the relentless pursuit of betterment, and it is unlikely any company can claim completion of continuous improvement and display the final results.

Progress toward ultimate goals can be tracked. The measures for continuous improvement are not outcomes, but rather an evaluation of how the process is proceeding. They include performance measurements and benchmarking, as discussed previously.

Measures of continuous improvement are important. Answers to the following questions may provide valuable insight:

1. What is working according to the plans?
2. What surprise benefits are happening?
3. What resistance to progress exists?

4. What problems occurred that were unforeseen?
5. What major decisions were required that were unforeseen?
6. What failed and why?

These questions should be asked often. The answers to these questions, and others, can help reshape thinking and plans for continuous improvement. A major reason for lack of progress is failure to modify plans regularly to reflect what has been learned.

Efforts rarely go as originally charted. Details need to be constantly evaluated and redesigned. This is due to the large-scale involvement of people in any company's continuous improvement efforts. This involvement drives details to be sharpened and modified until they best support strategic goals.

Employees need to learn, and they must be allowed to try different approaches. Some might fail, but the learning process will improve the next attempt. It is too optimistic to expect complete success the first time.

Occasionally, it may appear that efforts have stalled, but they may have only retrenched, awaiting renewed emphasis. A major copier manufacturer found that applying for the Malcolm Baldrige National Quality Award was a catalyst that rekindled continuous improvement efforts after having been on a plateau. Keeping momentum is a constant challenge for management.

Rigid attitudes must be avoided. Leadership must adapt to changing conditions and new ideas, if a company is to survive. Continuous improvement efforts should remain flexible enough to take advantage of new opportunities, and discard those no longer feasible.

Management can plan and revise the general process that motivates change, but the strategy of continuous improvement will remain the same. Only the details will change as learning occurs throughout the organization.

Even the vision for the company will change as new factors are recognized. This may require fine-tuning the strategic plans regularly.

For these reasons, continuous improvement is difficult. Change is an ongoing, fluid process. Details cannot be rigidly planned. Rather, they are based on projections, and are revamped as needed. The revisions are guided by new information learned during the process of continuous improvement. Much of the new information is gained from the cross-discipline improvement teams.

Expecting quick results would be a major error in judgment. Often, several years are required for results to reach the bottom line of financial reports. The path to continuous improvement is uncharted, and no company has reached the end.

Companies that have begun their effort have found the early stages chaotic. The journey was marked by constant change to reflect new factors uncovered, and the massive learning taking place. It is important to recognize this and avoid being discouraged when progress is slow.

AUDITS

Periodic measurements are helpful in gaging progress with strategic plans. Still other means are necessary to identify problems if progress is not as swift as possible. Some companies choose to have detailed discussions to work out trouble spots. Often, these discussions involve only top management.

These talks do not always find the causes for failing to address strategic plans. The managers involved in the discussion may not be close enough to situations to have great influence, and biases may inadvertently mask good solutions. That old cliche often comes true: "You can't see the forest for the trees."

Properly designed audits and surveys can help identify situations that may not be obvious to either top management or those directly involved. Reshaping these situations could be critical to success. Audits can be conducted by:

1. The Top Officer

    In the past few years, top company officers have found contact with others helpful in keeping continuous improvement on course. They made regular trips to offices, team meetings, suppliers, customers, and the factory floor. The practical side of issues was seen first-hand, unfiltered by layers of management. This realization is unlikely to occur in traditional meetings.

    Meetings of a cross-section of people are also used for this purpose. They usually consist of randomly selected representatives from different functions in the company, and sometimes include customers or suppliers. The sessions should be held in areas that are not close to the executive offices. Establish a positive perception of management among workers by going to their "turf." This is much better than summoning them to prearranged meetings. In this setting, a free flow of information is sought.

    The observations made during these visits and meetings comprise a learning process for top officers. The information gained provides additional, practical inputs to the decision making process at the very top of a company. Insight and understanding are gained about the level of performance measurements, and the reasons for both positive and negative influences on progress may be better understood and addressed.

    Benefits of visits by top officers are:

    a. The reality of situations is infused at the top level of management so it can be addressed in strategic plans.
    b. Measurements are better understood, and plans are appropriately modified to realize progress.
    c. Improved objectivity of information reaching the top officers.
    d. Improved critique of situations by top management through greater understanding of the practical realities.
    e. Contact by the top officer with the rest of the organization greatly improves human relations.
    f. Motivation of the company and suppliers is improved because of the

obvious personal interest of the top officer.
g. The perception of customers is improved by the personal interest of
    the top officer.

For the same reasons, it is a good idea if other top managers conduct
such visits. It is important that visits be made by one person alone.
If other members of the staff are included, information may be inhibited,
and vital contributions lost.

Visits should be planned to gain critical information that will clear up
confusion, and lead to better decisions and greater understanding.
Usually, visits are best when there is no formal agenda. A free
exchange of information in an unstructured environment often brings out
issues that would otherwise go unnoticed.

Encouraging open exchange of information may be a major challenge. Those
providing the information may feel inhibited by the possibility of
recourse by immediate management. Middle management may feel threatened
by the inability to immediately provide background information.

The perception of how information will be used is critical. It must be
carefully and openly discussed with all those concerned, either before
or during the initial contact. Using the information to improve business
processes, rather than blame people, is essential. Only then will trust
be developed, and needed information continue to flow freely.

2. Cross-Functional Audit Team

Often, a cross-functional audit team is very helpful in identifying areas
for improvement in companies and suppliers. The team may consist of
members from each major functional area. They should be experts, and
possess the ability to make good observations. Although they should be
trained in auditing fundamentals, it is not necessary that they be
experienced auditors.

In a company with several operating units, each unit may create a cross-
discipline audit team to review each other's operations, and share
improvement ideas. Each member on the team concentrates on their
functional specialty. For example, a manufacturing engineer will visit
the operations area. Ideas will be shared among all the team members for
critiquing and fine-tuning. After a thorough discussion, the ideas will
be shared with the operating unit that was reviewed. An additional
benefit is that each member of the team will also be likely to learn
something they can apply.

When a team audits suppliers, a great deal of expertise is focused on
offering suggestions for improvements. Several major companies have
found this technique more beneficial than using a sole audit
professional. The synergism among the audit team members, coupled with
the expertise available, results in superior improvement ideas that are
more readily accepted.

3. Auditors External to the Company

Often, audits and surveys are conducted by customers, third party
agencies, or persons external to the company, such as consultants. They

are an important source of improvement ideas, and often bring into focus
a fresh view of the company's activities.

Customer Audits or Surveys

First-time customer audits or surveys may be intended to provide
information to the customer on whether future business should be awarded.
Visits after the award of business are intended to improve future quality
performance by identifying areas for improvement.

Responding to customer audits and surveys is very serious. Future
business hinges on satisfying the customer.

A company that is audited by its customers also has suppliers. The
suppliers are audited with the same intent. For most companies,
suppliers form the foundation of their quality effort. In essence, a
company can be no better than what is furnished by their suppliers. The
information gained through audits or surveys of suppliers can be
invaluable in maintaining continuous improvement effort. A survey used
by a major automobile producer appears in the Appendix.

A major problem for most companies is the large number of customers
making audits and surveys. Accommodating frequent visits is a strain on
resources. Efforts are ongoing to reduce the number of visits by a
common assessment that is acceptable to all customers. This requires:

a. A specification for a quality system that is acceptable to most, if
   not all, customers and suppliers.
b. Auditors that are trained in acceptable audit procedures using the
   quality specification.
c. An organization that will assess the qualifications of the auditors,
   and certify their competence.
d. Independent third parties, or agencies, using auditors to administer
   the assessment, and report results. Usually, they will certify
   compliance to the quality specification.
e. Publication of relevant details from the audits that are readily
   accessible to customers.

Third Party Agencies

In Europe, the use of agencies making independent quality system
assessments was extensive by 1990. Such assessments are useful to many
companies seeking to place business, or to continue in a business
relationship, with specific suppliers. This avoids the necessity to make
separate audits or surveys by each company.

In essence, the approach meets the criteria discussed for a common
assessment. It is expected that many U.S. companies doing business
overseas will participate in such a program in the future. Motivating
this change is the multinational nature of suppliers and customers.
Geographical distances do not permit supplier audits by each customer.
This makes good business sense, avoiding a great deal of cost and
unwise use of resources.

Assessments are done using ISO 9000 standards with costs absorbed by the supplier desiring an assessment. Some U.S. companies have completed an assessment under these standards. There are also third party agencies in the U.S. performing assessments and registering the companies. During 1990, the third party agencies operated under the auspices of British and Canadian organizations. In the future, the ASQC is expected to be a dominant factor in the U.S. (There is a discussion of ISO 9000 standards presented in Appendix B. This paper was written by Edith Holmes.)

Assessment and registration is expected to become a "license" to do business with European companies. It may also spread to other parts of the world. Advantages to a supplier are:

a. The number of audits and surveys by major customers participating in the registration process is greatly reduced.
b. There is less disruption to normal operations, and less diversion of resources to accommodate audits and surveys.
c. Registered companies have a positive quality image that is widely known to potential customers participating in the registration process.
d. With a common standard, compliance is easier to consistently achieve.
e. Motivation of those in the country is likely increased in view of the new status.

The assessment could also contribute new means to realize continuous improvement.

Another way to obtain a third party evaluation is to apply for the Malcolm Baldrige National Quality Award. The guidelines for the process provide for an excellent self-assessment of preparedness for continuous improvement. This assessment becomes the application for the award. Finalists are visited by a team of inspectors providing additional input.

Auditing by Outside Consultants

Use of an outside consultant to evaluate the effectiveness of a continuous improvement effort may be viable for some companies. The view of someone not burdened by experiences within the company may freshen an effort that could be going stale. Issues of management commitment may surface more readily without reliance on input from employees. Another viewpoint may help in the reevaluation of priorities and assignment of resources.

4. Company Audit Professionals

Many companies have their own auditors. In larger companies this may be a full-time assignment. Typically, such an auditor identifies weaknesses in the quality system.

Maintaining the objectivity of a company auditor is a prime concern. Auditors who pursue factors of little consequence will loose credibility and effectiveness in their quest for more important factors.

Independence of the audit function is also paramount. Inhibiting the identification of inherent weaknesses in the quality system cannot be allowed. To minimize this possibility, the audit function is usually placed outside a functional area. A good case can be made for direct reporting of the audit function to the top officer.

GENERAL FORMS OF AUDITS

Audits are normally an ongoing activity. Their types can be thought of as either product, process, or system audits. Each is unique, but collectively they provide much insight about progress toward continuous improvement. More importantly, weaknesses are identified, and possible solutions suggested.

1. Product Audit

The product audit centers on the deliverables to the customers. The customer's point of view is adopted. The product is the tangible object delivered. Customers form a perception of the company based largely on the performance and quality of the product.

The product audit is conducted in addition to the normal final inspection and testing done in the plant. Its objective is not to find defects and reject shipments. Rather, the goal is to help identify possible improvements. A secondary objective is to check the effectiveness of final inspection and test.

Because the comprehensive evaluation may take some time, the number of samples taken is much less than what would be statistically necessary. In the majority of situations, this does not adversely affect the credibility of results. It is important, however, that the products are randomly selected.

This audit is a detailed examination of the product before acceptance by the customer. It may include measurements, performance testing, and durability testing. The conformance of the product to the requirements on drawings and specifications is evaluated. In addition, results of customer surveys are often reviewed, and remarks are sought from those individuals in direct contact with customers.

Occasionally, requirements are found to be inadequate or unclear during the audit. When this occurs, specifications and drawings are identified, and revised. Changes may also be prompted by the discovery of flaws with shipping methods and containers.

Products are audited in a variety of locations. Cars are often audited at railheads to determine their condition just before delivery to the dealer. Other products are obtained from shipping containers ready for loading onto trucks, and still others are audited at distributors and warehouses.

The audits are not performed by individuals involved in building or shipping the product. The result is an unbiased report. Reliance on a product audit report means looking at the bottom line--what the customer is receiving. This brings perspective to the situation. What is found in final inspection and test reports may be different from audit reports. However, improvements to designs, processes, and shipping methods can be identified by the audits, contributing to continuous improvement efforts.

2. Process Audit

Unlike the product audit, the process audit concentrates on examining the manufacturing processes. This verifies that the process, operators, and equipment are functioning as required. In doing this, ineffective business processes may also be identified for improvement.

This audit includes a detailed examination of the inputs, processing, and outputs of a process. The results are compared to the requirements defined.

It is important that process audits are done by individuals not involved in the process. This helps assure an unbiased view of the situation.

There are usually many processes involved in production. Only a few can be audited because of the time involved. They should be the processes most critical to the quality of the product and the productivity of the company. Processes for audit should not be selected in a random fashion. This way, ideas for improvement will have maximum impact.

Areas where requirements are lacking or unclear are identified, and the situation is corrected. Procedures, work instructions, and process sheets may need modification to reflect proper requirements.

This is a particularly troublesome area for most companies. Some parameters are difficult to define, and depend on the skill of the operator. Often, documented requirements do not produce better results than previous practices.

However, correct specification of requirements ensures consistency: when a new operator is assigned, for example. Neglecting to document the requirements promotes a chaotic situation, and causes chronic problems. Continuous improvement is best attained when conditions and parameters are well defined, and changes are based upon them.

3. System Audit

The system audit is the broadest type. Its purpose is to produce a detailed analysis of the business processes in the company or its suppliers. An example appears in Appendix A. Other names are often used for this type of audit. Despite the different titles, the general objectives and approach is the same. System audits are often called audits, reviews, or surveys of:

a. Management.
b. Systems and procedures.
c. Operations.

This type of audit may be internal, or external. Internal system audits are concerned with the business processes in the company. External system audits are conducted on the business processes of suppliers. When suppliers are evaluated, an abbreviated form of product audit and process audit also may be done simultaneously.

There are many business processes in a company or supplier. Obviously, it would be impossible to conduct a detailed audit of each. In reality, only a few can be evaluated. Those processes judged most critical should be audited; they should not be picked at random.

For example, many problems arising from engineering changes could signal an audit of the product engineering release procedure. Missed schedules may show that the material requirements planning system needs attention. Improvements identified will likely make a great contribution to the continuous improvement of the company or supplier.

Once business processes have been selected, members of a team or an individual may be identified to conduct the audit. Obviously, expertise in the selected processes is necessary. For internal audits, this may be perplexing because the person doing the audit must be unassociated with the business process to assure an unbiased evaluation.

System audits are often complex, requiring journeys along uncharted paths and the ability to accurately evaluate difficult situations. Special skills are necessary to successfully handle such an assignment. Detailed planning before the audit may reduce uncertainties and promote agreement on the best methods.

The auditor must compare actual conditions to desired methods and performance. Existing performance must be measured, and compared to desired results or requirements. It is desirable to check progress against strategic plans and objectives during the audit. Every effort must be made to provide the necessary background for comparisons prior to the audit.

In system audits, business processes may not be well defined, and desired performance may not be established as an ongoing measurement. This often contributes to the perceived problems of the business process.

GROUND RULES FOR AUDITS

There are several general rules in auditing that are applicable to all efforts. They will help assure positive results. The details of each audit or survey should be planned with these rules in mind:

1. Carefully define the customer, objectives, and scope of the effort prior to starting the audit or survey.

   In essence, the customer is the user of the information gained from the audit. The user is the activity that will make the improvements. For example, the customer could be the managers of the products, processes, and systems being examined. They must carry out the changes. Most audits and surveys are not done for the sole use of top management.

   After this, the needs of the customer can be sought. They form the objectives of the audit.

   Clearly defining the scope will establish the "turf" on which the audit will take place. This prevents the auditor or audit team from investigating activities of little relevance. If a scope is too large, the audit will take an unreasonable amount of time. Too narrow a scope may restrict the study, such that results are questionable. Scope also influences the resources needed and costs.

2. Prior to making the audit, performance measures should be established.

    Performance measures are the way in which the effectiveness of a product or process is judged. For a product such as an automobile, the minimum life should be a specific number of miles as measured by a durability test. An example using a business process is the level of engineering changes required for each product released. Often, goals for these performance measures are established by a company when planning for continuous improvement.

    Perhaps the ultimate goal for a company is to eliminate the need for engineering changes. Since this may not be achieved for sometime, goals to track progress are established. For example, a goal may be to reduce the level of engineering changes to four for each product released by the close of 1991.

    There can be no meaningful gage of progress without performance measurements and knowledge of the desired goals. Without a comparison of actual performance to goals, audits, or surveys may be conjecture. Allowing this destroys the creditability of suggestions and makes the carrying out of improvements difficult.

3. Details of methodology should be developed before the audit.

    Details must be finalized in advance. First, identify the information to be sought. Second, a method of organizing documents and notes on interviews must be developed.

    An audit checklist of items to be covered by the audit should also be drafted. Generic checklists can be purchased from various sources. Purchased checklists may help in drafting lists unique to the company and audit. They should not be used directly, for the following reasons:

    a. The way each company is organized and responsibilities assigned is different.
    b. Unique business system features are important to the evaluation, but are obviously not included.
    c. The purchased lists will probably lack an inventory of the criteria particularly important to a company.
    d. Preparation for the audit may be inadequate because the audit or survey lacks critical analysis of the items to be evaluated.

4. During the planning phase, there must be regular contact with the customer of the audit or survey. Once it is ready, there should be a formal launch.

    It is important that the audit be completely open, and beyond reproach. The existence of the audit cannot be a secret, or surprise to the customer. Those involved must be informed, and consulted ahead of time.

During planning, details should be reviewed by those involved. An open posture will foster attitudes that support the objectives of the audit. In addition, plans can be fine-tuned using input from the customer and those in the audit process.

Just before the audit is launched, a meeting should be held with the customer, the auditors, and others involved in the process. The role of each should be clearly defined. Additionally, the scope, objectives, and plans should be reviewed. An open discussion may clear up any confusion. This will do a great deal to set the stage for a successful audit.

5. During the audit, short, daily briefings should be held by the auditors and those concerned.

   Sharing results can be very beneficial. It helps develop an awareness of progress.

   Findings can be tested to assure credibility, and suggestions for improvements can be fine-tuned. Changes in plans to pursue specific aspects can be discussed, and agreement reached. This approach ensures there are no surprises at the end of the audit, or survey.

6. Audit results must be formally reported to the customer shortly following completion.

   The deliverable of the audit, or survey is the report. It must be presented to the customer as soon as possible. Often, a verbal discussion takes place simultaneously with the submission of a written report. This clears up confusion about findings, and suggestions.

   Typically, the report on the audit, or survey will include:

   a. The customer.
   b. The scope of the study.
   c. The objectives of the evaluation.
   d. A summary of the findings, and the effects on performance.
   e. Suggestions for improvement.

The next chapter summarizes this book.

BIBLIOGRAPHY

Arter, Dennis R., "Evaluate Standards and Improve Performance With a Quality Audit." Quality Progress, September 1989, p. 41.

Blache, Klaus M., "Success Factors For Implementing Change." Dearborn, MI: Society of Manufacturing Engineers, 1988.

Grieco, Jr., Peter L. and Gozo, Michael W., "Made In America: The Total Business Concept," PT Publications, 1987.

Hill, William J., "Assessing Quality Program Effectiveness," Quality Congress Transactions (Dallas). Milwaukee: American Society for Quality Control, 1988.

Ishikawa, Kaoru, "The Quality Control Audit." <u>Quality Progress</u>, January 1987, p. 39.

Juran, J.M., Quality Control Handbook, 4th ed. New York: McGraw Hill, 1988.

Lawler III, Edward E., "High Involvement Management," Jossey-Bass, 1988.

Lay, Henry G., "The Quality Audit: Who Does What?" <u>Quality Progress</u>, January 1987, p. 20.

Q.C. Trends, "Quality Audits - Why and How To Perform," May 1988.

Quality World Newsletter, Volume VIII, Number 4, International Chapter of American Society for Quality Control, December 1990.

Willborn, Walter, "Registration of Quality Programs." <u>Quality Progress</u>, September 1988, p. 56.

CHAPTER 17

SUMMARY

In this chapter. . .

A SUMMARY IS PRESENTED. CONTINUOUS IMPROVEMENT IS DISCUSSED.

17
Summary

A wide range of topics are covered in this book, and all are important. For some, such as the tools of continuous improvement, a lot is known, and guidelines are abundant. For others, this is not the case and improved methods are constantly being sought.

One thing is clear. Continuous improvement is a very complex process. It takes dedication from everyone inside an organization to succeed. It is more than SPC, or Design of Experiments. These are only a few of many tools that can put a company on the road to improvement.

Continuous improvement cannot be attained by focusing on inspection, product design, or operator education alone.

Improvement occurs from a balanced effort throughout the company. Quality activities must exist in all functions: marketing, product development, manufacturing, accounting, and others. They must work in harmony to satisfy the needs of customers and users.

Continuous improvement requires the participation of all employees. Management and white and blue collar workers must act as partners in the pursuit of improvement. This partnership should extend to suppliers and customers. In most companies, the broad focus requires a change in culture.

Continuous improvement will not work unless it is ingrained in the way a company conducts its business. Organizationally, this means eliminating top-down, autocratic management. Artificial walls between departments stifle teamwork, and must be removed. This is difficult because the walls may have existed for a long time.

For many companies, the only competitive strategy is continuous improvement. Those who believe in it recognize that the journey will be long, difficult, and probably without end.

Companies that survived the last decade had to change basic methods of conducting business. This involved "repouring" the foundations, or changing the culture of the companies. The changes were dramatic, and their cultures are still evolving today.

Much of the change involved humanizing the workplace.

Workers during the 1980s were much different from their predecessors. More have become involved in administration. Unskilled labor accounts for only 30% of the work force, down from 50% in the 1960s. College graduates now comprise 40% of the work force. They are well-informed, and technically oriented. They are also less willing to work in a hierarchical, autocratic business setting.

Companies have changed their style of management. Self-management is more widely practiced than rigid supervision. A team approach is used in problem solving, instead of looking to management for solutions.

In many plants, workers are allowed to stop production lines to ensure consistent quality. They can also switch tasks with others to help fight boredom. In many companies, the role of management has changed to that of a facilitator, helping employees make improvements. The result is better decisions, and workers who feel they are making a positive contribution.

Many companies are aware that better solutions are drafted by those involved in the process. If people are involved on teams, there is a high likelihood that better solutions will be found. There is also the recognition that you fix processes, and not people. People want to do a good job, but can't always due to factors beyond their control.

The use of teams is growing. They are often composed of members from each function such as product development and manufacturing. Suppliers may also be on the team. Teams have been very successful in early identification of problems, and timely resolutions.

A customer focused mentality needs to prevail. It is widely recognized that meeting the needs of the customer is the only way to survive in today's marketplace.

The change in culture of many companies was vital to improving quality. Many people believe this permitted manufacturing in the U.S. to maintain its competitive posture during the last decade. Change is the common thread that ties the chapters of this book together.

Quality has a competitive advantage in the marketplace. Because of this, a company must display equal, or better quality than its competitors. Competitor quality, however, is a moving target, constantly improving. This in turn drives a company to improve its quality continually to remain a viable force in the marketplace.

Gaps in quality between companies provide a huge competitive advantage to the leader. A large gap could result in the quality follower going out of business, or losing market share. Once the gap is recognized by customers, it takes a long time to regain confidence in the marketplace.

Once customer perceptions about inferior quality are formed, they are hard to change. Many companies improved tremendously during the last decade. Repair records verify this. Yet, Gallup poll results indicated that the perception of quality of American products didn't change.

The message is clear. Companies can no longer tolerate quality gaps. To prevent this, a viable program of continuous improvement is required. Some feel the most critical factor in ensuring quality relates to the caliber of a company's work force. The work force in the United States offers both good and bad news. One-third of the work force is better than elsewhere, but the remaining two-thirds could have better education, more skills, and improved motivation. One in five adults cannot read, write, or count on a seventh-grade level. This situation is expected to continue unless drastic, comprehensive action is taken.

Companies must be extensively involved in improving this situation. Long-time employees without basic skills should receive training in math and reading. The emphasis should be on improving the work force.

Support from industry may be forthcoming. In recent years, many companies have changed their views about their work force. Instead of seeing employees as a cost of doing business, they now recognize that they are a resource and an asset.

Spending to improve the performance of employees has never been greater. This is seen as affecting performance over a long period--perhaps the entire career of the employee. Like a capital investment, an investment in an employee can have a long and rewarding payoff.

The switch in focus from the short-term to the long-term has influenced this shift in viewpoint. From this perspective, investment in employees is not only justified, but it may be mandatory. Long-range success is strongly dependent on the quality of the work force.

Much of the investment is in training employees. It involves improving the ability of a person to do a job. This ranges from basic math and reading skills to approaches for continuous improvement. Many companies are doing this on company time.

To encourage professional employees to stay abreast of technology and improve themselves, continuous education programs are supported. These programs range from sending employees to seminars given by professional organizations to paying tuition for degree programs at universities.

The concept of continuous improvement is a strategy companies must adopt.

They must be involved in an ongoing effort to achieve better levels of performance. Once a new level is reached, efforts must continue toward the next. The journey for continuous improvement is expected to last forever.

Improvement efforts must be broad in scale, and applied wherever necessary. Continuous improvement involves more than just increasing the quality of products. It could refer to improving cash flow through better customer billing methods. Another example is reducing the lead time required to develop a product. Quality improvement is only part of the broader effort.

Continuous improvement mandates change in how we think, learn, govern, and operate any organization. Many past attempts to improve quality were fruitless because this basic change did not occur.

Each company must develop a vision of what it wants to become. Top management must have a vision. This must be translated into strategy and tactics. Measurable goals and objectives must be developed. Support and commitment must be gained from everyone in the company. As time passes, the vision will be adjusted to meet new challenges, causing further change. The process never stops.

Achieving the vision is not easy. It is much simpler to talk about change than accomplish it. Shared visions are difficult with politicking and empire building going on. Turf battles between activities still occur. Yet, for the vision to be realized, all activities in a company must work in unison.

Overcoming these barriers is a challenge for top management. Without their active involvement, removing the obstacles would be an immense task. There have been efforts to change from the bottom, but without a strategy for dealing with change at the top, the risk of failure is high.

A crucial element in any company is trust. Distrust causes people not to share ideas.

Cooperation also is lost when the spirit in which it will be used is unclear. Success in continuous improvement depends on using the creativity of each employee to solve problems. Unlocking this creativity is contingent on providing a climate of trust where individuals do not fear consequences that may result from the sharing of ideas.

In the past, trust did not exist widely. For example, workers were sent home for errors that may not have been their fault. The result of this ranged from doing as little as possible to not taking any chances. For these employees, it was more important to avoid risks than to make a contribution. The survival of companies today depends on the contribution of each employee. A company cannot afford to thwart employee contribution by a culture of distrust.

Trust cannot be mandated. It must be built over a period of time. The interaction of employees forms the trust inherent in a company. In a sense, it is part of the culture. Trust results from the way the company wants employees to treat others. It starts with top management, and extends throughout the company. Specific rules cannot be written down. Trust must be part of the value system of each employee.

Feelings of trust are more likely in a company where each employee receives support from the others. There must be mutual understanding and acceptance of individual differences. Risk taking must be encouraged, and failures accepted as a potential byproduct.

Trust promotes honesty. It is necessary to bring problems to the surface so they can be addressed. Many chronic problems today result from fear of the consequences if they are mentioned. In many ways, lack of trust is a cancer that can destroy the long-range viability of a company. More importantly, lack of trust limits the true potential of individuals. For a company to survive, a culture of distrust cannot be allowed.

Keeping continuous improvement in perspective requires recognition that the journey to a company's maturity is a long one. Ultimate goals are rarely visible. The concept of continuous improvement means the effort will last a long time, and perhaps never end. It is a relentless pursuit to better the company. It is unlikely that any company can claim completion of the continuous improvement effort, and display final results.

APPENDIX A

COST OF QUALITY

Use the following two sheets to organize your COQ elements.

PREVENTION COSTS

1. _____ $ _____
2. _____ $ _____
3. _____ $ _____
4. _____ $ _____
5. _____ $ _____
6. _____ $ _____
7. _____ $ _____

                                    TOTAL   _____

APPRAISAL COSTS

1. _____ $ _____
2. _____ $ _____
3. _____ $ _____
4. _____ $ _____
5. _____ $ _____
6. _____ $ _____
7. _____ $ _____

                                    TOTAL   _____

Cost of quality worksheet. *(Courtesy of Charney & Associates, Inc.)*

COST OF QUALITY WORKSHEET

Item	Disc. or Cons.	Definition	How to Measure	Method to Calculate Cost	$ Cost/ Month

Cost of quality worksheet (continued)

The following scale will be utilized to assess each question appearing from page A-4 to A-12.

RATING	DEFINITION

0   NONEXISTENT

        * Not included in the Quality System

1   POOR PERFORMANCE

        * Included in the Quality System
        * Planning and execution require
          substantial improvement

2   INADEQUATE

        * Included in the Quality System
        * Planning and execution require improvement

3   MEETS MINIMUM REQUIREMENTS

        * Included in the Quality System
        * Planning and execution meet minimum
          requirements

4   EXCEEDS MINIMUM REQUIREMENTS

        * Included in the Quality System
        * Planning and execution exceed requirements
        * Exhibits the Continuous Quality Improvement
           Philosophy

5   OUTSTANDING PERFORMANCE

        * Included in the Quality System
        * Planning and execution exceed requirements
        * Innovative
        * Utilizes maximum technology available
        * Optimizes the Continuous Quality Improvement
          Philosophy

Form used to evaluate quality systems of tool and equipment suppliers *(Courtesy of Chrysler Corporation)*

	POINTS AWARDED	REMARKS

I.   MANAGEMENT POLICY

1. To what extent does senior management actively support and participate in the Quality Improvement Process?   _____ _____

2. What level of commitment exists in senior management to effectively educate all respective personnel in the Quality Improvement Process?   _____ _____

3. What type of measurement is utilized by senior management to monitor continuous improvement and how effective is it?   _____ _____

4. To what extent has the Quality Improvement Process been implemented?   _____ _____

5. Are sophisticated project management techniques utilized to schedule project completion?   _____ _____

6. Are work areas well lighted and large enough to allow efficient and effective implementation of process control?   _____ _____

7. Does the supplier maintain housekeeping in line with the commodities being produced?   _____ _____

8. Is management committed to the use of statistical techniques?   _____ _____

9. Are supplier facilities monitored to assure capability of handling current/ future Product Program Requirements?   _____ _____

SECTION TOTAL   _____ _____

II. ADMINISTRATION

1. Are quality costs analyzed (i.e. trend charted, Pareto ranked) to show areas that require attention?   _____ _____

2. Are quality cost reports (price of conformance/nonconformance or prevention/appraisal failure) issued throughout the organization?   _____ _____

Evaluating quality systems of tool and equipment suppliers (continued)

II.   <u>ADMINISTRATION</u> (CONT.)

    3. What plans exist to improve quality costs?   _____   _____

    4. As products and processes are added or
changed, are the system plan and flow
charts updated and distributed as
required?   _____   _____

    5. What documented quality training programs
(some will include training in statistical
techniques) are provided for all management,
sales, quality, and production personnel?   _____   _____

    6. Are flow charts available and used, and do
they depict all manufacturing, inspection,
test and/or quality check points?   _____   _____

    7. Is the material identification system
sufficient to control material throughout
the manufacturing system?   _____   _____

    8. Determine what record retention system
exists for the maintenance of **all** quality
system documents and records.   _____   _____

    9. What specific person or department is
responsible for program management of new
products?   _____   _____

   10. Are documented quarterly "system" self-
audits performed with results and
corrective actions reported to and
reviewed by management?   _____   _____

   11. Is there a sufficient number of qualified
personnel to administer programs to meet
product requirements at this location?   _____   _____

   12. Is there a formal program which identifies
and upgrades insufficiently trained
personnel?   _____   _____

   13. Is an approved system plan defining the
total quality system available, maintained,
and properly implemented?   _____   _____

                               SECTION TOTAL   _____   _____

Evaluating quality systems of tool and equipment suppliers (continued)

III.	**QUALITY AND RELIABILITY PLANNING**	**POINTS AWARDED**	**REMARKS**

1. To what extent is the responsibility for quality planning and specification review on new and changed products and processes defined?

   _____ _____

2. To what extent are departments such as Manufacturing, Engineering, Marketing, and Quality Assurance involved in the quality planning activities?

   _____ _____

3. How is product reliability considered in the design review process?

   _____ _____

4. How are runoff characteristics determined in planning meetings prior to design and build?

   _____ _____

5. What department goals have been established as part of the quality planning process and how are they monitored?

   _____ _____

6. What employee participation processes have been developed and implemented to aid in quality planning and improvement?

   _____ _____

7. What statistical/analytical and **other** innovative planning techniques are used throughout the supplier's organization to improve "process/product" capabilities?

   _____ _____

8. What type of design, manufacturing, quality, feasibility reviews are conducted on future products and/or programs? (Up front prevention rather than current detection procedures.)

   _____ _____

9. Are Failure Mode and Effects Analyses (FMEAs) used within the supplier's organization?

   _____ _____

10. Are Failure Mode and Effects Analyses (FMEAs) updated to reflect changes in designs and processes?

    _____ _____

11. What system is used to monitor customer reliability complaints and how are these results used?

    _____ _____

12. What follow-up system is used to be sure corrective action is taken and is successful?

    _____ _____

Evaluating quality systems of tool and equipment suppliers (continued)

III.   **QUALITY AND RELIABILITY PLANNING (CONT.)**

    13. What preventive maintenance system is recommended for the equipment to optimize its use?   _____   _____

                                      SECTION TOTAL   _____   _____

IV.   **ENGINEERING**

    1. Who is responsible to ensure that the latest drawings, engineering standards, and specifications and materials are available for use, and are adequate?   _____   _____

    2. What controls exist to confirm distribution of all changes affecting drawings, specifications, process sheets, instruction sheets, etc., and the removal of all such obsolete materials from any affected departments?   _____   _____

    3. Are change request procedures used and understood when the supplier makes any changes to their product or processes?   _____   _____

    4. Are all engineering standard/specification requirements incorporated into the system?   _____   _____

    5. Do process inspection procedures adhere to the requirements in engineering standards/ specifications?   _____   _____

    6. What specific person or department is responsible to review specifications and standards to ensure incorporation into the design of the product?   _____   _____

    7. In the event of a failure to meet engineering standards/specification requirements, is there a written procedure to notify Engineering and Supplier Quality?   _____   _____

    8. What capabilities exist to transfer computer aided design (CAD) drawings into your system?   _____   _____

    9. What procedures exist to ensure timely incorporation of engineering revisions?   _____   _____

                                       SECTION TOTAL   _____   _____

Evaluating quality systems of tool and equipment suppliers (continued)

| | **POINTS AWARDED** | **REMARKS** |

V.   IN-HOUSE STATISTICAL/ ANALYTICAL TECHNIQUES

1. To what extent have appropriate personnel been trained in statistical methods?   _____ _____

2. Are appropriate statistical techniques utilized throughout the supplier's operation? (i.e., X bar and RCP charts, etc.)   _____ _____

3. Are production personnel knowledgeable in the maintaining and interpreting of control charts?   _____ _____

4. Do supplier personnel react in a timely manner to data provided by control charts? Do records include interpretation of control charts and actions taken?   _____ _____

5. Are process control charts reviewed by management? How are assignable causes identified, corrected, and documented to prevent future occurrences?   _____ _____

6. How effective are in-process control methods in the control of significant characteristics?   _____ _____

7. Where processes are stable and in control, evaluate the existing documented plans for continuous improvement of C_{pk} values.   _____ _____

8. Are statistical problem solving (SPS) techniques used throughout the supplier's organization?   _____ _____

SECTION TOTAL   _____ _____

VI.   GAGING, MEASURING AND TEST EQUIPMENT

1. What is the established program for the identification and control of calibration for all test/inspection equipment (including employee-owned equipment)?   _____ _____

2. Is the design level of gages and test equipment verified upon initial receipt and prior to use?   _____ _____

3. Is there traceability of all calibration masters to the National Bureau of Standards, or equivalent?   _____ _____

Evaluating quality systems of tool and equipment suppliers (continued)

		POINTS AWARDED	REMARKS

VI. GAGING, MEASURING AND TEST EQUIPMENT (CONT.)

4. For supplier owned or manufactured gages, what system is used to provide repeatability and reproducibility studies for equipment before incorporating into the system, and for existing gages/equipment?   _____ _____

5. Are checking aids and gages properly used?   _____ _____

6. What plans exist to reduce the use of attribute gaging in favor of variable gaging and/or to get "State of the Art" gaging (coordinate measuring machines, electronic gages, automatic feedback, etc.)?   _____ _____

7. Where would this facility rank in inspection technology?   _____ _____

SECTION TOTAL   _____ _____

VII. INCOMING

1. Are materials awaiting inspection properly identified and segregated from previously inspected material?   _____ _____

2. How are incoming materials approved and identified before release to production operations?   _____ _____

3. Are written inspection instructions, which include frequencies and sample sizes, available at the required control points or in the proper areas?   _____ _____

4. Is adequate measuring and testing equipment specified, present, and used?   _____ _____

5. Are sub-supplier certifications, including detailed test or statistical results, required in inspection instructions and are they periodically verified?   _____ _____

6. Do sub-suppliers follow your engineering standard and specification requirements?   _____ _____

7. Are approved sub-suppliers used where required?   _____ _____

8. What statistical techniques are sub-suppliers required to use?   _____ _____

Evaluating quality systems of tool and equipment suppliers (continued)

VII.   INCOMING (CONT.)

9. What systems are used to notify sub-
   suppliers of material rejections and are
   they required to submit a written cor-
   rective action plan?   _____ _____

10. How is the supplier purchasing activity
    kept aware of all sub-supplier survey
    results, ratings, and rejections?   _____ _____

                            SECTION TOTAL   _____ _____

VIII.   IN-PROCESS

1. Are adequate instructions available at the
   required control points or in the proper
   area?   _____ _____

2. Is adequate measuring and testing equipment
   specified, present, and used?   _____ _____

3. To what extent are visual aids provided for
   operators and inspectors and are they
   appropriate?   _____ _____

4. What type of set-up approval is required to
   ensure conformance to requirements before
   runoff? Is the responsibility clearly
   defined?   _____ _____

5. What type of routing sheets are used to
   control material throughout the manufacturing process?   _____ _____

6. Determine how the production control system
   is used to ensure complete traceability of
   the finished product back through the entire
   manufacturing system.   _____ _____

7. Is nonconforming material identified and
   held in properly designated and secure,
   segregated areas?   _____ _____

8. Are rework/repairs or scrap procedures
   defined, and are they approved by customers
   when required?   _____ _____

9. Are reworked/repaired or sorted materials
   subjected to the same operating controls,
   and are they resubmitted for inspection?   _____ _____

                            SECTION TOTAL   _____ _____

Evaluating quality systems of tool and equipment suppliers (continued)

IX   FINAL AUDIT AND RUNOFF

FINAL AUDIT

1. Does all finished equipment receive a final audit, inspection and/or other verification of product acceptance?   _____   _____

2. Is the final audit/inspection performed and/or monitored by the Quality Department?   _____   _____

3. Does the final audit include a review of spare parts required by the engineering specification?   _____   _____

4. Is adequate measuring and test equipment specified, present, and used?   _____   _____

5. What system exists to review packaging, labeling, change level and shipping procedures and is it adequate to preserve product quality?   _____   _____

6. Are final audit results reviewed and incorporated into the process to ensure continuous improvement?   _____   _____

7. What specific person or department is responsible to assure that the final product meets your company's requirements?   _____   _____

8. Does the equipment meet your safety and federal regulations as specified?   _____   _____

RUNOFF

9. Are process potential studies (C_p) conducted on new processes/machines as required by your runoff requirements?   _____   _____

10. What documentation is available showing the method or plan to reduce variation and achieve the minimum C_p requirements?   _____   _____

Evaluating quality systems of tool and equipment suppliers (continued)

IX. FINAL AUDIT AND RUNOFF (CONT.)

11. To what extent does the equipment conform
    to the 50/20 program test procedure in
    the supplier's facility and are adequate
    records available for process improvement?   _____ _____

12. Does the supplier request feedback from
    long term capability studies conducted
    at customer locations?   _____ _____

                                    SECTION TOTAL   _____ _____

Evaluating quality systems of tool and equipment suppliers (continued)

DESIGN
FAILURE MODE AND EFFECTS ANALYSIS

Subsystem/Name _____

Model Year/Vehicle(s) _____

Primary Design Responsibility _____

Other Depts Involved _____

Plants (and/or Supplier(s) Involved _____

⑥ Final Design Deadline _____

⑦ Prepared By _____

⑧ Reviewed by _____

⑨ FMEA Date (Orig.) _____

① P = Probability (Chance) of Occurence
② S = Seriousness of Failure to the Vehicle
③ D = Likelihood that the Defect will Reach the Customer
⑤ R = Risk Priority Measure (PxSxD)

1 = very low or none   2 = low or minor   3 = moderate or significant   4 = high   5 = very high or catastrophic

⑩ NO.	⑪ PART NAME PART NO. & PROCESS	⑫ FUNCTION PART & PROCESS	⑬ FAILURE MODE	⑭ MECHANISM(S) & CAUSES(S) OF FAILURE	⑮ EFFECT(S) OF FAILURE	⑯ CURRENT CONTROLS	⑰ P.R.A.				㉒ RECOMMENDED CORRECTIVE ACTION(S)	㉓ ACTION(S) TAKEN	㉔ P.R.A.				㉕ RESPONSIBLE DEPARTMENT (INDIVIDUAL)
							⑱ P	⑲ S	⑳ D	㉑ R			P	S	D	R	

Design failure mode and effects analysis

(Courtesy of Chrysler Corporation)

PROCESS
FAILURE MODE AND EFFECTS ANALYSIS

Subsystem/Name _____

Model Year/Vehicle(s) _____

Primary Design Responsibility _____

Other Depts Involved _____

Plants (and/or Supplier(s) Involved _____

Final Design Deadline _____

Prepared by _____

Reviewed by _____

FMEA Date (Orig.) _____

P = Probability (Chance) of Occurence
S = Seriousness of Failure to the Vehicle
D = Likelihood that the Defect will Reach the Customer
R = Risk Priority Measure (PxSxD)

1 = very low or none 2 = low or minor 3 = moderate or significant 4 = high 5 = very high or catastrophic

NO.	PART NAME PART NO. & PROCESS	FUNCTION PART & PROCESS	FAILURE MODE	MECHANISM(S) & CAUSES(S) OF FAILURE	EFFECT(S) OF FAILURE	CURRENT CONTROLS	P.R.A.				RECOMMENDED CORRECTIVE ACTION(S)	ACTION(S) TAKEN	P.R.A.				RESPONSIBLE DEPARTMENT (INDIVIDUAL)
							P	S	D	R			P	S	D	R	

Process failure mode and effects analysis

(Courtesy of Chrysler Corporation)

A-14

Part No. & Name					Char. Measured
Operation No. & Desc.					Date

SAMPLE DATA:

No.	Value	No.	Value	No.	Value	No.	Value	No.	Value
1		21		41		61		81	
2		22		42		62		82	
3		23		43		63		83	
4		24		44		64		84	
5		25		45		65		85	
6		26		46		66		86	
7		27		47		67		87	
8		28		48		68		88	
9		29		49		69		89	
10		30		50		70		90	
11		31		51		71		91	
12		32		52		72		92	
13		33		53		73		93	
14		34		54		74		94	
15		35		55		75		95	
16		36		56		76		96	
17		37		57		77		97	
18		38		58		78		98	
19		39		59		79		99	
20		40		60		80		100	

Remarks:

TALLY SHEET:

VALUE																
TALLY																
FREQUENCY																

Data collection for capability analysis. *(Courtesy of Ford Motor Company)*

CAPABILITY ANALYSIS SHEET

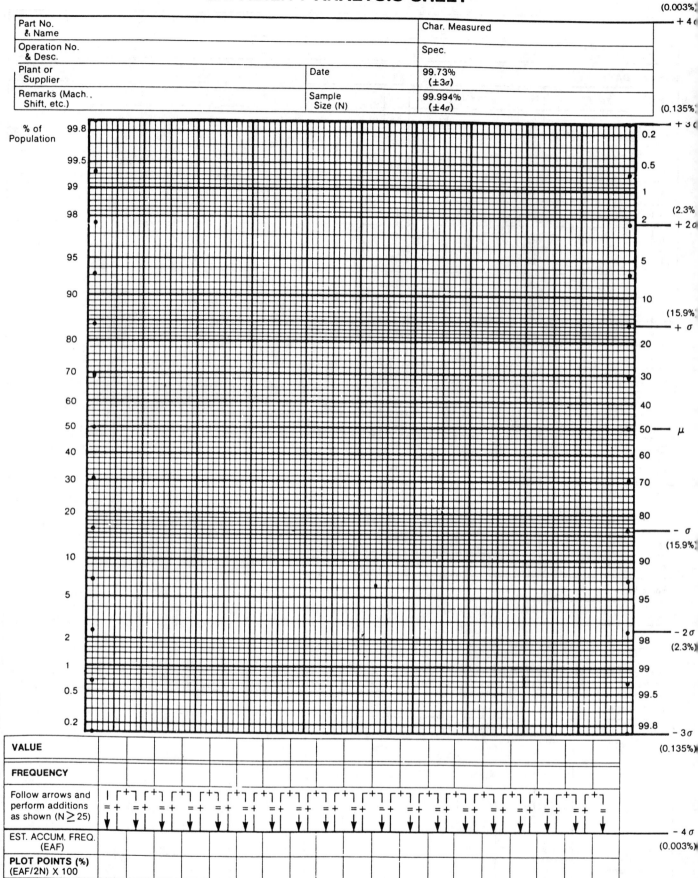

Capability analysis sheet. *(Courtesy of Ford Motor Company)*

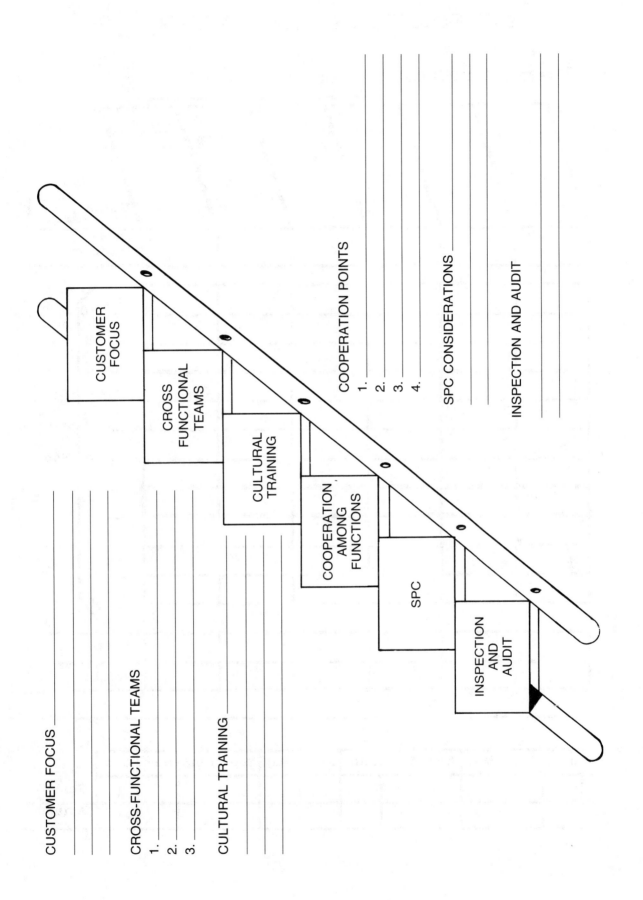

CUSTOMER FOCUS

CROSS-FUNCTIONAL TEAMS
1.
2.
3.

CULTURAL TRAINING

COOPERATION POINTS
1.
2.
3.
4.

SPC CONSIDERATIONS

INSPECTION AND AUDIT

CUSTOMER
FOCUS

CROSS
FUNCTIONAL
TEAMS

CULTURAL
TRAINING

COOPERATION
AMONG
FUNCTIONS

SPC

INSPECTION
AND
AUDIT

Ladder of culture change.

PERFORMANCE INDEXING

Department

						Month	
						Actual Performance	

						Scores
						... 10
						... 9
						... 8
						... 7
						... 6
						... 5
						... 4
						... 3
						... 2
						... 1
						... 0

						Score	
						Weight	
						Value =	

Jan	Feb	Mar	Apr	May	Jun	Jul	Aug	Sep	Oct	Nov	Dec	
												Goal
												Actual

Performance indexing. *(Courtesy of Charney & Associates, Inc.)*

LOCATING PERFORMANCE MEASUREMENTS
WORKSHEET
(See Figure 4-4 and Figure 4-5)

Customer:

Final Product:

Staff Involved:

Material Needed:

Equipment Needed:

Information to be Supplied:

Operations to be Performed:

    1.
    2.
    3.
    4.
    5.
    6.
    7.
    8.
    9.
  10.

Potential Locations of Performance Measures:

Locating performance measurements worksheet.

PARETO DIAGRAM

Using Pareto Diagrams

A Pareto diagram is a column graph used to present and analyze data. These diagrams are named after Vilfredo Pareto, an economist, who lived about one hundred years ago.

Pareto created the 80/20 rule, or the rule of the trivial many and the vital few. It is an excellent technique to help us focus on priorities and prevent us wasting time on trivia.

Why are Pareto Diagrams so useful?

Pareto diagrams are useful for analyzing data and in identifying problems to be solved. They can help us pinpoint the most frequent causes of problems.

Pareto Diagrams Used in the Problem Solving Process.

Pareto diagrams are used to Identify, Define, Investigate, Analyze, Solve, and Confirm or Monitor.

How is a Pareto Diagram Constructed?

The steps in the development of a Pareto diagram are:

Step 1   Prepare a table of data, prioritizing each item. The item with the greatest frequency or **dollar cost** is listed first. Miscellaneous items are listed last even if combined they have a higher number than the smallest problem.

Step 1a.   Calculate the percentage of each problem using the formula

$$\frac{\text{problem}}{\text{total}} \times 100 = \% \text{ of Total}$$

Problem	Cost	Percent Total	Cumulative Percent
1.	3000	30 %	
2.	2500	25 %	
3.	2000	20 %	
4.	500	5 %	
5.	500	5 %	
6. Misc.	1500	15 %	
Total	10000	100 %	

e.g. $\dfrac{3000}{10000} \times 100 = 30\%$

Pareto Diagram. *(Courtesy of Charney & Associates, Inc.)*

Step 1b.   Complete the cumulative column of this table by adding the percentage total in column three.

Problem	Cost	Percent Total	Cumulative Percent
1.	3000	30 %	30 %
2.	2500	25 %	55 %
3.	2000	20 %	75 %
4.	500	5 %	80 %
5.	500	5 %	85 %
6. Misc.	1500	15 %	100 %
Total	10000	100 %	100 %

Your data is now ready to be entered onto a Pareto diagram.

Step 2   Draw the horizontal and vertical axis of the Pareto diagram. Record the problems in order of priority along the horizontal axis. Label each axis.

Step 3   Construct a scale on the left hand vertical axis with the total number of occurrences or dollars at the top. On the right hand vertical axis list percentages with 100% opposite the total.

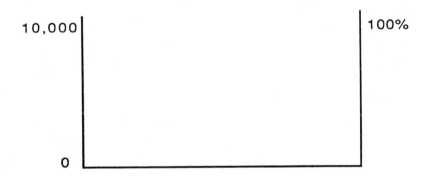

Step 4   Using the information recorded in the data table, construct a column graph on the Pareto diagram.

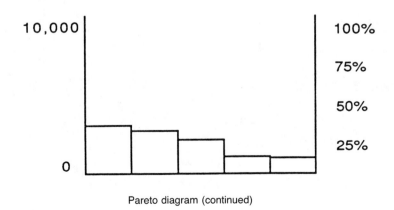

Pareto diagram (continued)

Step 5   Place a dot at the right hand edge of each column, cumulating the percentages until 100% is reached. This dot corresponds to the total percentage in the cumulative column of the data chart. Connect the dots.

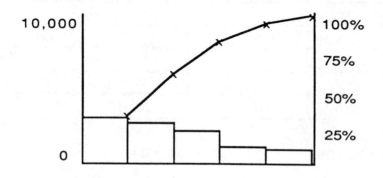

Step 6   Add a legend which will serve as a record of the data, who collected it, and where it was collected.

Pareto diagram (continued)

CONTROL CHART

PLANT	DEPT.	OPERATION	ENGINEERING SPECIFICATION	PART NO.		YES ☐ NO ☐
						CONTROL ITEM (∇)
MACH. NO.	DATES	CHARACTERISTIC	SAMPLE SIZE/FREQUENCY	PART NAME		

DATE CONTROL LIMITS CALCULATED

DATE CONTROL LIMITS CALCULATED

AVERAGES (X BAR CHART)

$\overline{\overline{X}}$ — Average $\overline{X}$ =

U.C.L. = $\overline{\overline{X}}$ + $A_2 \overline{R}$ =

L.C.L. = $\overline{\overline{X}}$ − $A_2 \overline{R}$ =

RANGES (R CHART)

$\overline{R}$ — Average R =

U.C.L. = $D_4 \overline{R}$ =

L.C.L. = $D_3 \overline{R}$ = *

ACTION
ON SPECIAL CAUSES

- ANY POINT OUTSIDE OF THE CONTROL LIMITS.
- A RUN OF 7 POINTS-ALL ABOVE OR ALL BELOW THE CENTRAL LINE.
- A RUN OF 7 INTERVALS UP OR DOWN.
- ANY OTHER OBVIOUSLY NON-RANDOM PATTERN.

ACTION INSTRUCTIONS

1.

2.

3.

4.

5.

SUBGROUP SIZE	A_2	D_3	D_4
2	1.88	*	3.27
3	1.02	*	2.57
4	.73	*	2.28
5	.58	*	2.11
6	.48	*	2.00
7	.42	.08	1.92
8	.37	.14	1.86
9	.34	.18	1.82
10	.31	.22	1.78

THE PROCESS MUST BE IN CONTROL BEFORE CAPABILITY CAN BE DETERMINED.

DATE						
TIME						
R E A D I N G S	1					
	2					
	3					
	4					
	5					
SUM						

X̄ — NO. OF READINGS
SUM
R — HIGHEST−
LOWEST

* For sample sizes of less than seven, there is no lower control limit for ranges.

A Variable Chart. *(Courtesy of Ford Motor Company)*

CONTROL CHART

PROCESS LOG SHEET

ANY **CHANGE** IN PEOPLE, MATERIALS, ENVIRONMENT, METHODS OR MACHINES SHOULD BE NOTED. THESE NOTES WILL HELP YOU TO TAKE CORRECTIVE ACTION WHEN SIGNALED BY THE CONTROL CHART.

DATE	TIME	COMMENTS

DATE	TIME	COMMENTS

Control chart process log. (*Courtesy of Ford Motor Company*)

CONTROL CHART FOR ATTRIBUTE DATA

PLANT		p ☐ c ☐	PART NUMBER AND NAME
		np ☐ u ☐	

DEPARTMENT	OPERATION NUMBER AND NAME	PRODUCT ENGINEERING DESIGNATED CONTROL ITEM (▽) ☐

Avg.▬   UCL▬   LCL▬

DATE CONTROL LIMITS CALCULATED:	Average Sample Size: Frequency:

Sample (n)	
Discrepancies **Number (np,c)**	
Proportion (p,u)	
Date (Shift, Time, etc.)	

ANY **CHANGE** IN PEOPLE, EQUIPMENT, MATERIALS, METHODS OR ENVIRONMENT SHOULD BE NOTED. THESE NOTES WILL HELP YOU TO TAKE CORRECTIVE OR PROCESS IMPROVEMENT ACTION WHEN SIGNALED BY THE CONTROL CHART.

DATE	TIME	COMMENTS

A Control Chart. (Courtesy of Ford Motor Company)

ATTRIBUTE CONTROL CHART FORMULAS

	Nonconforming Units	**Nonconformities**
Number	np Chart	c Chart

(Subgroup sizes must be equal.)

$$\text{UCL}_{np}, \text{LCL}_{np} = n\bar{p} \pm 3 \sqrt{n\bar{p} \left(1 - \frac{n\bar{p}}{n}\right)}$$

$$\text{UCL}_c, \text{LCL}_c = \bar{c} \pm 3 \sqrt{\bar{c}}$$

Proportion

p Chart

u Chart

(Subgroup sizes need not be equal.)

$$\text{UCL}_p, \text{LCL}_p = \bar{p} \pm 3 \sqrt{\frac{\bar{p}\,(1-\bar{p})}{\bar{n}}}$$

$$\text{UCL}_u, \text{LCL}_u = \bar{u} \pm 3 \sqrt{\frac{\bar{u}}{\bar{n}}}$$

DATE	TIME	COMMENTS

ACTION
On Special Causes

- Any Point Outside of the Control Limits

- A Run of 7 Points — All Above or All Below the Central Line

- A Run of 7 Intervals Up or Down.

- Any Other Obviously Non-Random Pattern

ACTION INSTRUCTIONS

1.

2.

3.

4.

5.

Attribute control chart formulas *(Courtesy of Ford Motor Company)*

Now that your group has listed it's steps to success in order of priority, indicate the forces that will help you attain that advantage. Use the force field analysis below.

ITEM _____

#C	POSITIVE FORCES	NEGATIVE FORCES	C#

A force field analysis worksheet. *(Courtesy of Charney & Associates, Inc.)*

CRITERIA	A TEXT BOOK RANK	B INDIV. RANK	A-B INDIV. SCORE	C GROUP RANK	A-C GROUP SCORE
Training	4				
Teamwork	8				
Steering Committee	10				
Management Commitment	1				
Union Support	3				
Middle Management Support	2				
Use of Outside Consultants	9				
Excellent SPC Co-ordinator	5				
Large Quality Control Dept.	14				
Staff with Math Training	12				
Breakthrough Thinking	6				
Informal Relationships on Floor	7				
Training Materials	11				
High Rework Rate	15				
Historical Quality Data	13				
TOTALS					

Scores of Each Group Member

High Individual Score   Average Score   Group Score

Criteria analysis worksheet. *(Courtesy of Charney & Associates, Inc.)*

ORGANIZATIONAL CULTURE SELF-ASSESSMENT PROFILE

UNSOUND

SOUND

1. ___ Poor communications with the emphasis on downward communications.

1. ___ Communications are open and candid; individuals are receptive to new ideas and the best procedure.

2. ___ Directives and orders are given in an authoritarian manner without previous participation and are expected to be carried out without question.

2. ___ There are definite team management concepts and practices where the decision makers seek and obtain the best solutions and the most productive activities, even they are not their own.

3. ___ There is a lack of trust between individuals. Individuals are suspicious of the motive behind actions taken, directions, policies, suggestions, and communications.

3. ___ Mutual trust and respect is evident. Employees ask, suggest, confide, and feel free to challenge and evaluate. Knowing that the bottom line of their efforts is that their subject(s) of discussion will be digested, evaluated, and implemented with appropriate recognition if the situation warrants it.

4. ___ A sense of insecurity with barriers causing a reluctance to suggest or fully report for fear of the response. The individual perceives his superiors as not being receptive to suggestions and change. No one listens.

4. ___ Each individual feels secure based on self-confidence and mutual respect. Employees practice good listening habits and are treated fairly. They also know what is positively delegated with mutual trust.

5. ___ There is a strong emphasis on work rule enforcement and disciplinary action procedures.

5. ___ Employees self-manage and police themselves through commitment, involvement, and group peer pressure. Work rules are minimal with disciplinary action seldom necessary. They appreciate management's empathy and treatment as participating human beings.

6. ___ There is a lack of goals. Top management may have goals but they have not communicated them throughout the organization.

6. ___ Goals are established in writing, agreed on, and are measurable throughout the organization through first level supervision. Also, they are consistently updated and reviewed quarterly.

Organizational culture self-assessment profile. *(From Management Vitality: The Team Approach)*

7. ___ With the lack of goals providing individual and group direction of activities, an excessive number of employees are required to meet production requirements.

8. ___ There are no goals, objectives, or Standards of Performance; therefore, time is poorly managed and is not recognized as an important resource.

9. ___ Workers, supervisors, and middle managers put in their eight hours and at the sound of the whistle or when the clock strikes four, all leave regardless.

10. ___ Supervisors and managers are unaware of their management style and/or are unconcerned about the impact they have on others.

11. ___ Status quo or the present trend is accepted as good enough. We made a profit last year, don't question or suggest we change and do differently.

12. ___ Employees are working within restrictive job descriptions, concerned only about oneself vs. the group.

13. ___ Delegation is poorly handled and is not considered as a means of developing people and an organization.

14. ___ Favoritism and discrimination is suggested with the practices being justified as a means to "get the job done."

15. ___ Conflicts are avoided or suppressed resulting in frustrations and anxieties.

7. ___ The lean organization manages by goals with group and team efforts designed to improve productivity.

8. ___ Time is considered a resource to be used effectively in achieving goals, objectives, and Standards of Performance.

9. ___ Output per manhour is important. Individuals will put in extra energy and time to achieve agreed upon goals or handle a crisis.

10. ___ Supervisors and managers have identified their management style and are aware of the positive/negative impact it has on others.

11. ___ Status quo is not good enough. What are our opportunities, are we properly managing for change, utilizing our capital, natural and human resources to our best advantage? What we did yesterday isn't necessarily good enough today.

12. ___ Job descriptions are non-existent. Employees work against goals, Standards of Performance, and objectives.

13. ___ Delegation is used to develop people and the organization to permit experienced workers to concentrate on the few vital activities that make the difference.

14. ___ All employees are treated in a fair and consistent manner. Employees are given an opportunity to grow by continuously learning new skills.

15. ___ Conflicts are confronted, discussed, resolved, and used as opportunities and learning experiences.

Organizational culture self-assessment profile (continued)

16. ___ Problems are avoided or concealed from superiors.

16. ___ Problems are solved and are considered opportunities for improving productivity. A monthly (quarterly) summary and solutions are communicated to all employees.

17. ___ Employees are put down and suppressed.

17. ___ Creativity is encouraged by seeking change and new ideas with time allocated for creativity, research and development.

18. ___ Decisions and practices are from above, there is no opportunity to critique performance.

18. ___ There is a practice of concurrent critiquing of performance activities and decisions, always toward seeking excellence.

19. ___ The tendency is to concentrate on what the employee is doing wrong and berate him or her in front of others.

19. ___ Employees are recognized for contributions through positive reinforcement techniques.

20. ___ Performance is seldom or infrequently evaluated.

20. ___ Poor performance is immediately identified with action taken to help the employee improve performance through additional training and coaching.

21. ___ Employees have little or no input into their jobs. Their procedures are established without participation from others.

21. ___ Worker-Supervision Productivity and Development Activities are in existence and are allowed the freedom and time for self-management, identifying and solving productivity problems, and setting goals and standards.

Self-assessment profile (continued)

QUESTIONNAIRE

Answer the following questions ranking your answers from 1 to 5.

1 - represents very poor,   4 - good and
2 - poor,   5 - very good.
3 - average,

- Do you have a formalized JIT process?
  1 - No,   4 - Have many aspects,
  2 - A little,   5 - Totally.
  3 - Somewhat,

- Are your vendors certified on the basis of their ability to deliver quality parts, on time?
  1 - Not at all,   4 - Mostly,
  2 - A few,   5 - Totally.
  3 - About half,

- Do you have a push or a pull manufacturing system?
  1 - Exclusively push,
  3 - Combination,
  5 - Exclusively pull.

- Are incoming parts held in a storage area, or are they sent directly to the floor?
  1 - All into storage,   4 - Mostly direct to floor,
  2 - Mostly into storage,   5 - All direct to floor.
  3 - Some into storage,

- Are operators allowed to shut down the line if they know that poor quality parts are produced?
  1 - Never,   4 - Most times,
  2 - With permission,   5 - Always.
  3 - Sometimes,

- Do operators monitor key dimensions of their process on a statistical process control chart?
  1 - Never,   4 - Most times,
  2 - Infrequently,   5 - Always.
  3 - Sometimes,

- Are you capable of producing lot sizes of one without lost time?
  1 - No,
  3 - Sometimes,
  5 - Yes.

- Do you make regular changes to reduce changeover times?
  1 - Never,   4 - Quite often,
  2 - Seldom,   5 - Regularly.
  3 - Sometimes,

- Do you use a multi-disciplined team approach to find ways of reducing setup times?
  1- Never,
  3 - Sometimes,
  5 - Always.

- Do you document changes to ensure that they are standardized and used?
  1 - Never,   4 - Most Times,
  2 - Seldom,   5 - Always.
  3 - Sometimes,

- Is your plant designed to minimize material handling?
  1 - No,
  3 - Somewhat,
  5 - Totally.

Questionnaire assessing culture at different levels of the organization
Reprinted from *Time to Market: Reducing Product Lead Time*.
Copyright 1991 Society of Manufacturing Engineers

- Are your shop floor people regularly consulted on process improvements?
  - 1 - Never,
  - 2 - Infrequently,
  - 3 - Sometimes,
  - 4 - Frequently,
  - 5 - Always.

-. Do parts arrive for assembly as needed?
  - 1 - Never,
  - 2 - Infrequently,
  - 3 - Sometimes,
  - 4 - Most times,
  - 5 - Always.

- Do you have a vendor certification program?
  - 1 - No,
  - 3 - Limited,
  - 5 - Total.

- What is your relationship with your suppliers ?
  - 1 - Hostile,
  - 2 - Somewhat adversarial,
  - 3 - Fair,
  - 4 - Good,
  - 5 - Excellent.

- What is the length of your contracts?
  - 1 - One year or less,
  - 2 - 1-2 year,
  - 3 - 2-3 years,
  - 4 - 3-4 years,
  - 5 - in excess of 5 years.

- Do your purchasing people spend time at the premises of existing and potential suppliers?
  - 1 - Less than 5% of time,
  - 2 - 6-10% of time,
  - 3 - 11-15% of time,
  - 4 - 16-20% of time,
  - 5 - 20% or more.

- Do you share data electronically with your suppliers?
  - 1 - Never,
  - 2 - Limited,
  - 3 - Some,
  - 4 - Many,
  - 5 - All.

- Do you inspect products from your suppliers?
  - 1 - Check 100%,
  - 2 - Check most,
  - 3 - Check some,
  - 4 - Check few,
  - 5 - No incoming inspection.

- Do you have ongoing joint problem solving/cost reduction teams with your suppliers?
  - 1 - None,
  - 2 - Very limited,
  - 3 - Some,
  - 4 - With many key suppliers,
  - 5 - With all key suppliers.

- Do your operators monitor their own quality?
  - 1 - No,
  - 2 - Infrequently,
  - 3 - Sometimes,
  - 4 - Most times,
  - 5 - Always.

- Do you document your manufacturing processes?
  - 1 - None,
  - 2 - A few,
  - 3 - Some,
  - 4 - Most,
  - 5 - All.

- Do you audit to ensure that your processes are followed?
  - 1 - Never,
  - 2 - Infrequently,
  - 3 - Sometimes,
  - 4 - Frequently,
  - 5 - Always.

Culture assessment at different levels of the organization (continued)

TOTAL SCORES

Interpretation

In relation to the element of World-Class Manufacturing:

- A score of 14 to 21 indicates that your quality process is very poor.
- A score of 22 to 35 indicates that your quality process is poor.
- A score of 36 to 49 indicates that you are doing a reasonable job.
- A score of 50 to 63 indicates that you are doing a fairly good job on quality
- A score in excess of 64 indicates that you are doing a superb job on your quality process.

Culture assessment at different levels of the organization (continued)

PROJECT PLANNING PROCESS

HELP	#	OBSTACLE	SOLUTION	C	P	WHEN	WHO

Project planning. *(Courtesy of Charney & Associates, Inc.)*

Steps in Designing a PERT Network

Putting a PERT diagram together is a 4 step process:

Step 1
List (a) all activities/events that must be done for a project and (b) the sequence in which these activities/events should be performed.

Step 2
Determine how much time will be needed to complete each activity/event.

Step 3
Design a PERT network that reflects all of the information contained in steps 1 and 2.

Step 4
Identify the critical path.

Project Planning Process

The Project Planning Process is commonly used to ensure that projects are implemented. To do this, it identifies possible obstacles, ensuring that these are dealt with effectively.

Construction of a Project Planning Process

Like all effective tools, the Project Planning Process works best when it is used systematically. The steps are as follows:

Step I   Construct the appropriate diagram (see below)

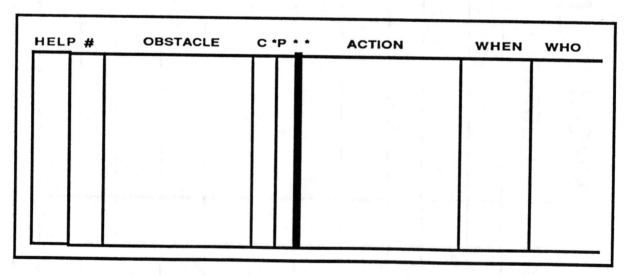

HELP #		OBSTACLE	C *P **			ACTION	WHEN	WHO

*   **C** stands for control

      1 = full control by numbers

      2 = partial control

      3 = no control

**   **P** stands for priority

Steps in designing a PERT Network. *(Courtesy of Charney & Associates, Inc.)*

Step II List all possible obstacles. These items will prevent the project's success. List items that can help you.

EXAMPLES

HELP	#	OBSTACLE	C *	P * *	ACTION	WHEN	WHO
Man support	1	Untrained people					
Training programs	2	Lack of time					
Budget $	3	Little mid-management support					
	4	Downtime					

Step III Decide who has control over the obstacles.

HELP	#	OBSTACLE	C *	P * *	ACTION	WHEN	WHO
Man support	1	Untrained people	1				
Training programs	2	Lack of time	1				
Budget $	3	Little mid-management support	2				
	4	Downtime	2				

Problems you have full control over are given as 1
Problems you have partial control over are given as 2
Problems you have no control over are given as 3

PERT Network (continued)

Step IV   Prioritize items in terms of their impact on the problem or project. Get a consensus. You may use the nominal group technique.

HELP	#	OBSTACLE	C*	P**	ACTION	WHEN	WHO
Man support	1	Untrained people	1	2			
Training programs	2	Lack of time	1	1			
Budget $	3	Little mid-management support	2	3			
	4	Downtime	2	4			

Step V   Make a judgement whether to continue or not. You may decide to abandon the project or solution if there are important obstacles which are outside of your control. If not, proceed.

Step VI   Develop actions to deal with all obstacles. Utilize the resources listed in the 'Help' column. Follow these simple principles:

- start with the most important obstacles first
- involve people outside the group for type 2 problems
- don't try and do everything at once. Work on the obstacles one at a time, being realistic about your resources (time, money, etc.)
- get commitments for activities and completion dates from people

HELP	#	OBSTACLE	C*	P**	ACTION	WHEN	WHO
Man support	1	Untrained people	1	2	Provide training program in problem solving	July 1	Mac
Training programs	2	Lack of time	1	1	Time management program	June 5	Pete
Budget $	3	Little mid-management support	2	3	Presentation to middle management	June 18	Group
	4	Downtime	2	4	Preventative maintenance schedule	July 19	Marsha

PERT Network (continued)

TRAINING EFFECTIVENESS QUESTIONNAIRE

Training Course or Program _____

Course Completion Date _____

Today's Date _____

INSTRUCTIONS

Please read the question and mark the circled number which best describes your opinion about the training course or program. Then give a few specific examples to illustrate how the course or program has made a difference in the way you carry out your job, manage or supervise. Please fill out both sides of this questionnaire.

To a very great extent
To a great extent
To some extent
To a little extent
To a very little extent

QUESTIONS

1. Did the training increase your technical, supervisory or managerial skills?
   ① ② ③ ④ ⑤

2. Did the training increase your knowledge or base of information?
   ① ② ③ ④ ⑤

3. Did the training increase your self-confidence?
   ① ② ③ ④ ⑤

4. All things considered, was the course worth the time you spent?
   ① ② ③ ④ ⑤

5. Please give two or three specific examples which show how the training has helped you do your job more effectively (improvements in job performance measures are very useful).

_____

_____

_____

_____

_____

_____

_____

_____

_____

_____

(over)

A training effectiveness questionnaire (Copyright 1989. Ann Arbor Consulting Associates)

TRAINING EFFECTIVENESS QUESTIONNAIRE (Con't.)

To a very great extent

To a great extent

To some extent

To a little extent

To a very little extent

Have you put the training into practice:

6. In personal planning, problem-solving and decision making ① ② ③ ④ ⑤

7. In one-on-one coaching, training, problem-solving, planning, or reviewing with subordinates/supervisor ① ② ③ ④ ⑤

8. In meetings and team activities ① ② ③ ④ ⑤

9. In taking initiative and providing leadership ① ② ③ ④ ⑤

10. In areas outside the company or organization, i.e., family, community, profession, etc. ① ② ③ ④ ⑤

11. What changes, if any, would you suggest to improve this training course or program? _____

_____

_____

_____

12. What personal comments or observations would you like to share with the instructor(s)? _____

_____

_____

_____

Training effectiveness questionnaire (continued)

Sample Agenda

Objective: Reduce Downtime by 15%

Meeting Time: 2 hours

AGENDA

WHAT	HOW	TIME
1. Agreement on Objective	Consensus	5
2. Agreement on Agenda	Consensus	5
3. Appointment of Recorder & Timekeeper	Volunteer	1
4. Review of Problem	Presentation of Data	4
5. Input & Reaction of Members	Feedback by Round Robin	10
6. Establish all Causes	Cause & Effect Diagram	20
7. Choose Most Important	Nominal Group Technique	10
8. Identify Solutions	Brainstorm	20
9. Choose Best	Nominal Group Technique	20
10. Develop Implementation Plan	Action Plan Planning Graph	20
11. Summary	Presentation	5

A Sample Agenda. *(Courtesy of Charney & Associates, Inc.)*

SAMPLE AGENDA

Meeting of _____   Date _____

_____   _____

Attendees _____   _____

Objective(s) _____

_____

Item	Process	Time

Sample agenda (continued)

SAMPLE

Minutes of Meeting

Organization _____

Department Team _____

Participants _____   _____
                 _____   _____
                 _____   _____
                 _____   _____
                 _____   _____

Summary of Discussion

Action Plan

<u>Who</u>   <u>What</u>   <u>When</u>

Date : _____   **Signed :** _____

Sample agenda (continued)

In order to make sure that we run a good meeting, one of us should keep a score sheet and provide us with feedback during the last five minutes of the meetings.

MEETING EVALUATION CHECKLIST

	YES	NO
* Before the Meeting Did You:		
Inform the right people of the time, place?	____	____
Prepare your flip charts?	____	____
Check equipment?	____	____
* At the Start of the Meeting Did You:		
Agree to an objective with the participants?	____	____
Agree how the meeting would be run? The technique you will be using - eg. Brainstorming, Cause & Effect, N.G.T., Project Planning Process, etc.	____	____
Agree on a time limit?	____	____
Use others to keep time and do chart writing?	____	____
* During the Meeting Did You:		
Keep the Agenda Visible at all times?	____	____
Follow the Agenda?	____	____
Keep on Track?	____	____
Keep everyone involved?	____	____
Ask questions instead of giving your opinion?	____	____
Get agreements when necessary?	____	____
* At the End of the meeting Did You:		
Summarize?	____	____
Set an action plan?	____	____

Things we want to do better next meeting:

1._____

2._____

3._____

Sample agenda (continued)

Division/Operations Group	System Survey Rating =	Survey No.	Date
To	Producer personnel contacted		
Producer name Producer code			
Plant Phone			
Address	Description of products		
City and state			
Producer in conformance with Ford Q-101 Yes ☐ No ☐	Survey representative signature(s)		
Corrective action required Yes ☐ No ☐			
Purchasing assistance required Yes ☐ No ☐			
Producer acknowledgement signature			

Copies to

Purchasing:

Product Engineering:

Customer Plants:

For each question, provide complete descriptive comments. Then assign a rating using the System Survey Scoring Guidelines.	Rating

PLANNING FOR QUALITY

1. Is the responsibility for quality planning on new products clearly defined? Does the definition of responsibility make sense for the processes involved?
   - Describe the responsible organization.
   - Indicate reporting relationships.
   - Indicate the key contact personnel/department for quality planning and quality concern resolution.

2. Are Control Plans, Process Failure Mode and Effects Analyses, and other documented methods used as a basis for establishing quality programs for new (and specifically-identified existing) products?
   - Does the producer perform feasibility analysis on potential new products?
   - Assess the adequacy of the producer's quality planning effort.

3. Does the producer have available and use a procedure for reviewing design and process changes prior to implementation?
   - Are FMEAs and Control Plans reviewed and updated as part of this procedure?
   - Is customer approval obtained prior to implementing change?
   - Is there a procedure for updating operator instructions and visual aids for process and product changes?

   TOTAL PLANNING FOR QUALITY (Total points available = 30) =

STATISTICAL METHODS

4. Is Statistical Process Control (SPC) utilized for significant and Critical (   ) product characteristics and process parameters?
   - How are the significant characteristics chosen?
   - Describe the SPC methods used? Are they appropriate to the processes being controlled?
   - Evaluate the producer's reaction to out-of-control conditions. Is the reaction as specified in the Control Plan? What is the role of the operators? Of the supervisors?

   Evaluate the producer's application of SPC, based on the evidence of the control charts, process logs, and other appropriate documentation.

A quality system survey report *(Courtesy of Ford Motor Company)*

	Rating
STATISTICAL METHODS (Continued)	

5. Are preliminary statistical studies conducted on new product characteristics and process parameters? _____

6. Are control charts being used effectively to monitor the processes? Do the charts indicate that statistical control has been achieved and that process capability has been demonstrated?
   - In all cases where process capability has not yet been demonstrated, is there a plan to improve the process? Is appropriate interim action (i.e., 100% inspection) being taken to prevent shipment of nonconforming parts. _____

7. Does the producer have a definite program to bring about continual improvement in quality and productivity?
   - Describe the program. Indicate the statistical methods and other tools used to promote continual improvement.
   - Are there improvement priorities identified and project teams established? _____

8. Does the producer have an effective system for assuring the quality of incoming products and services (e.g., plating, heat treating).
   - Are suppliers encouraged to meet Q-101 requirements?
   - Are suppliers encouraged to use SPC? Is evidence of statistical control and capability required from producers?
   - Assess the adequacy of the incoming material quality system? _____

   TOTAL STATISTICAL METHODS (Total points available = 50) = _____

GENERAL

9. Are process/product auditing functions and responsibilities clearly defined?
   - Indicate which plant activities conduct process/product auditing (e.g., quality inspectors, production operators, laboratory technicians).
   Assess the adequacy of the producer's auditing program. _____

10. Are written procedures defining the significant quality-related functions available (i.e., a quality manual)?
    - Are these procedures appropriate to and adequate for the producer's operations? (e.g., is there an adequate procedure for reacting to ES test failures?)
    - Are the procedures implemented as written?
    - Is there a formal review system to verify implementation? _____

11. Are written process monitoring and control instructions available for incoming, in-process, laboratory, layout inspection and outgoing auditing?
    - Are all Critical and Significant characteristics included, specifically those affecting function, durability and appearance?
    - Are Control Items, their Critical Characteristics and related operations identified with the inverted delta symbol?
    - Are sample sizes and frequencies adequate?
    - Is appropriate statistical analysis specified? _____

12. Are appropriate gages, measuring facilities, laboratory equipment, and test equipment available to facilitate process control?
    - Is the selection of significant characteristics effectively incorporated in gage planning and design?
    - Are gages and test equipment and personnel appropriately located throughout the producer's operations?
    - Are adequate, well-lighted areas available for gaging, measuring, and testing the product?
    Evaluate the producer's gage planning and execution. _____

Quality system survey report (continued)

Rating

GENERAL (Continued)

13. Does the producer have an effective gage and test equipment maintenance program?
    - Are new gages/test equipment inspected to design specifications, calibrated and approved before being used?
    - Do records indicate that gages and test equipment are periodically inspected and calibrated?
    - Does the producer use statistical methods to determine the stability and capability of gages, measuring, and test equipment?

    Assess the adequacy of the producer's gage and test equipment maintenance program.   ———

14. What controls does the producer use to indicate the processing and inspection status of products throughout the producer's system?
    - Are effective controls in place to provide accurate part number identification throughout processing, storage, packaging and shipping?
    - Are controls adequate to prevent movement of rejected incoming materials into the production system?
    - Are nonconforming products separated from the stream of production? Are there effective controls to prevent their movement?   ———

15. Does the producer have complete records supporting initial sample certifications?   ———

16. Does the producer react appropriately to customer concerns?
    - Are in-plant and customer quality concerns effectively communicated to all members of the organization?
    - Are nonconforming parts returned by customers analyzed? Is the root cause of failure determined, verified, and corrective action taken?
    - Is a disciplined method of problem solving (the Eight Discipline Method) utilized?

    TOTAL GENERAL (Total points available = 90) =   ———

IN-PROCESS AND OUTGOING

17. Are inspections, measurements, and tests being performed according to the instructions?
    - Are there adequate records of inspections, measurements, and tests?   ———

18. Are documented rework and/or scrap procedures and standards available? Are reworked or sorted products audited for conformance to <u>all</u> customer requirements? Assess the adequacy of rework and sorting operations.   ———

19. Are the handling, storage and packing adequate to preserve product quality?
    - For production and service parts, does the producer meet applicable packaging specifications?
    - Are effective controls in place to assure correct service part identification?   ———

20. Are plant cleanliness, housekeeping, environmental, and working conditions conducive to quality improvement?
    - Are there working conditions that could be detrimental to quality improvement?
    - What actions have been taken to mitigate these factors?   ———

    TOTAL INCOMING, IN-PROCESS and OUTGOING (Total points available = 40) =   ———

    TOTAL RATING POINTS FROM QUESTIONS 1-20 (Maximum = 200 points) =   ———

Quality system survey report (continued)

APPENDIX B

Presented at the SME Fabricating Composites '90 Conference
October, 1990

Quality—Both Home and Abroad

By Edith I. Holmes
Section Head
Physical Testing Department
Wacker Silicones Corporation
Adrian, Michigan

INTRODUCTION

The American dream was and still is to have a chicken in every pot, a TV in every home, and a car in every garage. Well, we did it! We now have chicken, well parts of chicken, served to us in a restaurant or a fast food place, one to three TVs in every home, and two-plus cars in every garage. Unfortunately some of the chicken, a lot of the TVs, and many of the cars are not performing to our expectations.

People today are willing to pay for a quality service or product. But they expect the service or product to meet their expectations. Everyone wants quality.

In our search to improve quality in our products and service, it is easy to become lost in trying to meet the quality requirements of many customers. Automotive, military, FDA, aerospace, all have different quality perceptions. To meet the varying requirements keeps everyone in an uproar and causes industry to maintain several quality systems dependant on to whom they are selling. This is time-consuming and costly.

If you examine the requirements of many standards, you will find that there are basic systems common to all. The following discussion will be a review of basic principles and systems needed to meet the demand of today's market. To what degree you would implement the systems within your company will depend on the requirements of your industry.

WHAT IS QUALITY?

If asked, many people would say, "I can't put quality into words, but I know it when I see it. It is easier for me tell you when something doesn't have quality. It's when it doesn't meet my expectations."

Quality is a moving target. It depends on customers and their expectations of the product or service. Probably the simplest definition for quality would be a product or service which is entirely suitable for use and is available when needed.

Defining what is quality for your customer and determining if you are capable of producing the service or product to meet your customers' expectations, on time, is your first and most crucial step in providing quality goods and service.

Too often a company doesn't understand what the customer wants or commits to far more than it is capable of delivering. When this happens, the company spends a tremendous amount of time, money, and resources to determine why it is having problems when in reality the company didn't even have a chance of delivering quality from the outset.

COMPANY COMMITMENT

Before systems needed to produce quality products and service can be instituted, there must be a commitment from upper management to:

* make quality everyone's job,
* seek input from the most knowledgeable,
* establish a quality plan and policy,
* establish procedures,
* commit capital,
* commit human resources,
* provide programs and training,
* establish final quality verification independent from manufacturing, and
* foster inspection at the point work is done.

From this point forward whenever product quality is discussed, service quality also should be understood in the same context.

THE MAKING OF A QUALITY PRODUCT

In your company, you want to work on prevention rather than detection. You need to establish systems that build quality into the product from the beginning.

Systems which are needed are:

* Advance Quality Planning;
* Raw Material Controls;
* Lot Traceability;
* Standardized Job Analysis and Operating Instructions;
* Preventative Maintenance Program;
* Statistical Process Control (SPC), and
* Process Control.

QUALITY CONTROL

Once a product has completed the production cycle, the product needs to be tested to determine if it will meet expectations. Systems which are needed for quality control are:

* Manufacturing Specifications must be established.
* Test procedures need to be written and followed.
* Calibration systems must be established.
* Repeatability and Reproducibility studies need to be performed.

MEASURE OF QUALITY

Whenever working on a major program within the company, methods to measure improvement, etc., need to be available.

Reports which can be useful are:

* Production Quality Index;
* QA Quality Index;
* Cost of Quality Report;
* Return Goods Authorization Report (RGA);
* On-time Deliveries Report;

and others to suit your individual needs.

CONTINUOUS IMPROVEMENTS

Quality is a journey, not a destination. There is no finish line. Quality must be a part of every department of a company. You need quality in your Sales/Marketing Department all the way through to your warehouse. A company will be as strong as it's weakest link. If anyone does a substandard job, your customers will eventually be effected.

Depending on your company, some of the following activities will facilitate continuous improvement:

* Quality Through Participation - allowing workers in the production area to work on quality and work life issues.
* Product Improvement Committee - a group consisting of production and technical representatives allowed to work on improving existing products or processes.
* Quality Improvement Initiative - a group allowing managers and directors to discuss items which would be considered by QTP or PIC.
* Common Areas of Cooperation - a group allowing directors, vice-presidents and the president to discuss items which cannot be agreed upon in the previously listed groups. This group would approve proposed policy changes, capital, and human resource needs.
* Statistical Process Control - A company needs to determine how to intelligently apply SPC in all areas - not just production.
* Manufacturing Resource Planning - A company may want to consider implementing a (computer) system which would monitor and tie together such departments as Order Entry, Inventory, Scheduling, Ordering, Quality Control, and Shipping to maximize the efficiencies and resources of a company.
* Laboratory Information Management Systems (LIMS) - A company may want to consider a LIMS system to computerize data used in quality control to derive the most benefit from the expenses associated with

gathering this data. Without such a system manual extraction of all of the valuable information contained is impossible.

LIMS establishes a computer database which can determine if material passes or fails a manufacturing specification, determine if a material is certifiable, create the certification letter, provide trend analysis, SPC, etc.

* New Testing Technology - A company must constantly look for new equipment which can increase efficiency, reduce testing, improve accuracy and reproducibility, and provide test capabilities not presently possessed.

DOCUMENTATION

There needs to be a document control system to cover the creation, modification, and deletion of documents used in quality. The following are examples of types of documents requiring control:

> Drawings,
> Specifications,
> Blueprints,
> Inspection Instructions,
> Test Procedures,
> Work Instructions,
> Operation Instructions,
> Quality Manuals,
> Inspection Reports,
> Test Data,
> Audit Reports,
> Calibration Data,
> Quality Cost Reports.

There should be a record retention program to retain records for a specified period of time so as to be retrievable upon need. While in storage, quality records should be protected from damage, loss, and deterioration due to environmental conditions.

I will now discuss some quality systems which have been developed outside of the United States.

ISO-9000 SERIES

People abroad want quality at least as bad as we do. The Europeans have taken a different approach to establish a quality system within their industries. The International Standards Organization (ISO) have written the ISO-9000 series which consist of five standards which define different parts of a quality system. The standards define the minimum requirements a company must meet to assure customers of a good product. With the establishment of a set of standards which bind European trade and which will be used world-wide, companies can be audited by an independent third party. This gives several advantages:

1. The audits have to be performed only once to establish to which level a company can be certified. The audits are accepted and available upon request for any customer from any country.

2. This reduces the cost of being audited by 10-20 different companies per year to one audit which is accepted by all.

3. The possibility of industrial espionage under the pretext of a quality audit is eliminated.

4. Objectivity is an additional advantage of an audit performed by a third party. These auditors have been trained and perform the audit to one standard, - ISO-9000.

Beginning in 1993, ISO-9000 ratings will be required to export to the European community. Since it takes up to 18 months to become certified to the ISO-9000 standards, American companies need to prepare now if they wish to export to anyone in the future.

These standards have been adapted by many nations worldwide as national standards. In the United States the ISO-9000 series corresponds to ANSI/ASQC Q-90 series.

ISO - 9000

The first document, ISO 9000, is the "road map" for the series. The main purpose of this standard is to provide guidelines for the selection and use of the series for quality systems.

ISO - 9001

This standard specifies quality system requirements for use where a contract between two parties requires the demonstration of a supplier's capability to design and supply product.

The requirements specified in this standard are aimed primarily at preventing nonconformity at all steps from design through servicing.

ISO - 9002

This standard specifies quality system requirements for use where a contract between two parties requires demonstration of a supplier's capability to control the process that determines the acceptability of products supplied.

The requirements specified in this standard are aimed primarily at preventing and detecting any nonconformity during production and installation and implementation of the means to prevent its recurrence.

ISO - 9003

This standard specifies quality system requirements for use where a contract between two parties requires demonstration of a supplier's capability to detect and control the disposition of any product nonconforming during final inspection and test.

ANNEX

Cross-reference list of quality system elements

Title	Corresponding Clause No. in		
	ISO 9001	ISO 9002	ISO 9003
Management responsibility	●	◐	O
Quality system principles	●	●	◐
Auditing the quality system (internal)	●	◐	--
Economics - Quality-related cost considerations	--	--	--
Quality in marketing (Contract review)	●	●	--
Quality in specification and design (Design Control)	●	--	--
Quality in procurement (Purchasing)	●	●	--
Quality in production (Process control)	●	●	--
Control of production	●	●	--
Material control and traceability (Product identification and traceability)	●	●	◐
Control of verification status (Inspection & test status)	●	●	◐
Product verification (Inspection and testing)	●	●	◐
Control of measuring and test equipment (Inspection, measuring & test equipment)	●	●	◐
Nonconformity (Control of Nonconforming Product)	●	●	◐
Corrective Action	●	●	--
Handling and post-production functions (Handling, storage, packaging and delivery)	●	●	◐
After-sales servicing	●	--	--
Quality documentation and records (Document Control)	●	●	◐
Quality records	●	●	◐
Personnel (Training)	●	◐	O
Product safety and liability	--	--	--
Use of statistical methods (Statistical Techniques)	●	●	◐
Purchaser supplied product	●	●	--

Key   ● - Full Requirement
       ◐ - Less stringent than ISO 9001
       O - Less stringent than ISO 9002
       -- - Element not present

Figure 1. Cross-reference list of quality system elements.

ISO - 9004

This standard describes a basic set of elements by which quality management systems can be developed and implemented.

The selection of appropriate elements contained in the ISO standards and the extent to which these elements are adopted and applied by a company depends upon factors such as market being served, nature of product, production processes, and consumer needs.

The basic elements are covered in the quality loop is found in Figure 2.

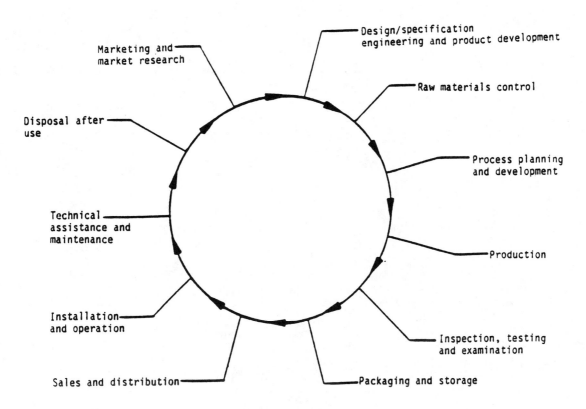

Figure 2. Quality loop.

For now, ISO 9000 standards are a European phenomenon. As soon as the advantages are realized and it's proven that the system works, many other countries will begin to adopt the standards. It is unfortunate that in the United States some important industries (automotive for example) are maintaining their own particular quality systems. Until these industries align with the rest, the systems cannot be universal.

The bottom line is, "Quality is here to stay. Are you?

Index

A

Accounting, 277
Action plans, 119, 206
Activity on arrow approach, 138
Activity on node approach, 137, 142
Ad hoc improvement teams, 163, 169
Aging stage, 110, 111
Allocation by resource, 148
Allocation by task, 145
Analytical problems, 233
AON, See: Activity on node
  approach
Appraisal costs, 35
As-new condition, 18
Assembly, 54, 72, 74, 78, 79
Assessment, 268
Attribute charts, 95
Attribute check sheets, 87
Attribute data, 93
Auditors
  checklists, 272
  by consultants, 268
  external, 266-267
  general forms, 269-271
  ground rules, 271-273
  internal, 268-269
  results, 273
Audits, 42, 46, 265, 266-267,
  268-269, 271-273
Avoiding failure, 253-259

B

Bathtub curve, 16
Benchmarking, 17, 63, 65, 75, 76,
  115, 121, 228-230, 263
Bench test, 135, 142, 143, 145
Bonuses, 244
Brainstorming, 67, 90, 216,
  234, 236, 239
Breach of express warranty, 35
Breach of implied warranty, 35
Budgets, 211
Business plans, 37, 42
Buy-in, 37, 103, 121, 127,
  129, 166

C

Cafeteria plan, 248

Capability analysis, 19-20
Capital investments, 254, 279
Cash flow, 51, 212
Cause and effect, 89, 236
Certification, 41
Change agents, 33
Common market, 117
Communication, 202
Company maturity, 263
Company vision, 280
Company-wide quality control, 51
Compensation issues, 244
Competition, 3, 4, 5, 7, 17, 75,
  103, 115, 125, 132, 177, 218,
  227, 228, 243
Computer-generated CPM
  chart, 140
Computers, See: Software
Conceptual traits, 104
Conflict, 132, 202-203
Constant failure-rate period, 16
Constituent groups, 106, 107
Consultants, 184
Continuous quality improvement,
  49-68, 69-100
Control chart process logs, 97
Control charts, 21, 94, 97, 168
Costs
  accounting, 213-215
  activity, 214
  appraisal, 35
  avoidance, 213
  breakdowns, 149
  centers, 214
  cumulative, 149
  data, 149
  direct materials, 212
  external failure, 35
  factory, 223-224
  failure, 6, 73, 131, 215, 225
  fixed, 214
  graph, 148
  internal failure, 35, 215
  inventory, 116
  investment, 212
  labor, 212
  of living, 248
  monitoring, 168, 171
  operations, 214
  prevention, 32, 35
  product, 116, 215

project, 149, 213
real, 214
reductions, 168
reports, 168
resource, 144
scrap, 226
targets, 129, 130
techniques, 215
training, 176
variable costs, 214
Counseling, 244
CPM, See: Critical path method
Crashing projects, 146
Crash ratio, 147
Critical path method, 136-138,
  141, 143, 147
Cross-discipline improvement
  teams, 55, 57-58, 60, 66, 202,
  256, 264
Cross-functional audit team, 266
Cross-functional improvement
  teams, 57, 58, 60, 66
Cross-training, 247
Cultural changes, 12, 55-56, 187
Cultural influences, 7
Culture self-assessment
  profiles, 114
Cumulative cost graph, 149
Customer audits, 267
Customer billing methods, 51
Customer clinics, 75
Customer focus, 32, 55, 163,
  253
Customer needs, 64, 71, 76
Customer perceptions, 5, 13,
  46, 227, 278
Customer satisfaction, 4, 37, 39,
  63-65, 73, 76-77, 217, 218, 226

D

Damage, 41, 42
Decision making, 165
Defects, 16, 35, 78, 79, 269
Deliverables, 189, 206
Deming, Edwards W., 244-245
Demise stage, 110-111
Department objectives, 121
Design
  for assembly, 78, 79
  and effects analysis, 39, 40, 42,
    58, 82
  of experiments, 80, 227, 277
  failure mode, 39, 40, 42, 58, 82
  for manufacture, 78-80

parameters, 80-81
phase, 71, 73
process parameter, 82
product, 4, 11, 115-126, 33, 37,
  54, 59-61, 76, 132, 277
requirements, 76
specifications, 143, 145
Detection/correction system, 32
Development phase, 16, 41
Direct labor 212, 214-215
Disclaimer of warranty, 35
Distrust, 280
Domestic products, 4
Downtime, 46, 60, 141, 199
Durability testing, 269, 272

E

Education, 186, 277
Educational institutions, 186
Effects analysis, 39, 42
Employee involvement
  teams, 33, 52, 198
Engineering economic
  techniques, 218
Engineering economy tools, 213
Europe, 5
Exports, 5
External customers, 17, 37
External factors, 106, 114, 121,
  153, 215, 234, 248, 253
External failure costs, 35
External failures, 35, 215
External system audits, 270

F

Facilitators, 204, 206-207, 238,
  257-258, 278
Factory floor, 3, 11-12, 52, 54,
  82, 132, 168, 176, 180, 198,
  201-202, 212, 234, 236, 265
Failure analysis, 46, 215
Failure costs, 6, 73, 131
Failure prevention analysis, 42
Fault tree analysis, 39
Feedback, 62, 64
Financial plans, 120
Financial rewards, 245-246
Fishbone diagram, 168, 236,
  238-239
Formative stage, 110
Fringe benefits, 248
Full-time teams, 198

Functional boss, 159
Functional organization, 157-159,
 161, 163, 170

G

Gage capability, 43
Gage controls, 42
Gage error, 23
Gage repeatability and
 reproducibility report, 24-25
Gantt Charts, 133-136, 147
Goal setting, 104-105, 223

H

"Halo" effect, 193
Hard data, 224
Hazard analysis, 39
Hierarchies, 104-105
Histograms, 92
Holism, 104-105
Human resources, 63-64

I

Ideal traits of a company, 104,
 114
Imports, 4-5, 7
Improvement organization, 164
Improvement teams, 94
Industry customs and traditions,
 106-107
Infant mortality period, 16
In-house classes, 185
In-house teardown and testing, 75
In-process control, 42
Input and outputs, 6, 35, 38,
 42, 58-59, 61-62, 104-105
Inspection, 11, 32-33, 41-43, 45,
 51, 55, 86, 269, 277
Internal customers, 17, 37
Internal factors, 253
Internal failure costs, 35, 215
Internal system audits, 270
Inventory management, 229
ISO 9000 standards, 267

J

Japan, 4-5, 76, 89, 153
JIT, See: Just-in-Time
Job classifications, 247
Judgmental problems, 234
Just-in-Time, 74, 78, 215

L

Lead time, 51
Learning objectives, 189
Legal climate, 109
Legal liability, 35
Legal protection, 244
Location check sheets, 87
Low-priced items, 15
Loyalty, 15

M

Mail and telephone surveys, 75
Maintenance, 17
Malcolm Baldrige National Quality
 Award, 57, 63, 65, 264, 268
Management
   commitment, 165
   insight, 254
   inventory, 229
   philosophy, 165
   policies, 155
   project, 127, 130, 141-144,
     161-163
   top, 254
   top-down, 277
Manufacturing Quality Plan, 42,
 45, 120
Market share, 4-5, 57, 225, 278
Market studies, 227
Marketing plans, 119
Material review boards, 45
Matrix approach, 76-77
Matrix organization, 159-161
Mature stage, 110
Measurement devices, 22
Meetings, 206, 256
Mental blocks, 234
Merit raises, 244, 247
Mission statements, 115-116, 121,
 128, 205

MIT Commission on Industrial
  Productivity, 52
Motivation, 26, 245-246

N

NC, See: Numerical control
Negative rewards, 246, 249
Net present worth, 212-213
Networks, 137-139
New appraisal processes
  characteristics, 245
NIH, See: Not Invented Here
  Syndrome
Nominal group technique, 216
Nominal values, 78, 80, 82
Not Invented Here Syndrome, 229
Not natural variation, 83
Not random variation, 83
NPW, See: Net present worth
Numerical control, 178

O

Offshore competition, 3, 5, 12,
  57, 179, 187, 197
Operating principles, 205
Operator education, 33
Order activity, 134-135, 138,
  141-143, 145
Organizational changes, 162, 165,
  167, 171
Organizational performance, 225
Outputs, 6, 17, 35, 58, 61-62
Overhead pool, 214
Overloaded resources, 126

P

Parameter design, 80, 81
Pareto Charts, 86
Part characteristics, 76
Part deployment, 76-77
Part-time teams, 198
Payback, 218
Perception features, 13-14, 235
Perceptions of customers, 224
Perceptions of employees, 224
Performance appraisal systems,
  243-249
Performance-based plans, 246
Performance indexing, 61

Performance measures, 3, 15, 17,
  34, 37-39, 41, 46, 51, 60-61,
  64, 80-81, 117, 121, 129-130,
  189, 193, 224, 243, 263, 265, 272
Performance testing, 74, 269
PERT, See: Project evaluation
  and review technique
PFMEA, See Process failure mode
  and effects analysis
Plan-Do-Check-Act cycle, 66
Platform skills, 193
Policy making, 156
Precedence diagrams, 139, 141
Prevention costs, 32, 35
Priorities, 211-212, 216-218
Priority assessment, 218
Problem solving
  brainstorming, 237
  cause, 238-239
  computers, 233
  creative, 235-236
  evaluation, 239
  failure, 236
  problem types, 233-234
  steps, 238-239
Problem statement, 238
Process audits, 270
Process capability index, 21
Process capability, 3, 11, 21, 37,
  39, 82
Process capability studies, 82
Process control charts, 43, 244
Process failure mode and effects
  analysis, 42-44, 58, 82
Process flow charts, 85
Process parameter design, 82
Process planning, 71-72, 76-78
Process validation methods, 42
Product
  assurance, 51
  audit, 269
  design process, 4, 11, 33, 37, 54,
    59-61, 76, 115-126, 132, 277
  development phase, 80
  development teams, 33, 37, 39,
    42, 71, 74-76, 82, 119
  durability, 43
  engineering, 3, 132
  failures, 6, 51
  features, 15
  performance, 218
  variation, 4
Production, 59, 76-77
Professional growth, 156
Professional societies, 184

Profile 21, 3
Profits, 4, 6, 14, 57, 212, 226,
 247, 254
Profit-sharing, 246-248
Project boss, 159
Project costs, 149, 213
Project evaluation and review
 technique, 136-137
Project management, 127, 130,
 143-144, 161-163
Project scope, 126-127, 205
Promotion considerations, 244
Public information, 75
Public opinion, 106, 108

Q

QFD, See: Quality Function
 Deployment
Quality assurance, 51, 63-64
Quality circles, 153, 199
Quality control reports, 224
Quality cost study, 168
Quality cost techniques, 215
Quality council teams, 168, 199
Quality councils, 36-37, 163-164,
 166-169, 171, 199
Quality Function Deployment, 76,
 180, 181, 183-184
Quality measurements, 64-65
Quality systems, 31, 35, 38, 64
Quick change tools, 215

R

Random variation, 83
Rating system, 216-217
Recognition, 155, 245
Repeatability, 22-23, 26, 43
Reproducibility, 22-23, 26, 43
Resource leveling, 144, 146
Retention and discharge
 decisions, 244
Return on investment, 36, 117,
 213
Revenue enhancement, 215
Rewarding performance, 243
Reward systems, 167, 243
Risk taking 165, 255, 280
Roadblocks, 126, 133, 167, 170,
 202, 245
ROI, See: Return on investment

S

Safety, 34-35, 38, 56, 64
Sales, 3, 52, 126, 254-255
SBU, See: Small business units
Scatter diagrams, 90
Schedule charts, 143, 137
Seriousness classification of
 characteristics, 42-43
Shewhart Cycle, 66
Simultaneous engineering, 37, 73
Skill-based pay scales, 247
Skunk works, 198
Small business units, 162-163
Small car manufacturing, 5
Software, 78, 80, 135, 142-144, 146
SPC, See: Statistical process
 control
Staffing, 129, 244
Stages in a company's life, 110
Standards, 34, 64
Statistical process control, 34,
 42-43, 45, 52, 55, 61, 244, 277
Steering committees, 205-207,
 253, 256-257
Strategic planning, 37, 52, 56, 63,
 65, 111, 112, 113, 115-118, 120-121,
 125, 176-177, 179-180, 182, 224,
 253, 256, 264-265
Stratification charts, 90
Successor activity, 141
Suppliers, 12-13, 17, 31-33, 35,
 38, 41, 45, 53, 59, 64-65, 74,
 129, 161, 204, 215, 265-268, 270,
 277-278
System audits, 270

T

Taguchi Method, 78, 80, 82, 95, 180
Task and milestone forms, 145, 147
Teaching styles, 192
Team building
  approach, 205-206
  effectiveness, 204
  trust, 199-201
Teams
  adhoc improvement, 163-169
  advantages, 197
  development. 33, 37, 39, 42, 71,
   74-76, 82, 119
  disadvantages, 198

employee involvement, 33, 52, 198
full-time, 198
improvement, 94
leader, 171
life cycle, 206-207
part-time, 198
quality council, 168, 199
resources, 170
selecting, 170-171
sponsor, 170
tasks 169
training, 171
Technical studies, 227
Test specifications, 134-135, 143, 145
Testing, 17, 18, 39, 43, 45, 46, 75, 86, 269
Testing agencies, 75
Theory X, 154, 156
Theory Y, 154
Third party agencies, 267-268
Tolerances, 11, 15, 16, 21, 23, 39, 43, 74, 80., 82, 227
Tooling, 17, 45
Top-down management, 277
Top management insights, 254
Top officer, 265
Total involvement, 33
Total quality control, 51
Total quality management, 51
Training
approachs, 187-189
computers, 178, 181-182
continuing education, 180-182
cost of, 176, 186, 198
delivery, 189-190
employees, 182
human resources, 188
for improvement, 173-194
individuals, 178-180
learning, 190-192
objectives of, 176-178, 188
plans, 189

U

Unskilled labor, 278
Use features, 13

V

Validation of selection techniques, 244
Value analysis, 82
Value systems, 14, 201, 253
Values, 54, 57, 65, 106, 108
Variable charts, 95
Variable check sheets, 88
Variable control charts, 193
Variable gage study, 23
Variable histogram, 93
Variables control charts, 96
Variability, 84

W

Warning labels, 46
Wear, 22
Wearout period, 16
Win-lose syndrome, 244
Win-win culture, 244-245
Work breakdown, 139, 140, 147
Work breakdown charts, 140, 147
Working conditions, 155